... a profound grasp of the Indus

Ron Peltier
CEO, Home Services of America

... the industry's premier Report.

Lennox Scott
CEO, John L. Scott Real Estate

One of the best jobs of 'Pulling It All Together' that I have seen.

Dale Stinton
CEO, National Association of REALTORS®

... gives you the edge on the competition.

Dirk Zeller
President, Real Estate Champions

... a new standard for research on industry trends.

Bob Hale
CEO, Houston Association of REALTORS®

... where you go to find out what is GOING to happen.

Terry Watson
Speaker and Trainer

... a must read, every year.

Mark Willis
CEO, Keller Williams Realty International

TRENDS TRANSFORMING 2013 AND BEYOND

SWANEPOEL
TRENDS REPORT 2013

Stefan J. M. Swanepoel
Jeremy Conaway, Rob Hahn, Matt Cohen,
Marc Davison & Tom Mitchell

SWANEPOEL TRENDS REPORT

COPYRIGHT © 2012 BY REALSURE, INC.

MANGING AUTHOR
Stefan J.M. Swanepoel

CONTRIBUTORS
Jeremy Conaway,
Rob Hahn,
Matt Cohen,
Marc Davison, and
Thomas Mitchell

EDITOR
Thomas M. Mitchell

GRAPHICS
Brittany Engh

COVER
D.J. Swanepoel

LAYOUT AND DESIGN
Tinus Swanepoel

FIRST PUBLICATION ON TRENDS IN 1990
Printed in the United States of America with all rights reserved. Except as permitted under the United States Copyright Act of 1976, no part of this publication may be reproduced or distributed in any form or by any means or stored in a database or retrieval system without the prior written permission of the publisher.

ISBN
978-0-9704523-5-1

PRICING
$ 149.95 USA $ 149.95 CAN   € 114.95 EUR

BOOKS AND REPORTS BY THE AUTHOR
- *Real Estate Handbook (1987)*
- *A New Era in Real Estate (1990)*
- *Swanepoel Top Real Estate Firms (1993)*
- *Real Estate Confronts Reality (1997)*
- *Real Estate Confronts Technology (1999)*
- *Real Estate Confronts the e-Consumer (2000)*
- *Real Estate Confronts the Banks (2001)*
- *Real Estate Confronts Profitability (2003)*
- *Real Estate Confronts Customer Acquisition (2004)*
- *Real Estate Confronts the Future (2004)*
- *The Domino Effect (2005)*
- *Real Estate Confronts Bundled Services (2005)*
- *Real Estate Confronts Goal Setting vs. Business Planning (2006)*
- *Swanepoel TRENDS Report (2006 Edition)*
- *Real Estate Confronts the Information Explosion (2007)*
- *Swanepoel TRENDS Report (2007 Edition)*
- *Swanepoel TRENDS Report (2008 Edition)*
- *Swanepoel TRENDS Report (2009 Edition)*
- *Swanepoel SOCIAL MEDIA Report (2010 Edition)*
- *Swanepoel TRENDS Report (2010 Edition)*
- *Swanepoel TRENDS Report (2011 Edition)*
- *Surviving Your Serengeti: 7 Skills to Master Business & Life (2011)*
- *Swanepoel TRENDS Report (2012 Edition)*
- *Swanepoel TRENDS Report (2013 Edition)*
- *Swanepoel TECHNOLOGY Report (2013 Edition)*

OWNER AND PUBLISHER
RealSure, Inc.
P O Box 7259
Laguna Niguel, CA 92607
Tel: 949.681.9409
www.RETrends.com

IMAGES AND PHOTOS
All images are protected by copyright and licensed by Shutterstock

Table of Contents

12   TREND #10 - SALVAGING OF THE HOUSING MARKET

Are We Heading in the Right Direction? Wherever the number of home sales goes up, home values follow a year or two later. Well, sales numbers are nudging up and in 2012 rising home values already pushed nearly one million homeowners above the low tide mark. That, my dear real estate professionals, is a strong confirmation that we are heading up. Now we just need to stay away from those cliffs!

24   TREND #9 - ON THE EDGE OF A FISCAL CLIFF

Is Real Estate on the Precipice Too? The political squabbling will most certainly have an effect on the economy in 2013. With significant numbers of Americans already facing difficult personal financial challenges the continuing blame game has reached beyond the irritation stage for most of us. Meanwhile we know it's going to have substantial and far reaching implications residential real estate industry. Join us as we analyze both sides so you can be better prepared.

42   TREND #8 - RESCUING HOMEOWNERSHIP

Is Government For or Against It? There is a long history of federal involvement in homeownership in the United States. Notably we are the only large developed county in the world in which the government plays a significant role in housing. And now, once again, it is getting involved. This time the Mortgage Interest Deduction is destined for modification. Right or wrong? You decide after reading this trend chapter.

54   Trend #7 - REVISITING ORGANIZED REAL ESTATE

Love Me, Leave Me or Sue Me? Last year On the Brink of Irrelevancy was our #1 trend. What a perplexing and mysterious year it's been for Realtor® associations since that time. This year we review the unexpected and noteworthy court cases, the scenarios identified, do a little introspection and then, given the other trends discussed the year, look at the impact on the future of Realtor® associations.

66   TREND #6 - REDEFINING REAL ESTATE PROFESSIONALISM

Hello, Capital. Are You Coming In? And so the debate continues: Professions, Professionals or simply being Professional. Who really cares? Being a real estate professional is not dead, but capital and investors are redefining the rules regarding how you will work and play in the future. The slowly adjusting real estate business model that has resisted change for too many decades now needs to pick up pace or it will be left behind, along with those stuck it.

Table of Contents

84   **TREND #5 - THE VALUE PROPOSITION OF BRANDS**
Do Brands Still Matter in Real Estate? Brands… those symbols or names that identify personal or company products and services as distinct from others. Strong brands have the ability to influence the choices made by consumers and power to generate profits for its owner, while other brands fade into obscurity, sometimes due to no more than the luck of the draw. And in the fierce battleground of real estate, what does a brand really mean? We analyze exactly that.

96   **TREND #4 - BIG DATA: THE NEXT FRONTIER**
Do We Really Want a National MLS? Which of the current stakeholders, franchises, brokers, agents, associations or vendors are really motivated to create a national MLS? What is the real danger that could threaten the existing structures and the very lucrative and mysterious world of MLS? Join us for a candid and deep dive as we try to find the answers on this reoccurring and provocative question.

110   **TREND #3 - THE GENTLE REVOLUTION**
What Happens When Smart Young Buyers Connect with Wise Old Realtors®? Quietly we have experienced the most dramatic and widespread changes in consumer behavior since the mid-70s. As a result, we have evolved consumers who are no longer vulnerable nor in need of third-party protection. They are bright eyed, computer savvy and very well connected. Whether a matter of history, poetic justice or divine intervention, real estate is the next big American business economy to undergo the consumer revolution.

122   **TREND #2 - THE REAL ESTATE OFFICE OF THE FUTURE**
The Options: Starbucks, Amazon.com or Target? Large bullpen zones, dividers, a plethora of top agent offices along the windows, oversized conference rooms that double up for training facilities and back office MLS tech rooms are all yesterday's news. Hello to uncluttered and inviting reception areas with high tech viewing lounges and see-through glass walls. However, virtual offices with cloud computing and enormous one-stop Superstores with everything also are in high demand. Agents, your choices have never been so good.

Table of Contents

136 TREND #1 - BERKSHIRE HATHAWAY TAKES ANOTHER HUGE STEP INTO REAL ESTATE

Merely a Big Investment or is this a Game Changer? For a almost two decades residential real estate has only had to contend with one really big colossus in the industry, but in October 2012 that changed when the "Oracle of Omaha" made a very strategic move and significantly expanded the scope of his existing real estate brokerage portfolio. Even more noteworthy is the unexpected decision to attach the highly respected Berkshire Hathaway brand to real estate agents. This is our take on what this means to you.

150 REFERENCES

157 ABOUT THE AUTHORS AND CONTRIBUTORS

161 FIFTEEN YEARS OF TRENDS AND TRACKING

162 SWANEPOEL TECHNOLOGY REPORT 2013

163 T3 SUMMIT 2013

164 SERENGETI INSTITUTE

Foreward

Fiscal cliffs, Obamacare, the Mayan's 'end of the world', Greece and the Eurozone collapse, Global Warming, North Korea testing long range missiles.... and that's just for openers. This decade is setting itself up to be a doozy: The Geopolitical climate is providing a seemingly endless supply of water cooler chatter and cocktail party fodder. Only now there are few, if any, water coolers and cocktail parties - having given way to organic, virtual forms of exchange with limitless capabilities for group and individual expression. The challenge now is to sift through, or perhaps better said – 'filter in' the information of most use at the right time.

My strategy is to confine or organize how and what gets through by industry – in this case the 'Real Estate' industry. It is hard for me to imagine an industry that has experienced more sustained turmoil in the last half dozen years and there appears to be little to suggest it will abate any time soon. As long as I care to remember, the conversation has always come back to 'profitability' or lack thereof. There are a host of very important topics and trends to consider (filtering in) that offer ample opportunity to better understand how tens of thousands of real estate enterprises drive towards that elusive bottom line affectionately referred to as 'the company dollar'. And that in a nutshell is the purpose of this publication.

Franchises, Independents, Large vs. Small, Boutique, Consolidation, Virtual, Fee for Service, Concierge, the list of Brokerage/Business models are the subject of endless opining and debate. Add to this a substantial dose of 'enlightened consumerism' and let's not forget our 535 friends in Congress and we have the makings of a first class business case study for the ages. But let's leave the academic autopsy to the class of 2025. For now it is enough to know that, large or small, affiliated or not, the company dollar is under more pressure than ever.

And to be an honest broker of my own opinions, I must declare my bias – I come from organized real estate. I have a strong prejudice for the collective voice that has stood for homeownership (ne: property ownership) in this country for over a century. I believe it is not misguided patriotism to suggest that organized real estate and the right to own, use, and transfer real property is one of the pillars this great country built itself on in the 20th century. I think the invention of 'cooperation and compensation' by otherwise competitive parties to the benefit of their clients, stands toe to toe with any game changing invention of the last 100 years.

It is also fair to say the real estate business is one of the toughest there is to make a living. There are few professions where you literally don't get paid until the deal is totally closed. There are also not many careers where the word "professionalism" is such a lightning rod of debate for its advocates and detractors.

So as the age of 'Consumer' finds its full bloom, and talk of invention and reinvention once again becomes the mantra of all good 'out of the box' thinkers – study this book from cover to cover – take what truth you can from it, discard what you will – and like all of us, do the very best you can to make a positive difference for the industry that has given us so much.

Dale A. Stinton
Chief Executive Officer
National Association of REALTORS®

Preface

This is an exceptionally special year for our Real Estate Trends research and writing, and specifically the *Swanepoel TRENDS Report*.

Firstly, I have for the first time formally invited and few industry thinkers to join me as authors and contributors in delving even deeper into the trends, shifts and changes that are shaping our beloved industry. To each and everyone that gave of his or her knowledge and time to help make this an even more comprehensive Report, you have my sincere appreciation and gratitude. This Report has become the annual official industry anthology and definitive work, and for that I salute you.

Secondly, the huge volume of ongoing change and the enormous growth of technology, the Internet and mobile innovation have driven us to birth a second annual report titled the *Swanepoel TECHNOLOGY Report*. Both annual Reports will be approximately 160 pages; TRENDS being published early February and TECHNOLOGY early April…collectively some 20 authors and contributors working to bring you the best strategic research and information.

Thirdly, and as you have become accustom to, both Reports carry no advertising. A stunning bonus, starting in 2013, will be that both Reports are now full color, making the read and thought-provoking diagrams so much more appealing.

Fourthly, in celebration of the fact that these two Reports in 2013 are our 19th and 20th publications tracking real estate trends, (that's well over 2,000 pages of published strategic trends research on our industry) we have decided to release the most recent 1,000 pages on our website, RETrends.com, as a gift to the industry. Thi information will be free to our subscribers; will be searchable, viewable in HTML and downloadable in PDF format.

Fifthly, we have received thousands of enquiries as to when we would be holding a live event to facilitate the quality discussion and strategic thinking on the subjects and topics covered in our Reports. Well, we are pleased to announce that the inaugural event will be held in 2013. This serious—no trade fair, no advertising—event is for those visionaries, leaders and rainmakers who are serious and seek the opportunity to debate and network with other like-minded individuals in a non commercial atmosphere. If you care about this industry and wish to make a difference, we will see you there. The two-day event will be known as the Swanepoel T3 Summit, and will be tucked away on the outskirts of Las Vegas from April 17-19. For more details visit T3Summit.com.

See why I started by saying an exceptionally special year… and I haven't even mentioned anything about the 10 trends that are covered by the *Swanepoel TRENDS Report* this year. As usual we discuss the topics that need to be covered in mind-bending detail, as well as other outside-the-box, thought provoking topics.

All I can say is "Enjoy the read" and all the very best with the numerous decisions you will be taking in 2013 and beyond. We are grateful to contribute to your continued success.

Stefan Swanepoel
New York Times Best Selling Author
December 2012

Introduction

WHAT IS AND WHAT CONSTITUTES A TREND?

A generic term used to describe any consistent pattern or change in the general direction of a stock, a market or an industry that over the course of time causes a statistically noticeable change.

It is sometimes hard to distinguish between a "Fad" and a "Trend;" between those events that will have longevity and substance compared to those that will fizzle out and fade away. Identifying a trend is not an exact science but rather an art based on facts, patterns, change and time.

Trends are generally not products and services; nor are they the companies that deliver them. They are instead concepts, beliefs or philosophies; the fundamental reasons that often cause a market to change direction.

Trends are more often than not interwoven with one another and one trend often encapsulates part of another. Trends are frequently born as a result of other events that have changed or shifted a paradigm, allowing the evolution of a new trend.

TRENDS IN REAL ESTATE

Some trends in the real estate industry evolve internally to meet a specific need while others develop when new products or solutions are created to solve problems that may or may not exist. Many times a successful trend in another industry spills over into the real estate industry and after trial and error it is adopted.

Many new trends, concepts, companies, products and services are not included in the *Swanepoel TRENDS Report*. The following factors are taken into consideration when evaluating trends:

- Origin of the concept or trend;
- The driving force behind it;
- Its lifecycle and maturity;
- The industry demand or need for the result;
- Its growth pattern; and
- Its potential long term impact on the industry

CONFIDENTIAL INFORMATION

No confidential sources were used in this Report and no information identified as confidential under any existing NDA was included without permission from the appropriate parties. This Report is a result of extensive research, articles that are readily available through the media, the study of hundreds of websites, Social Media pages, forums, surveys, whitepapers, and one-on-one discussions with industry decision makers, leaders, brokers, agents and vendors.

TRADEMARKS

Most of the companies mentioned in this Report own numerous trademarks and other marks and this Report, the publishers, the author, the contributors or any other party involved in this Report in any way seeks to challenge or dilute any of these marks. Specifically Realtor® is a registered trademark of the National Association of Realtors®.

LIMIT OF LIABILITY / DISCLAIMER OF WARRANTY

While the publisher, authors, contributors and editors have used their best efforts in preparing this Report, they make no representation or warranties with respect to the accuracy or completeness of the contents of this report and specifically disclaim any implied warranties. The advice, strategies and comments contained herein may not be suitable for your market or situation.

Although the authors and contributors may, from time to time be an investor in companies mentioned in the Report, and most certainly serve as a consultants and/or advisor to numerous companies and organizations stated in the Report, the Report is written as a neutral, accurate and reasonable view of the industry and its participants. References to any companies, products, services and websites do not constitute or imply endorsement and neither is any reference or absence of reference intended to harm, place at a disadvantage or in any way affect any company or person. Information contained in this Report should not be a substitute for common sense, thorough research and competent advice.

As far as possible all statements, statistics and information included in this Report were verified with the parties mentioned or a credible source. Information is not treat and casually and great pride is taken to provide accurate information. The advice, strategies and comments contained herein may not be suitable for your market or situation and readers are urged to consult proper counsel or other experts regarding any points of law, finance, technology and business before proceeding. All conclusions expressed herein are also of course subject to local, state and federal laws and regulations. Neither the publishers, authors, contributors nor editors shall be liable for any loss or any other commercial damages, including but not limited to special, incidental, consequential, or other damages.

COMPLIMENTARY COPIES

Trends do not appear, disappear or apply to only one year, and therefore do not only apply to one year in the *Swanepoel TRENDS Report*. Trends always span many years, even decades, and the *Swanepoel TRENDS Report*, covers trends as they evolve. Trends in one year should be read together with trends in preceding and subsequent years. Depending on the trend a 3 – 5 year range of Reports should be read on a specific topic. Free copies of previous editions of the *Swanepoel TRENDS Reports* are available on RETrends.com for your viewing pleasure.

© 2012 RealSure, Inc.

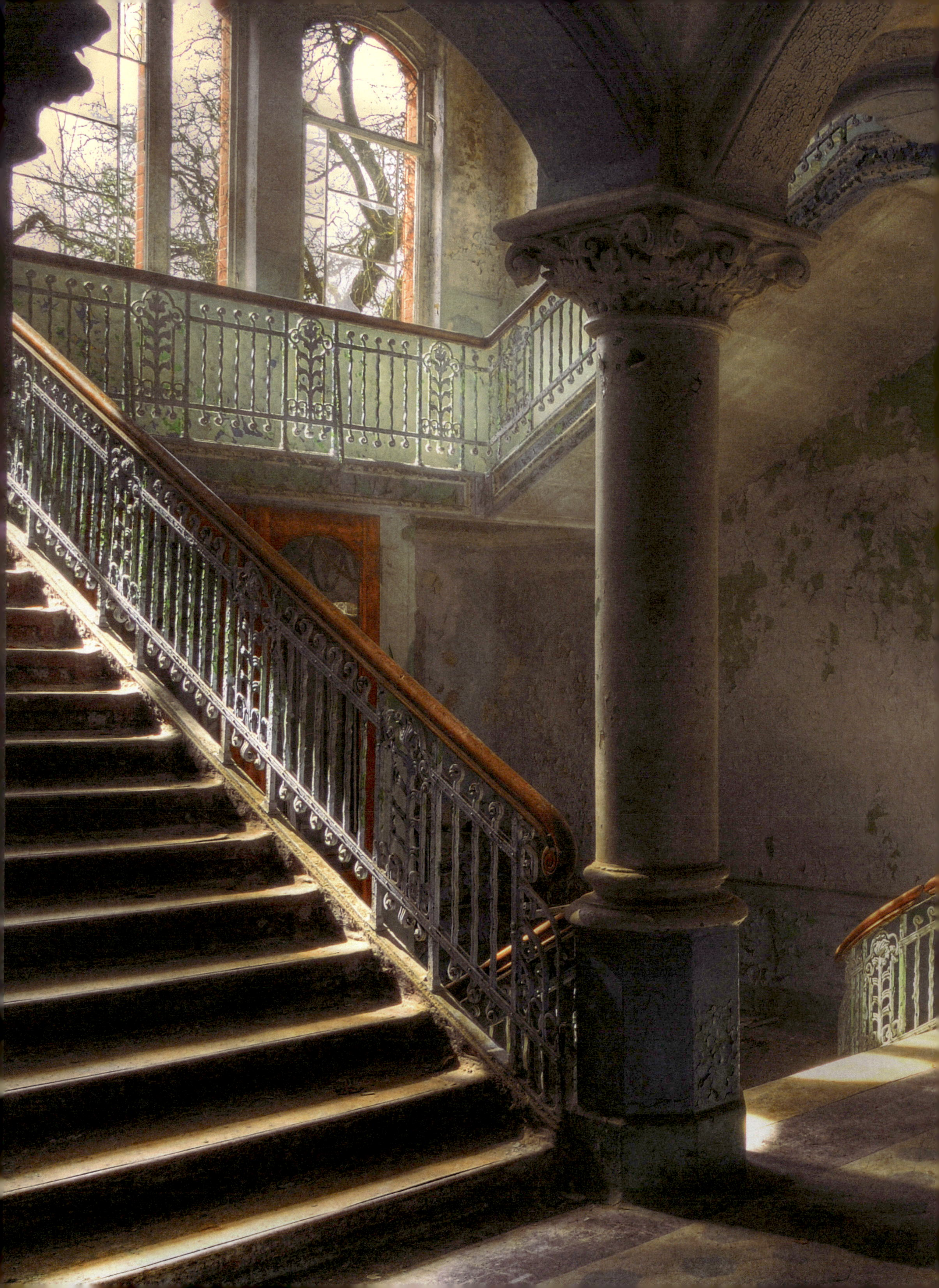

10 Salvaging of the Housing Market
Are We Heading in the Right Direction?

Salvaging of the Housing Market

Those who are looking at our residential real estate market from the outside like *The Economist* (economist.com) tend to place a strong emphasis on the overall health of the economy as a driver for real estate: The US economy has lost momentum. GDP growth slowed to 1.5 percent at an annual rate in the second quarter from 2 percent in the first. We now expect the weaker growth trend to continue into the third quarter and, possibly, into the fourth.

As a result, we have cut our forecast for average GDP growth in 2012 to 2.1 percent (from 2.2 percent). We have also cut our 2013 forecast to just below 2 percent. Should a deeply divided Congress fail to extend tax cuts and take other action in late 2012 to steer the economy away from the looming "fiscal cliff" of massive and unintended fiscal tightening, we would need to lower our 2013 growth forecast substantially.

At home we get various estimates of just how big our market is. The Federal Reserve (federalreserve.gov) estimates that the residential real estate market accounts for an estimated $18.1 trillion, or about three-fourths of the total U.S. property market. According to a report by IBISWorld (ibisworld.com) real estate sales and brokerage revenue for 2012 should hit $93.7 billion yielding a net of $8.2 billion and residential sales represent 48 percent of that pie; $44.9/$3.93 billion.

What's clear is that residential real estate is a huge part of the picture (see chart) and a very significant part of the solution. But neither the outsiders nor those who are closer to home tend to view our industry from anywhere below thirty thousand feet. Generalizations are a great place to start but without the specifics we won't get down low enough to find the answers and solutions.

Every year we have provided a synopsis of the housing market and this year we have called upon three of the country's leading real estate economists to provide us their insights. We are encouraged by the number of the positive points on which they seem to agree. They are also very clear on the difficult issues we will continue to face in 2013. Here then, in alphabetical order, are the views on where we stand today and what 2013 will look like of Zillow's Stan Humphries, Stewart Title's Ted Jones and NAR's Lawrence Yun.

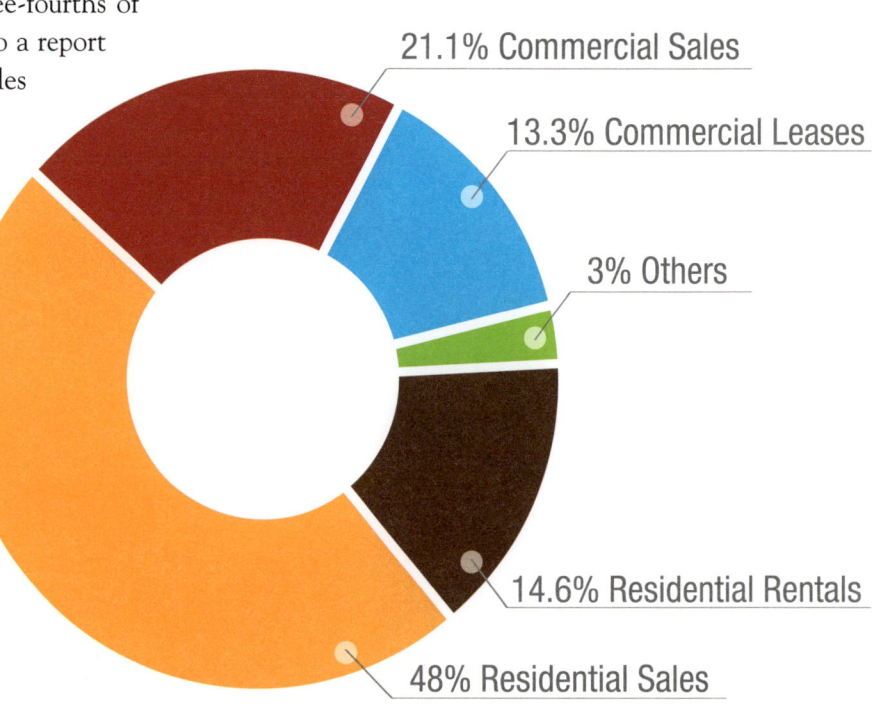

- 21.1% Commercial Sales
- 13.3% Commercial Leases
- 3% Others
- 14.6% Residential Rentals
- 48% Residential Sales

SOURCE IBISWORLD

STAN HUMPHRIES
Chief Economist, Zillow

Where Are We?

Home values reached their post-bubble trough levels in late 2011 after almost five years of the greatest housing recession since the 1930s. In October 2012, according to the Zillow Home Value Index, they increased 1.1 percent from the prior month and 4.7 percent from year-ago levels. It also marked the twelfth consecutive month of home value appreciation, confirming a housing market recovery.

While the real estate market showed brief signs of stabilization in 2009 and 2010, during the time when Federal homebuyer tax credits of up to $8,000 were available to buyers, this policy-induced stabilization proved artificial and transient, and the market correction continued apace after the tax credits lapsed.

This time stabilization appears to be driven more by market fundamentals, which have come back into alignment as a result of the natural market correction. Chief among these fundamentals is affordability, fueled both by huge resets in prices and by historically low mortgage rates. Between 1985 and 2000 Americans spent, on average, about 20 percent of their household income on mortgage payments. That percentage fell to 13 percent by the second quarter of 2012; 35 percent below the pre-bubble average.

Of the nation's 25 largest metro areas covered by Zillow only Chicago experienced monthly home value declines in October 2012. Additionally, 21 of these top metros experienced year-over-year value increases.

Negative Equity

The large decline in home values has led predictably to widespread negative equity in the U.S. As of the third quarter of 2012 roughly 14 million homeowners were still underwater. Of all homeowners with or without a mortgage, 20 percent are underwater (roughly one-third own their home free and clear).

The robust appreciation experienced in many regions during that period, when home values notched their strongest quarterly gain since 2006, pushed negative equity levels down from 30.9 percent in the second quarter. Much of that appreciation occurred in hard-hit areas like Arizona, Florida and California. However, "underwater homeowners" still owe $1 trillion more than their homes are worth.

- More than 42 percent of underwater homeowners (11.9 percent of all homeowners with a mortgage) owe 20 percent or less than their home is worth.

- On average, U.S. homeowners in negative equity owe $73,163 more than what their house is worth; 42.5 percent more.

- Roughly a quarter of homeowners with a mortgage are underwater but 90.3 percent of them remain current on their mortgage payments.

The plight of negative equity is not equally distributed across the nation. High rates of negative equity

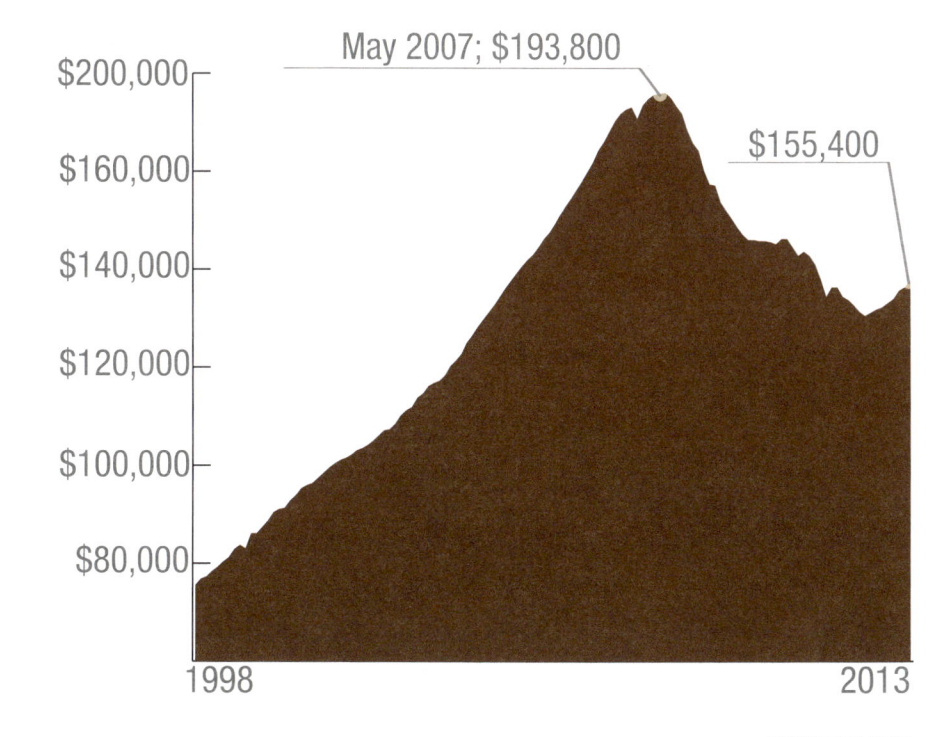

SOURCE ZILLOW

have accumulated in states such as California, Florida, Nevada, Arizona and Georgia where home values have fallen dramatically from their peak—some of the hardest hit areas of the housing recession. However, many of these hard-hit regions also experienced strong home value appreciation in the third quarter of 2012 on the back of high affordability and shortages of for-sale inventory.

The Rental Market

Even as the housing market picks up steam again the rental market remains strong. As of October 2012 nationwide rents were up 5.4 percent year-over-year, and they rose on an annual basis in all but three of the largest metros surveyed. Overall the Zillow Rent Index covers 449 metropolitan areas and it indicated year-over-year gains for 294 metropolitan areas in October. Las Vegas, however, appears to be an exception among the top 30 metros. Its rents declined on a year-over-year basis by 1.8 percent while its home values steadily appreciated, currently growing at an annual rate of 8.6 percent.

> Nationally, we believe that housing has finally turned a corner and is showing signs of a consistent and durable recovery, driven by strong fundamentals such as high affordability; measured either relative to rents or incomes.

Elevated foreclosure rates are keeping rental demand high, which in turn is continuing to draw investors into the marketplace to purchase distressed inventory and convert it into cash flow positive rentals. The large investor presence in hard-hit markets like Phoenix, Miami and Las Vegas has contributed substantial demand to the purchase side of the market, thus stabilizing home prices. In fact, these markets are now experiencing acute inventory shortages, particularly in the lower price tiers, which are most attractive to investors.

While renting has looked more attractive than owning in recent years—while home values have been plummeting—the reset in home prices has now created an environment in which owning is more financially advantageous than renting in many places. We regularly compute a "breakeven horizon" for cities and metro regions, which indicates the number of years before buying is more financially advantageous than renting.

At the precise breakeven horizon one is financially indifferent concerning buying versus renting. It considers all the costs associated with buying a home (e.g., down payment, transaction costs, maintenance and price appreciation) and renting the same home (e.g., rental payments and rent appreciation). For the third quarter of 2012, 152 out of 257 metros (59 percent) have a breakeven horizon of less than three

Metro Regions by Category

Largest 2012 Home Price Increases	
Phoenix, AZ	22.3%
San Jose, CA	11.4%
Denver, CO	10.4%
San Francisco, CA	9.5%
Miami, FL	8.8%

Largest 2012 Negative Equity	
Las Vegas, NV	63.0%
Modesto, CA	56.5%
Stockton, CA	55.5%
Atlanta, GA	50.4%
Riverside, CA	47.3%

years. Among the 30 largest metros New York has the longest breakeven horizon at close to 5 years, making it a better place to rent for many people. On the other hand Detroit has a breakeven horizon of 1.7 years, the lowest horizon among the top 30 metros, making it an attractive place to buy for most consumers.

Looking Forward

Nationally, we believe that housing has finally turned a corner and is showing signs of a consistent and durable recovery, driven by strong fundamentals such as high affordability; measured either relative to rents or incomes. Our home value forecast calls for 1.5 percent appreciation nationally from October 2012 to October 2013. Most of the 256 markets for which we produce a forecast have already hit a bottom, with only 19 not projected to reach a bottom within the next year. Among the top 30 metros only New York has not yet reached a bottom. Forty of the 256 markets covered are forecasted to experience home value appreciation of 3 percent or higher.

Negative equity is on a downward trend and is already below 30 percent nationally. The year-end "fiscal cliff" (read all the details on the "Fiscal Cliff" in Trend #9) is a risk factor in our forecast as it will likely create uncertainty with consequences for consumer confidence and employment growth and, if not successfully navigated, will create real disruptions in the economy.

We know from the previous debt ceiling debate that general economic uncertainty can sap consumer and employer confidence, which affects job growth and household formation, in turn impacting home sales.

In general, we continue to believe that high levels of negative equity paired with higher than normal unemployment will keep foreclosure rates higher than normal for at least the next 2-3 years. In some markets we believe this combination will temper near-term price appreciation and lead to a U-shaped recovery in home values.

However, in other markets we believe the trajectory of home values will look more like a step-function characterized by cycles of price spikes and plateaus. In these markets negative equity-induced supply constraints in combination with mainstream buyer demand and robust investor demand will lead to the short-term price spikes we're now seeing in Phoenix and Miami. These price spikes will free some homeowners from negative equity, allowing them to sell and thereby easing supply constraints and dampening prices until the cycle is repeated.

Downside risks to our outlook are that the pace of foreclosures increases more than expected, job growth becomes more sluggish or we have a political train wreck on the budgetary and tax issues going into 2013. However, we remain optimistic that low mortgage rates, high levels of affordability, rising rental prices and slowly improving conditions in the overall economy will combine to keep the housing recovery on track. We expect that both existing and new homes sales will be strong in 2013, tempered only by low inventory levels (versus anemic demand).

Largest 2012 Quarterly Declines in Negative Equity (% Pts.)	
Phoenix, AZ	-6.2
Las Vegas, NV	-5.5
Denver, CO	-4.9
Sacramento, CA	-4.6
Orlando, FL	-4.2

Strong Rental Appreciation in 2012	
Indianapolis, IN	10.7%
Austin, TX	9.5%
Chicago, IL	9.5%
Baltimore, MD	8.7%
San Francisco, CA	7.0%

SOURCE ZILLOW

Salvaging of the Housing Market

TED JONES
Chief Economist, Stewart Title

Heading Back to Normal in 2013 but Still a Great Upside

After the wild roller coaster ride in the housing markets since 2004, residential markets will continue a trajectory towards normal in 2013. So what is the definition of "normal" today? While existing home sales broke into the 7 million range in 2005 (an unsustainable level supported by subprime loans to many people that had close to zero probability of repayment), the "new normal" is probably in the mid five-million range. That means that housing sales, which hit an annualized pace of 4.6 million in 2012, must have an almost 20 percent upside growth rate potential just to get back to "normal."

The last time we saw a normal market was 2002 with an average 5.5 million existing home sales. This was following the recession of 2001 and prior to the stupidity of the mass subprime lending that commenced in 2004. That level of sales, which at the time was accompanied by an average of 130.3 million jobs, is probably the same today, even though we now have 133.1 million jobs. Increased mortgage underwriting requirements, the trend towards 20 percent down payments, the lingering short-term memory of declining home prices and for some, significant reduction in wealth and credit worthiness, redefines normal. And in the midst of this redefinition a mega trend emerged in 2007 that is shifting many individuals from being predisposed as homeowners to now being renters.

And while normal for new home sales is one million dwelling units, the current new-home sales numbers tally less than 400,000 per year—ditto big-upside potential.

Residential Markets

Only three types of people buy homes that do not have jobs: they have either gray hair, blue hair or no hair and we call them retirees.

Jobs are everything to the economy—period. Current job growth is at an anemic pace. Approximately 120,000 to 140,000 net new people enter the job market each month while the latest 12-month period only experienced an average job increase of 162,000—barely enough to satisfy the current demand with no room to make up for the existing back log.

There are still 4.4 million fewer jobs in the U.S. when compared to the peak as of January 1, 2008. While some economists talk glowingly of a jobless recovery I am of the set that believes you cannot have a growing economy without both matching the new job seekers entering the market and replacing those jobs that have been lost in the recent economic stumble.

Housing markets bottomed in mid-2011 but they have been recovering ever since. I believe that in the next 18 months we will look

US Existing Home Sales
Prior 12 Months Monthly Average

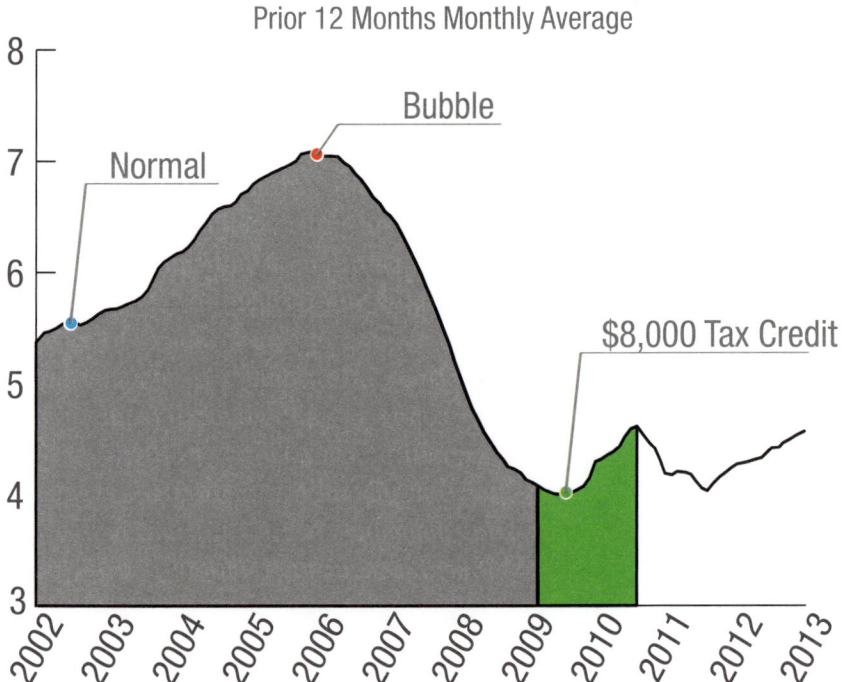

SOURCE NATIONAL ASSOCIATION OF REALTORS® AND STEWART TITLE

back to 2011 and 2012 and wished that we had bought more real estate. The graph shows the 12-month moving average of the seasonally-adjusted annualized rate of sales for existing homes. By averaging over 12 months the trends are more readily visible as the monthly noise in the data is tempered. Realize that the latest month of sales data is pulling up the prior 11 months, indicative of the strength of the recovery in housing markets today.

Both new and existing home sales should increase 8 percent in 2013 from 2012 levels.

Two questions arise regarding the $8,000 homebuyer tax credit from 2009 through mid-2010. Did we sell more homes or did we merely cannibalize future sales. The answer is yes. We did both. Without question, however, housing markets have continued to recover since mid-2011.

If you want to know where home values are heading, simply look at the trend in the number of home sales. Wherever the number of home sales goes, likewise prices will follow, but they lag 12 to 24 months. The graph shows the 12-month moving average of median U.S. home prices (again the moving average removing month-to-month noise in the data revealing the trend of prices).

TINSTAANREM:
There Is No Such Thing As A National Real Estate Market

Without question home values will continue to escalate. They will be driven by rising rents, minimal new construction, increasing jobs and with some but muted influence from an increasing population. Since not all markets are the same I always invoke the TINSTAANREM clause. Except for destination recreational properties, the demand for housing is a function of the local economy and respective supply and demand conditions.

Housing prices fell 29 percent below their 2006 peak before beginning a recovery. Although they are still down 27 percent they continue to improve. But the real story in housing is the minimal supply available for sale. Normal inventory for existing home sales is six months—today we sit in the upper five-month range. Many markets, Phoenix for example, have less than three months inventory, setting the stage for continued price increases.

The latest 12-month moving average of U.S. median home price is up 4.3 percent and, assuming continued job growth going forward, that is expected to approach a 5 percent increase in 2013. Housing will most likely once again outperform many stock market indices. In comparison, over the past 10 years the S&P 500 rose 4.3 percent per year; compounded annually.

Rental Market

More jobs, a growing population, increased demand for rental housing (recall the mega trend towards many individuals that in the past may have been tilted towards homeownership

Median Price in Thousands
Average Prior 12 Months

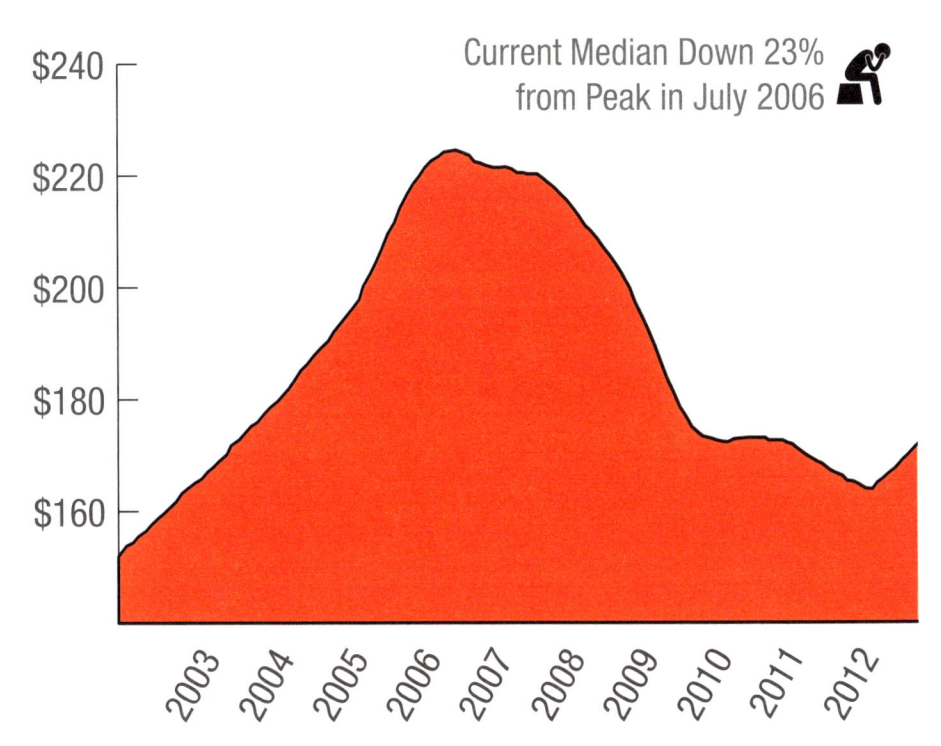

Current Median Down 23% from Peak in July 2006

SOURCE NATIONAL ASSOCIATION OF REALTORS® AND STEWART TITLE

Building Permits

[Chart showing Single Family and Multi Family building permits from 1980 to 2012, ranging from 0.0 to 2.0]

SOURCE NATIONAL ASSOCIATION OF REALTORS®

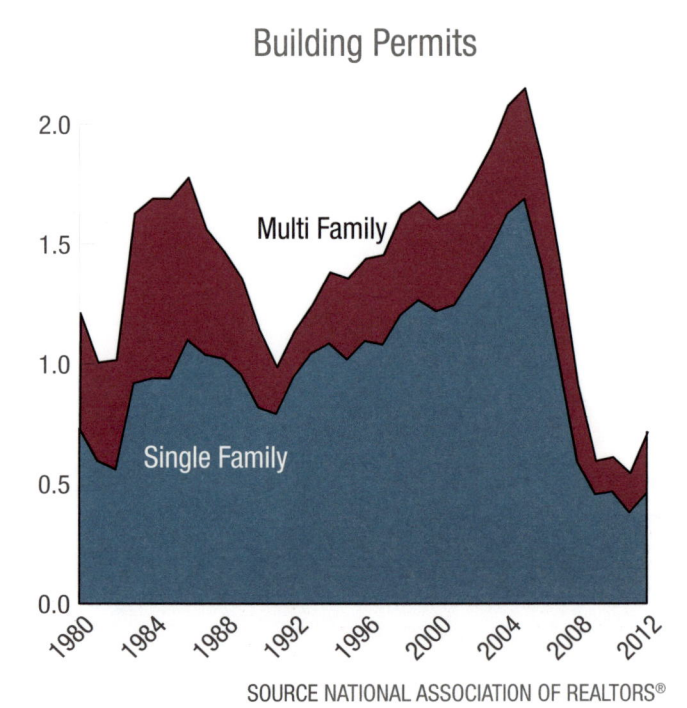

but today are relegated to being renters) and minimal new construction form a catalyst assuring rising rents.

In the last 12 months, 441,000 single-family residential building permits were issued along with 265,000 multi-family permits for a total 706,000 thousand new dwelling units as shown in the graph (see next page). During that same period the U.S. added 1.95 million net new additional jobs. Thus, 2.8 net new jobs were created for each dwelling built in the past 12 months. Normally you only need 1.25 to 1.5 net new jobs per new dwelling unit. Therefore, the U.S. is systematically under building new homes and rental properties by one-half. While we have lived off the excess inventory built during the housing bubble, that surplus has been consumed—in many instances by investors transitioning properties from owner-occupied dwellings to rental properties.

Further constraining a quick recovery in new construction is a dearth of developed, builder-ready lots. Essentially there has been zero new land development during the last six years, and what was available at the time has in a large part been consumed.

All of these factors combine to push up rental rates. Minimal vacancy levels and increased demand will see rents rise in most markets from 2.5 percent to 6 percent in 2013.

Interest Rates

The question is not if rates will rise but when, and "when" will be triggered by the return of consumer confidence. And that won't return until the politicians in Washington, D.C. define the rules for the future regarding taxes, entitlements and health care (note the difference between politicians and leaders).

Since mid-2008 we have seen the largest increase in the M1 money supply in the history of the U.S.—up 69 percent. M1 consists of currency, demand deposits and checking accounts, which literally earns zero interest. Historically the velocity of M1 (GDP divided by M1) is almost nine. That means that M1, on average, is spent nine times each year to cover the total value of all goods and services produced by the U.S. Today M1 velocity hovers in the upper sixes. That means that when the velocity of M1 returns to normal (which it will when consumer confidence returns) the U.S. economy has the potential to grow 29 percent—and that is without one additional dollar in money supply. When consumers and business America start spending this money the Federal Reserve will step in to tighten and slow the economy and interest rates will rise. Today consumers need to lock in interest rates with fixed-rate loans to avoid being squeezed by inevitable rising rates. But don't be enticed by adjustable rate loans in this record low interest rate landscape.

The Bottom Line

Housing will continue its recovery into 2013 with forecasts as follows:

- Existing and new home sales up

We will all look back in 2014 and wished we had purchased more real estate from 2011 – 2013.

8 percent.

- Home price increases approaching 5 percent.

- Residential rents increasing from 2.5 percent to 6 percent (depending on the market).

- Continued under-building of new construction constrained by developed lot availability and lenders.

- Interest rates rising—no place to go but up.

The good news is that rising home values are now moving some underwater homeowners to positive equity, with the likelihood of another $1 trillion of added homeowner equity in the coming twelve months. This will allow many owners that today cannot refinance at record low rates to do so in 2013—hopefully prior to interest rates rising.

Prerequisites for these forecasts are straightforward:

- Continued job growth.

- Continuity in the deductibility of both mortgage interest and property taxes on primary dwellings.

- Leadership rather than politics from Washington, D.C.

Looking back at 2013 we will most likely wish we had purchased more real estate during the period 2011 – 2013. Housing, while always a place to live, will once again provide attractive investment returns in many markets… TINSTAANREM.

LAWRENCE YUN
Chief Economist & SVP of Research, National Association of REALTORS®

The Big Picture

Home sales finally broke out of the lows in 2012 and the improving momentum will most likely continue into 2013. In fact, the improvement could be the start of a multiyear recovery lasting four to six years. The key reasoning is that the factors that generally support housing will continue to build. Jobs are on the rebound, rents are rising with no sign of a slowdown and the stock market wealth has nicely rebounded, thereby helping the second home market and the older generation possibly helping out the younger family members with down payments. Home price recovery is also a positive in the sense of providing confidence for hesitant buyers to get into the market. Most importantly, household formation is bound to recover after four years of suppression as people simply cannot continue to double-up or live with their parents. A recovering economy will help household formation to not only double from recent years but may even exceed historical normal for few years.

One optimistic sign is that buyer interest has been rising as measured by qualitative factors that are not yet hard-coded. A survey of Realtors® revealed that their foot traffic, phone inquiries and the seriousness of buyers have all climbed higher.

However, Washington policy changes can greatly impede the recovery. Changes to the mortgage interest deduction will harm

Household Rentals

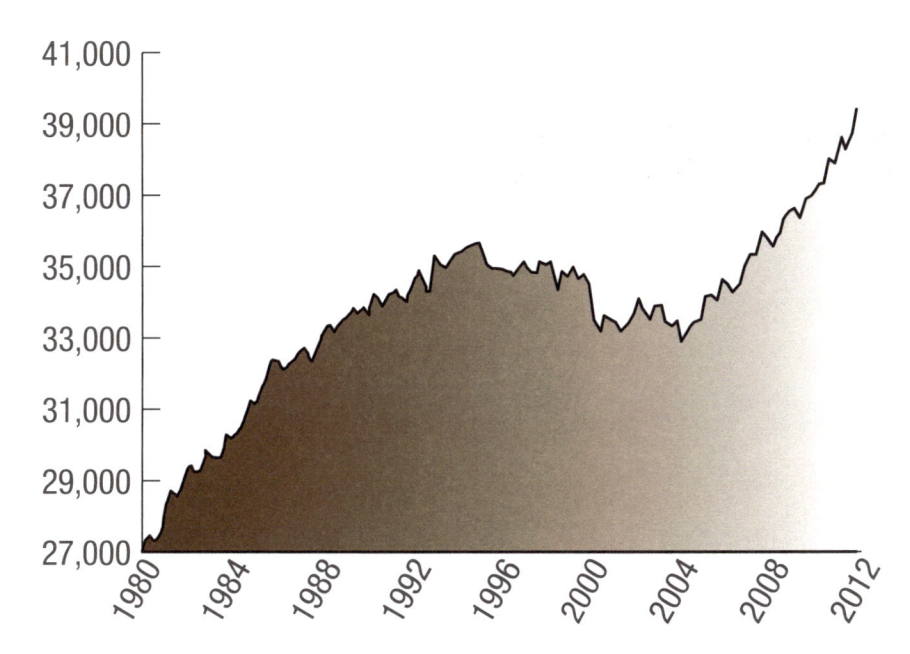

SOURCE NATIONAL ASSOCIATION OF REALTORS®

confidence and cost of purchase. Changes to mortgage credit accessibility and the resulting requirement for higher down payments can potentially shut out 20 percent of the buyers that would have qualified in a very normal housing market year like 2000. In addition, the troubling aspects of the economy and employment are always important factors. High deficits could lead to a sudden rise in long-term interest rates for 30-year mortgage rates and those rates could be pushed up to close to 5 percent in a few years by high inflation.

Visible Housing Inventory

SOURCE NATIONAL ASSOCIATION OF REALTORS®

The Rental Market

Rental demand will be solid in the upcoming years as many unfortunate homeowners that went through foreclosures will not be able to buy for nearly 10 years. For many, their credit has been damaged as a result of the recession of the last couple of years. Rising rental demand, however, does not mean there will be lower homeownership demand. What will happen is that the anticipated rise in household formation will lead to higher demand for both rentals and for ownership. If there is a bubble, the bubble is related to the purchase price of multifamily apartment units as investors have chased yields (rental income) because of the exceptionally low interest rate environment. In addition, I expect rents will rise 4 to 5 percent in conjunction with a continuing low vacancy rate, due in part to the difficulty of obtaining multifamily construction loans. There will be no quick relief to falling vacancy rates.

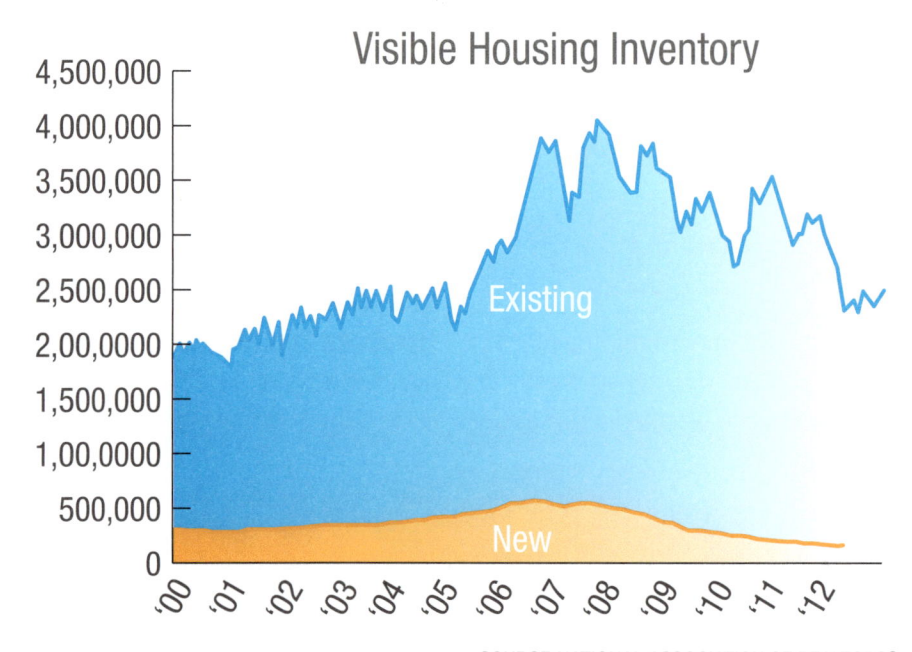

Shadow Inventory is Diminishing

The good news is that the shadow inventory is no longer a major threat. Although the overall size of the shadow inventory is still high, it has been falling for two straight years. Furthermore, the number of new mortgage defaults is very low. The only remaining question is how long will it take to flush out the mortgages originated during the bubble years?

New Construction

Although new housing starts are likely to have risen by about 30 percent—reaching

Sector	2011 History	2012 Forecast	2013 Forecast
NAR Forecast			
Existing Home Sales	4.26 million	4.64 million	6.5 million
New Home Sales	301,000	368,000	575,000
Housing Starts	612,000	776,000	1,128,000
Existing Home Price	$166,100	$176,100	$185,200
GDP Growth	+1.8%	+2.1%	+2.5%
Payroll Job Gains	+1.7 million	+1.7 million	+2.2 million
Fed Funds Rate	0.1 percent	0.1 percent	0.1 percent
30 Year Mortgage	4.7 percent	3.7 percent	4.0 percent

SOURCE NATIONAL ASSOCIATION OF REALTORS®

close to 800,000 new units—by the time the final numbers are in, there is still an inventory shortage in a growing number of markets across the country. The existing home inventory is at an 8-year low, while the newly constructed home inventory is at a 50-year low.

What is needed is to get back to 1.5 million housing starts per year; otherwise the inventory shortage will impact supply and demand, driving home prices up at a rapid and unhealthy pace.

One advantage from the recession is that the homebuilding industry is today dominated by large, publicly listed companies such as Lennar, KB Homes and Toll Brothers that can tap Wall Street funds to build fast and on an enormous scale.

Mortgage Rates Can't Go Lower

The Federal Reserve's actions have brought mortgage rates down to the 3.5 percent range and further downward movement is unlikely. A high budget deficit and the continued printing of money (QE) with the accompanying inflation will in a few years mean higher mortgage rates that could climb back to 5 percent by 2014 to 2015; but the rise will be gradual.

Underwriting standards are more important than small changes in mortgage rates and therefore, if underwriting standards were to return to normal even as the mortgage rates rise, the rise is not expected to have any significant impact on the residential market.

The Future

Looking back we can see that there has been improvement or stability in all the major categories and growth can be expected in 2013. Significant improvement will be seen in both existing and new home sales. On the economic front we should see an improving employment situation and a slight uptake in GDP.

9 On the Edge of The Fiscal Cliff
Is Real Estate on the Precipice Too?

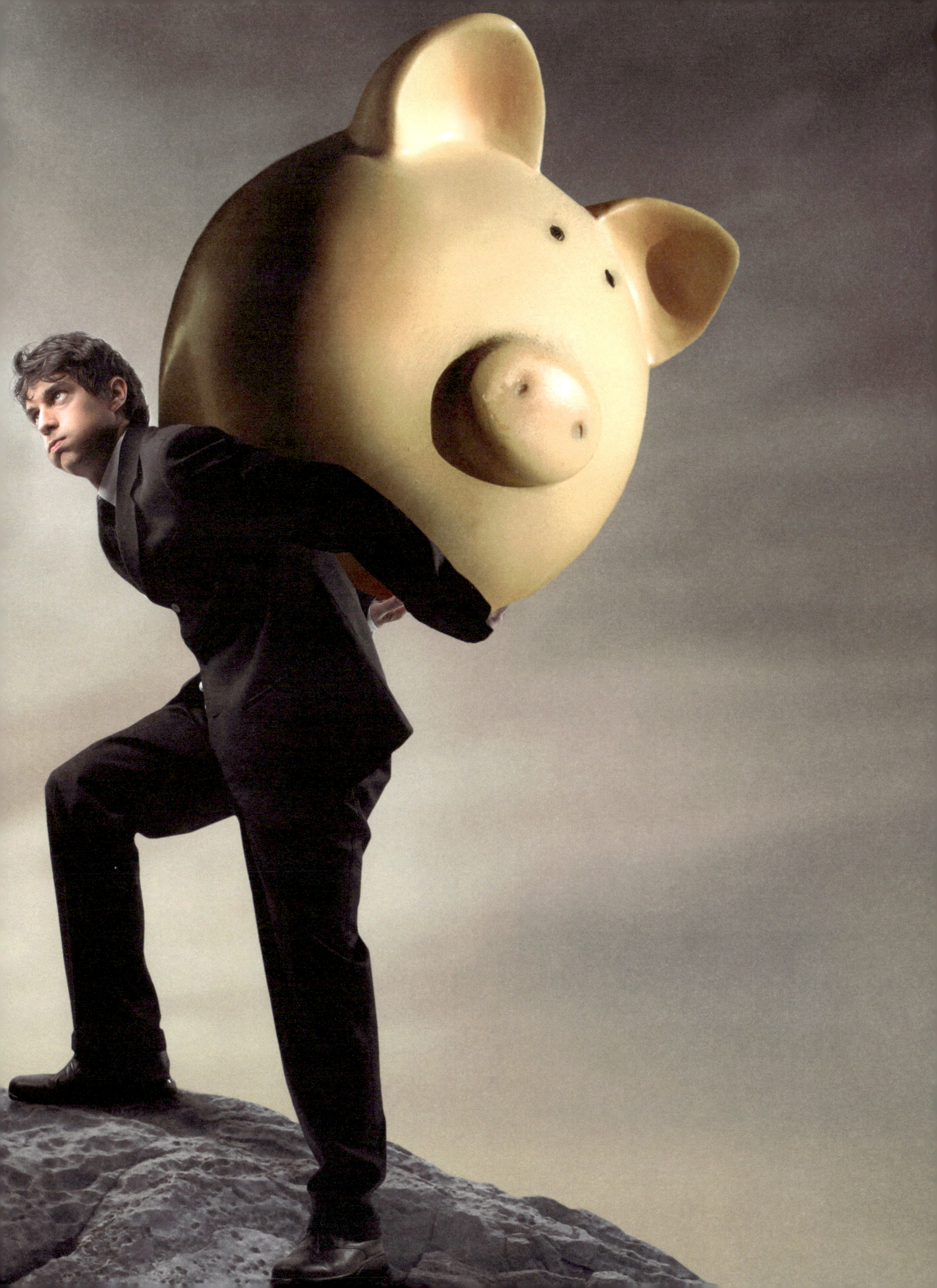

On the Edge of The Fiscal Cliff

Call it a Federal Deficit, a Debt Crisis or a Fiscal Cliff, there is no question—we have a huge problem and it's growing stronger with each passing day. America is standing on the precipice and if the tax increases and government spending cuts scheduled to be implemented in January 2013 take place the Congressional Budget Office (CBO; cbo.gov) predicts that the economy will once again slip back into recession with unemployment growing past 9 percent.

The CBO also predicted that it would result in the federal deficit being cut in half by the end of 2013, falling to under 1 percent of GDP by 2016.

With most Americans that are already facing the difficult personal financial challenges of unemployment, rising costs and pending foreclosures that's a tough pill to swallow. The numbers are so staggering that it's almost impossible to put them in perspective. For some clarity on the subject and what it means for those of us in the real estate industry we have explored where we are and what the future impact of the debt crisis will be on real estate.

That the U.S. has a debt problem is not a particularly controversial proposition, but what caused it, what to do about it and what the debt means represent very controversial political positions. In this Trend we try and make sense of this quandary as we take as neutral a look as possible, touching on politics only when necessary, but never in a partisan manner. Let's start with the factual information as it stands at the close of 2012.

THE FACTS

As of late 2012 here is what we know about the federal debt as reported by various sources:

- The Federal Debt as of December 31, 2012 was $16,352,586,144,900 — $52,053 for every citizen— and growing at some $3.82 billion per day.

- In the last three years, the Federal Government has borrowed $4 trillion and FY 2012 ended with $1.1 trillion in deficit spending.

- The top three holders of federal debt are the Social Security Trust Fund (ssa.gov), the Federal Reserve (federalreserve.gov) and China.

- In 2011 the Federal Reserve purchased 61 percent of all U.S. debt as demand from other buyers declined— particularly foreign governments.

Put it in Perspective	
U.S Tax Revenue	$ 2,170,000,000,000
Federal Budget	$ 3,820,000,000,000
New Debt	$ 1,650,000,000,000
National Debt	$ 14,271,000,000,000
Recent Budget Cuts	$ 38,500,000,000

Remove 8 Zeros and Its Your Household Budget	
Annual Family Income	$ 21,700
Money the Family Spent	$ 38,200
New Debt on the Credit Card	$ 16,500
Credit Card Balance	$ 142,710
Total Budget Cuts	$ 385

SOURCE SILICON INVESTOR

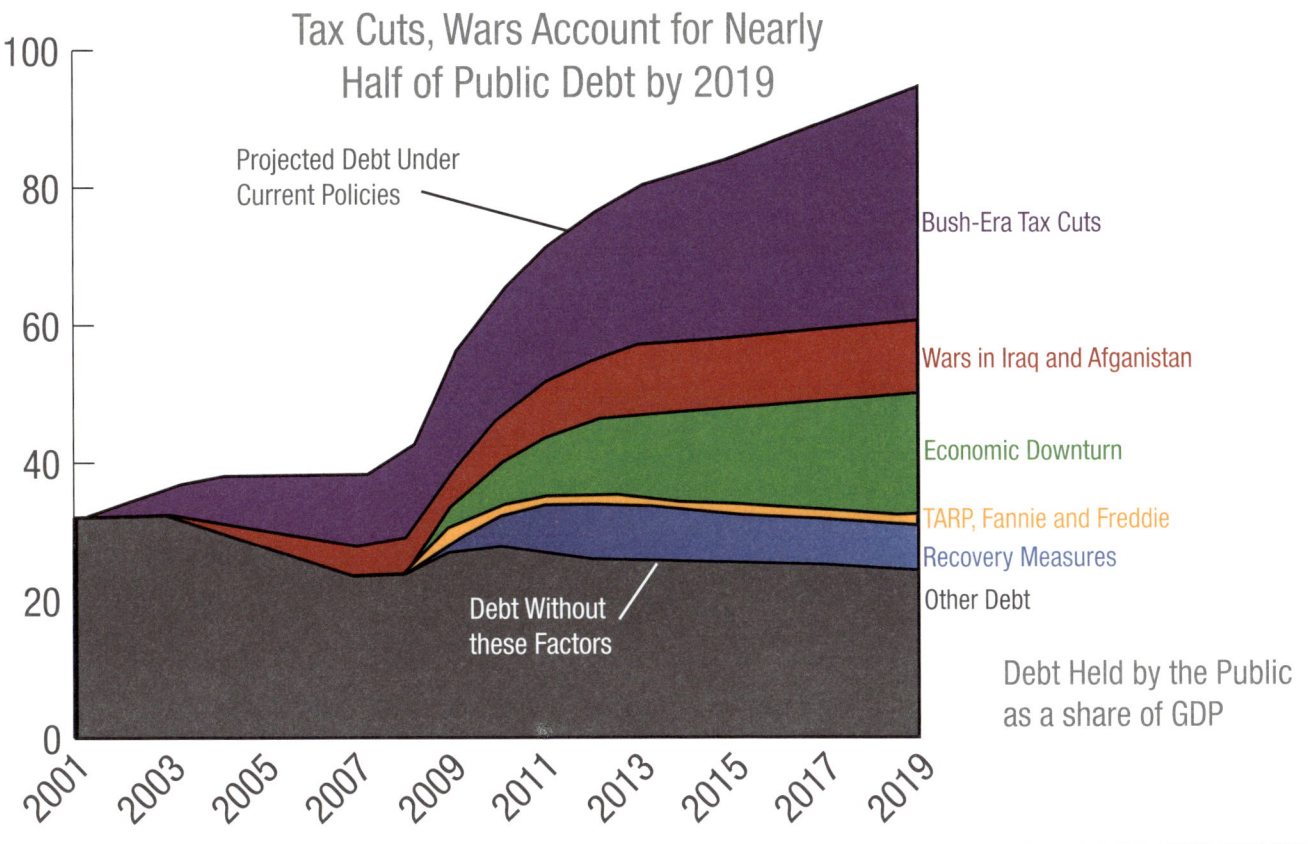

Tax Cuts, Wars Account for Nearly Half of Public Debt by 2019

Projected Debt Under Current Policies

- Bush-Era Tax Cuts
- Wars in Iraq and Afganistan
- Economic Downturn
- TARP, Fannie and Freddie
- Recovery Measures
- Other Debt

Debt Without these Factors

Debt Held by the Public as a share of GDP

SOURCE CBPP ANALYSIS BASED ON CONGRESSIONAL BUDGET OFFICE ESTIMATES

- The sixth largest holders of U.S. debt are state and local governments, with $504.7 billion; the tenth largest are state, local and federal retirement funds with $320.9 billion.

One of the most significant facts about the federal debt is how much of it was purchased and continues to be purchased by the Federal Reserve. Why? Because it's a sign that other bond investors (those willing to lend) have become soured on the U.S. debt.

China, the largest foreign holder of our debt, continues to buy Treasuries but not as an excited buyer because it doesn't have much of a choice. The large trade imbalance means that China ends up with a huge amount of dollars. They can't use them in China as those dollars have to be converted to Chinese Yuans and that would cause the value of the Yuan to rise, which would impact both their domestic economy and exports. So they buy U.S. Treasury Bonds by the hundreds of billions. They have nowhere else to park the money. This dynamic led to the Chinese government—through its state-owned media—to chastise the U.S. for "addiction to debt."

The U.S. government has to come to terms with the painful fact that the good old days when it could just borrow its way out of messes of its own making are finally gone, read the commentary, which was published in Chinese newspapers. (New York Times)

The influential finance blog, The Big Picture (ritholtz.com/blog), noted that foreigners are not buying anywhere near the amount of U.S. Treasuries as they were before:

> Since mid-2008 foreign purchases of Treasury securities have been under 50 percent of securities auctioned, and the Chinese have bought less than 10 percent of the amount auctioned. Even though foreigners have almost doubled their buying of Treasuries in the last few years, they have not kept pace with growing Treasury issuance over the same period. As a result, foreign purchases now account for less than half of what has been issued since mid-2008. Domestic purchasers of Treasuries are now buying more than half of the amount auctioned.

Furthermore, there is strong evidence that domestic investors aren't buying Treasury bonds either. Bill Gross of PIMCO (pimco.com), the world's largest bond fund, has gone on record about his fears of inflation, which makes investing in long-term Treasuries a losing proposition.

Mr. Gross has warned that the Federal Reserve's highly accommodative monetary policy and a lack of fiscal responsibility could spark inflation in coming years, making regular Treasury bonds vulnerable to a decline in value. Treasury Inflation Protected Securities (TIPS), on the other hand, would rise in value along with higher price pressure.

In an interview with Dow Jones earlier this month, Mr. Gross said he held Treasury bonds with no more than a 10-year maturity; the longer the maturity the bigger the losses that a bond can incur due to inflation. (Wall Street Journal)

Following that advice, at the end of September 2012 PIMCO reduced its holdings of U.S. debt from 21 percent to 9 percent.

The result is that the Federal Reserve—an entity that has the power to create money out of thin air—has been forced to step in and buy up the bonds that foreigners and bond investors have been unwilling to purchase at the rates that they were offered. Their reasoning is to keep rates low to stimulate the economy, and they have committed to do so until the employment situation improves.

Indeed, the statement from the policy unit, the Federal Open Market Committee, once again emphasized that it remained prepared to expand its efforts "if the outlook for the labor market does not improve substantially." Eleven members of the committee supported the decision. (New York Times)

There is significant disagreement across the political spectrum as well as among economists about how long the Fed can keep doing this. It does appear, however, that no one believes this can go on forever, with the federal government borrowing from a central bank that exists only because the federal government gave it the power to print money. At some point inflation will become a reality.

INFLATION TRENDS
One reason for the significant disagreement among economists is that they don't necessarily agree on whether there is inflation going on today or not.

The "official" inflation rate, based on data published by the Bureau of Labor Statistics (bls.gov), shows that it is historically low and relatively flat. If anything, there is deflationary pressure on the economy as prices contracted by 0.34 percent in 2009. From 2000 to 2011 the annual inflation rate ranged from the low of -0.34 percent to a high of 3.85 percent in 2008. However, there is significant disagreement on whether or not the official statistics are an accurate measure of inflation.

The American Institute for Economic Research (AIER; aier.org), for example, suggests that real inflation was 8 percent in 2011, not 3.1 percent. It arrived at this higher number by excluding prices of large purchases, such as homes and cars, and included the volatile food and fuel prices. That report resulted in commentary like this one from ETF Daily News (etfdailynews.com); How the Government Lies About the Real Inflation Rate:

Economic consultant John Williams, an outspoken critic of the government's economic statistics, contends things are even worse. Using the government's old methodology from 1980—before politicians started to monkey with the formula—he calculates the real inflation rate is north of 10 percent; more than triple the government's figure.

Furthermore, even if there isn't significant argument about what the "real" inflation rate is, economists differ on whether inflation is or is not a problem. For example, in the New York Times you have two economics professors disagreeing.

The Fed's hypersensitivity to inflation comes in large part from memories of the 1970s, but there is very little to justify worries that the inflation problems of the 1970s will be repeated. Inflation has been running at or below target, financial markets have not displayed any inflation jitters and the Fed can increase the interest rate it pays on bank reserves, a tool it did not have in the 1970s, which keeps funds idle in bank vaults and helps keep inflation under control. Even if the fight against unemployment does cause inflation, a long-run problem is far from inevitable and the costs of moderate, short-lived inflation are not that large. (Mark Thomas, University of Oregon)

And on the other side…

Inflation remains a danger, but not so much because of what the Fed is doing. U.S. debt is skyrocketing, with no visible plan to pay it back. For the moment, foreigners are still buying prodigious amounts of that debt. But they are mostly buying out of fear that their governments are worse. They are short-term investors, waiting out the storm, not long-term investors confident that the U.S. will pay back its debts. If their fear passes, or they decide some other haven is safer, watch out. The inflation some are hoping for will then come with a vengeance. It's not happening yet. Interest rates are low now but so were mortgage-backed security rates and Greek government debt rates just a few years ago. And inflation need not happen, if we put our fiscal house in order first. But if it happens, it will happen with little warning, the Fed will be powerless to stop it, and it will bring stagnation rather than prosperity. (John Cochrane, University of Chicago Booth School of Business)

Recent trends, however, suggest that both investors and everyday consumers are worried about inflation.

After the Fed's QE3 program was implemented, *Financial Times* reported that "investors pushed a key measure of U.S. inflation expectations to their highest level since 2006." And PIMCO released a gloomy investment outlook in October of 2012:

> *So on the question posed earlier: How can the U.S. not be considered the first destination of global capital in search of safe (although historically low) returns?*

Easy answer: It will not be if we continue down the current road and don't address our "fiscal gap." If we continue to close our eyes to existing 8 percent of GDP deficits, which when including Social Security, Medicaid and Medicare liabilities compose an

The Road to The Cliff

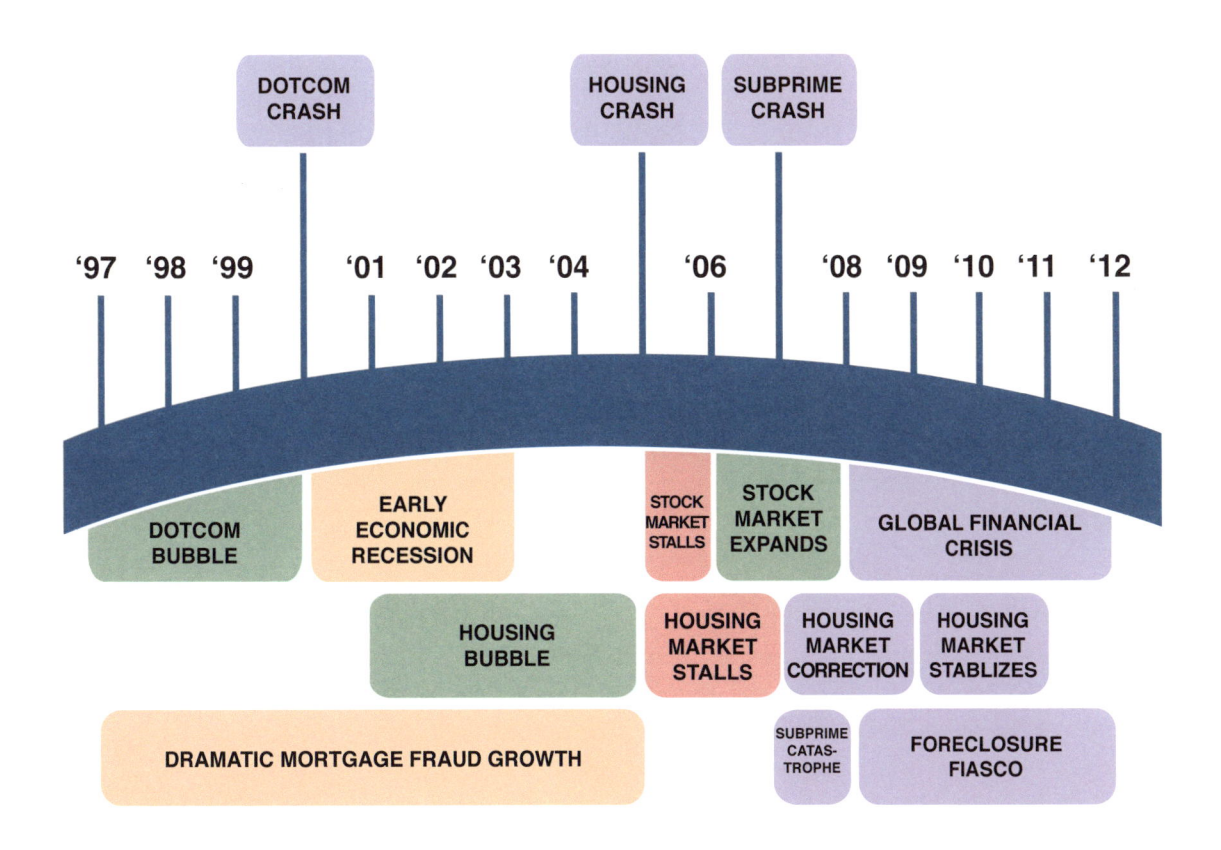

average estimated 11 percent annual "fiscal gap," then we will begin to resemble Greece before the turn of the next decade.

Unless we begin to close this gap, then the inevitable result will be that our debt/GDP ratio will continue to rise, the Fed would print money to pay for the deficiency, inflation would follow and the dollar would inevitably decline. Bonds would be burned to a crisp and stocks would certainly be singed; only gold and real assets would thrive within the "Ring of Fire."

If that be the case, the U.S. would no longer be in the catbird's seat of global finance and there would be damage aplenty, not just to the U.S. but to the global financial system itself, a system which for 40 years has depended on the U.S. economy as the world's consummate consumer and the dollar as the global medium of exchange. If the fiscal gap isn't closed even ever so gradually over the next few years, then rating services, dollar reserve holding nations and bond managers embarrassed into being reborn as vigilantes may together force a resolution that ends in tears. It would be a scenario for the storybooks, that's for sure, but one, which in this instance, investors would want to forget. The damage would likely be beyond repair (emphasis in the original).

All of this is very complicated, intelligent people are arguing about it, so why should real estate people care?

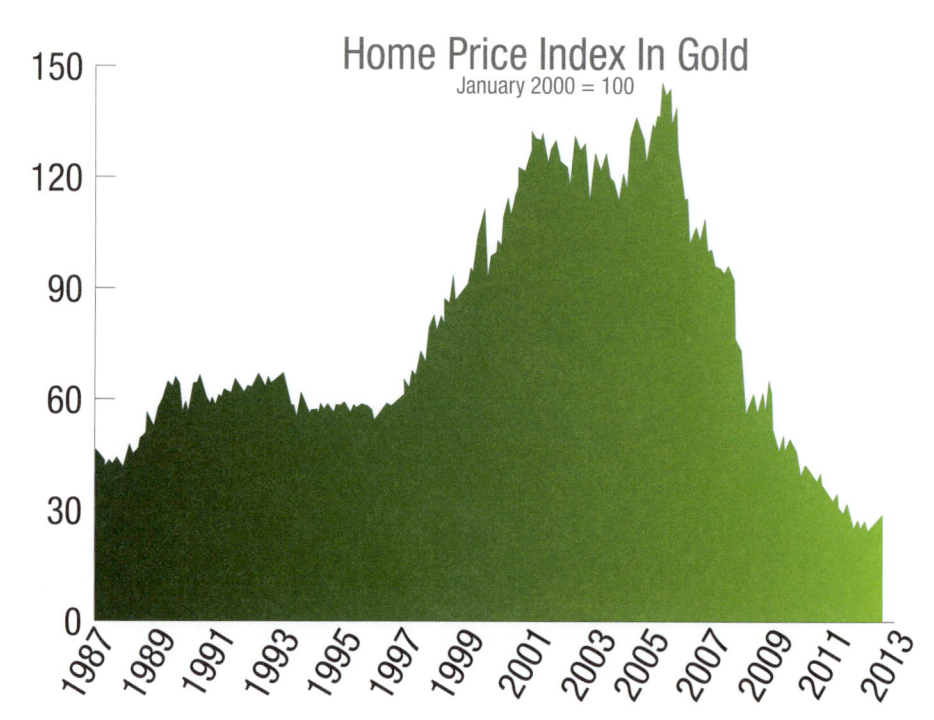

Home Price Index In Gold
January 2000 = 100

SOURCE CASE-SCHILLER

THREE OBVIOUS IMPLICATIONS

There are three implications for real estate that stem directly from the national debt situation.

1. Zombie Apocalypse

The first obvious implication is that, as those on the extremes of the issue fear, we will have a total economic collapse. Under that scenario it is unlikely that any of us would care all that much about the housing market, as we'll have Greek-style social unrest caused by currency collapse. As happened in Argentina after its currency collapsed, we'll be more concerned about rechargeable batteries, antibiotics, food, gasoline and ammunition.

2. Home Prices Will Rise in the Near Term

Assuming that the U.S. doesn't devolve into a full-blown zombie apocalypse scenario, the second implication of high inflation is that home prices will rise. In fact, the 2012 rise in home prices—usually reported as a recovery in the housing market—may be attributable almost entirely to fears of inflation.

Consider this chart of U.S. home prices; the Case-Shiller Home Price Index, expressed in ounces of gold. It is an extended analysis of house prices data going back to 1890, reflecting that the value of a house is actually below what it was in 1890 if priced in gold.

The very high investor activity in real estate in recent years is normally explained as the result of low prices, rental income and the like. NAR Chief Economist Lawrence Yun said investors with cash took advantage of market conditions in 2011.

"During the past year investors have been swooping into the market to take advantage of bargain home prices. Rising rental income easily beat cash sitting in banks as an added inducement. In addition, 41 percent of investment buyers purchased more than one property."

However, the other half of the equation that makes real estate an attractive investment is the lack of alternatives for people with money. There is absolutely no point in holding cash that pays 0.01 percent interest, nor is there any point in investing in a bond that pays less than inflation. The purchasing power that the investor seeks is constantly eroded.

Commodities and other actual physical goods become far more attractive simply as a holder of economic value if nothing else. Fear of inflation and dollar devaluation explains the incredible rise in prices of precious metals, and the near-constant advertising by gold and silver merchants on cable TV and radio stations. It also explains the incredible investor appetite for bricks, mortar and land.

There is, however, a bonus for real estate investors.

3. Renter Nation

If the short-term consequence of debt is a rise in house prices (at least in dollar terms if not in purchasing power terms), and the long-term consequence of debt crisis is currency collapse, then the medium-term consequence will absolutely be a reduction in buyer demand for real estate; except by investors.

The primary reason is that interest rates have to go up once the money printing stops. They have to go up or risk collapse of confidence in the dollar, which would lead to outright hyperinflation and the resulting social unrest. But, since we are assuming that the zombie apocalypse scenario will not come to pass, the only other alternative is that rates will go up as the Treasury will be forced to offer higher rates to attract investors other than the Federal Reserve.

Since the employment picture, even with recent announcements of new jobs being created, still remains bleak, there is also little reason to believe that actual employment will grow as sharply as needed for real economic growth. The salaries of even those employed are unlikely to keep pace with the rising interest rates, especially as inflation on everyday items—including food and fuel—eats away at disposable income.

At today's historically low interest rates, the "rent vs. buy" tilts in favor of buyers in many markets. But begin to increase the interest rate and that tilts in the other direction as monthly payments resulting from a home purchase—the key number for the consumer—increase. Many landlords, however, own their property outright or on a low fixed-rate mortgage and don't need to raise rents dramatically to earn a return.

As a result of higher mortgage rates there will be significantly higher rental demand and significantly lower buyer demand, assuming credit loosens up, which is unlikely as detailed below. In the medium term home prices will fall even in dollar terms.

THE POLITICS OF REAL ESTATE: TRENDS IN GOVERNMENT POLICY

The 2012 elections were, on the surface, a vote for the status quo. Obama won re-election, the Democrats held the Senate but did not get enough seats for the filibuster-proof majority and the Republicans kept the House. By the time you read this, Congress would have acted (*or not*) on the "fiscal cliff" that was approaching at the end of 2012. All that is known as we go to print is that

> The Federal Reserve can't spark a recovery in the housing market by itself because mortgage rates don't predict where home prices are going.
>
> **Robert Shiller**
> Yale University – Case-Shiller Home Price Index

Speaker of the House John Boehner agreed to new taxes "under the right circumstances" the day after the election.

As the exploration of the issue of national debt makes clear, at the heart of the debt crisis is the mismatch between revenues and spending. The proper balance between the two may be the subject of partisan bickering all across the country, but it is clear that monetary policy by the Fed cannot kick the can down the road much longer.

According to the Voice of America News (voanews.com), the Chairman of the Federal Reserve, Ben Bernanke, has warned recently that Congress and the President must get their act together:

- The U.S. central bank chief is pressing Congress to control the government's chronic deficit-ridden spending.
- U.S. lawmakers must soon find ways to put the federal budget on a sustainable path, but not so abruptly as to endanger the country's sluggish economic recovery. Congress and the White House will have to resolve the country's impending "fiscal cliff," a series of sharp spending cuts and tax increases set to take effect in January unless the lawmakers reach a compromise on a new economic path.

- Analysts agree that if Congress does not resolve the issue, "it would likely throw the economy back into a recession." Republican and Democrat lawmakers have long been at odds over the government's annual deficits, adding to a growing long-term debt that totals $16 trillion.

The connection between the fiscal decisions of the political branches and the monetary policy decisions of the Fed is little understood. It is often subject to debate and opaque but it's important for our purposes to delve into it briefly.

FISCAL DECISIONS VS. MONETARY POLICY

Normally, fiscal policy and monetary policy would go hand in hand in managing the economy. Government spending—including the critical elements of government employment, transfer programs like Social Security and general spending on what the government needs, whether fighter jets or low-income housing units—is a large part of the American economy. Monetary policy controls the supply of money in the economy, manipulating the interest rates and inflation (value of the money itself). The two are related, but remotely in normal circumstances.

The main issue today is that monetary policy appears to be driven by fiscal policy. The government of the U.S. can't afford to have its checks bounce. The retiree who goes

1993
Property listings become publically available on the web
Worldwide Web goes mainstream when it is offered free to everyone

1994
Amazon.com is founded
Clinton becomes President

1995
HFS (now Realogy) enters real estate with acquisition of Century 21
Realtor.com goes live

1997
First Harry Potter novel released
Realtor.com posts one millionth real estate listing

1998
House impeaches President Clinton
Google is founded
First transaction management systems introduced into real estate

1999
Existing home sales top 5 million for the first time ever
Warren Buffet enters real estate and HomeServices of America is formed
Gramm-Leach-Bliley Act repeals Glass Steagall Act deregulates banking industry

2001
Terrorists destroy World Trade Towers on 9/11
Economic recession follows stock market meltdown

2002
American Idol airs

2004
NAR membership surpasses 1 million for the first time
Homeownership rate peaks at all time high of 69.2%
Facebook is launched

to deposit a Social Security check can't have the bank reject it for insufficient funds; the paychecks for the armed forces must clear and so on. The entire economy, and quite possibly social order itself, would collapse if the checks of the United States of America were no good.

But deficit spending by definition means that the expenses are higher than income. As any family or business would do in such a situation, the government must borrow the money it doesn't have so that its checks will clear. But, like the family or business, there comes a time when it can no longer borrow.

The 61 percent purchase of U.S. Treasuries by the Fed essentially means that the Fed is making sure that the checks of the federal government will clear. And they accomplish this by printing money, a power it has through the grant from the federal government. In the long run—and the length of the "long run" is subject to partisan debate—simply printing more will devalue the money. It's a simple fact of supply and demand. Devaluation of money, of course, is another way of saying inflation.

The Fed has explicitly committed to supporting the housing market with its current stance toward stimulating the economy. QE3 specifically aims at buying enormous amounts of mortgage-backed securities, for example, and the last Fed meeting made it clear that it intends to support the nascent recovery in housing:

- The Fed will buy $40 billion in mortgage securities each month until the jobs outlook improves; a significant expansion of its stimulus campaign. It also intends to keep short-term interest rates near zero at least until mid-2015.
- The new policy is aimed specifically at helping the housing market by reducing interest rates on mortgage loans. The more people that buy homes the greater the benefit to the housing market and to the economy in general.

However, the concern is that the Fed will not be able to keep doing this if inflation becomes a real issue. If it can't keep printing money without the price of basic goods like food, clothing and iPods going through the roof (there are signs of inflation in the general economy today), then it will have to rein in all of the purchases of various financial instruments.

The problem is that the government's need to have its checks clear will not go away until deficit spending is eliminated. And there is

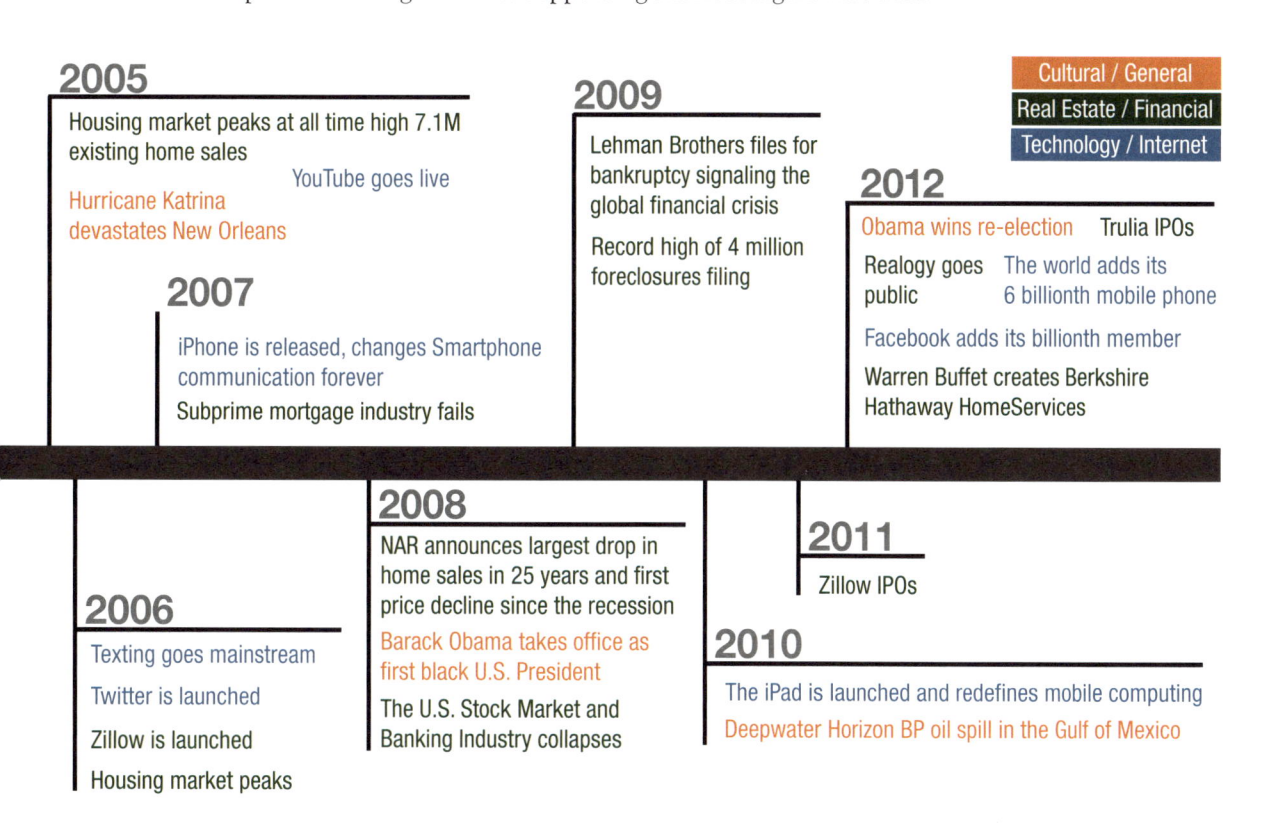

2005
Housing market peaks at all time high 7.1M existing home sales
YouTube goes live
Hurricane Katrina devastates New Orleans

2006
Texting goes mainstream
Twitter is launched
Zillow is launched
Housing market peaks

2007
iPhone is released, changes Smartphone communication forever
Subprime mortgage industry fails

2008
NAR announces largest drop in home sales in 25 years and first price decline since the recession
Barack Obama takes office as first black U.S. President
The U.S. Stock Market and Banking Industry collapses

2009
Lehman Brothers files for bankruptcy signaling the global financial crisis
Record high of 4 million foreclosures filing

2010
The iPad is launched and redefines mobile computing
Deepwater Horizon BP oil spill in the Gulf of Mexico

2011
Zillow IPOs

2012
Obama wins re-election
Trulia IPOs
Realogy goes public
The world adds its 6 billionth mobile phone
Facebook adds its billionth member
Warren Buffet creates Berkshire Hathaway HomeServices

Legend: Cultural / General | Real Estate / Financial | Technology / Internet

From the Vault: Swanepoel TRENDS Report (2006)

As a result of the market downturn several hundred thousand new licensees will leave the industry. For many the gravy train has come to an end and real estate professionals will have to accept that more of them will be fighting for fewer transactions; transactions carrying a lower commission. Professionals that are committed to being successful will have to take their career much more seriously.

no sign whatsoever that we will cut over $1 trillion from federal spending overnight or take in another $1 trillion in tax revenues. If the Fed has to make a decision between buying more Mortgage Backed Securities (MBS) to prop up the real estate industry or buying Treasuries to make sure that the federal government has money in its bank account, there is no doubt which it would choose.

At the end of the day, for real estate, the key decisions will be fiscal rather than monetary. The political branches, not the Fed, will ultimately decide on how to deal with the $16 trillion in debt and the $1.1 trillion in deficit spending.

There are, however, some real issues in terms of fiscal policy actually reducing the debt, even if the president's second term brings more cooperation from the House Republicans.

Limitations on Fiscal Policy

Federal spending falls into three main categories:

1. **Mandatory spending** – includes entitlements such as Medicare, Social Security and certain other payments that are required by law. In FY 2011 mandatory spending totaled $2.0 trillion.

2. **Discretionary spending** – constitutes most of what we think of as "government"—i.e., the armed forces, the FBI, TSA, salaries of government workers, purchasing programs whether of weapons or supplies for FEMA, Department of Education, the national parks, Air Force One, etc. In FY 2011 discretionary spending totaled $1.3 trillion.

3. **Interest payments on the outstanding debt** – must be paid. Nonpayment means default, which would instantly trigger an economic crisis as it would mean that the U.S. is a deadbeat. In FY 2011 interest payments totaled $454.4 billion.

The important point here is that interest payments and mandatory spending *cannot be touched* by Congress without either defaulting on the debt for the former or writing new laws changing entitlement legislation. Only the discretionary spending of $1.3 trillion is subject to any deals between the Republican House and the Democrat Senate and the Administration.

Here's the problem. Revenues in FY 2011 totaled $2.3 trillion but after making the legally required payments under mandatory spending and the impossible to avoid interest payments on the debt, the U.S. was in the hole for roughly $154.4 billion. Even if the President and Congress cut the entirety of the discretionary budget—what we all think of as government—the deficit would still have been $154.4 billion.

Since Senate Majority Leader Harry Reid has made clear that Social Security won't be touched, repealing entitlement reform does not appear to be on the agenda for 2013 at the very least. So what might be on the table? Higher taxes, of course, at least for high-income earners, since President Obama ran on that platform and Speaker Boehner agreed to it in principle. What else?

LOSING FAITH IN HOUSING

So now we come to the signature trend for real estate. Over the past few years it is evident that the elites have lost faith in housing and by extension have misgivings in the longstanding policy of the U.S. to encourage and support homeownership (read more on the government's support or lack thereof in Trend #8 – Is The Government for or Against

Homeownership?).

A review of academic literature on housing, housing economics and government support for housing shows a sharp departure from the overall supportive narrative pre-Bubble and post-Bubble. For the sake of space we limit the evidence to three prominent and influential think tanks and the words and actions of actual policymakers.

The left-leaning Center for American Progress (americanprogress.org) came out with its plan for housing reform; *A Responsible Market for Housing Finance*. It recommends, among other things, abolishing Fannie Mae (fanniemae.com) and Freddie Mac (freddiemac.com) and creating Chartered Mortgage Institutions backed by the explicit guarantee of the U.S. government. The details are interesting and worth reading, but this paragraph under the heading "Time for Reform" is the most relevant for us (emphasis added):

- Shortly, housing and finance policymakers in the Obama administration and on Capitol Hill will be deep in debate about how to reform the nation's housing finance system, which imploded by the fall of 2008 and is now functional only because the government effectively guarantees about 90 percent of all new mortgages. Major reforms are necessary, both to rein in the systemic risks to our housing and financial markets that became apparent over the past decade, and to recalibrate the balance between homeownership and rental housing. These reforms will have enormous impacts on U.S. households.

On the political right, we have the American Enterprise Institute (aei.org) with its major position paper in 2011: *Taking the Government Out of Housing Finance: Principles for Reforming the Housing Finance Market*. The white paper starts with this:

- Given the spectacular failures of U.S. housing finance and the enormous cost to taxpayers of two massive bailouts in twenty years, the housing industry should be required to show why it needs government support again. No other developed country provides anything that approaches the support for housing provided by the U.S. government, and—as shown below—many of these other systems produce higher homeownership rates, lower mortgage interest rates and fewer losses when defaults occur.

Even in the middle, among centrist libertarian types, government support for housing is being questioned if not opposed outright. Reason Foundation (reason.org), a think tank that calls itself libertarian, released a white paper in 2010 called *Rethinking Homeownership: A Framework for 21st Century Housing Finance Reform*. In it they take this position under the heading "What is the Role for Government in Housing Finance:"

- The role for government in the housing finance system is to support a legal structure for private sector financing of mortgages, and to enforce laws and regulations that ensure the market is a fair field for competition. However, there should be no federal government (i.e., American taxpayer) dollars available to support housing finance on a market-wide basis.

Journalists have also done their part post-Bubble to undermine the idea of homeownership. Here's a prime example from Time (time.com), which published an article called *The Case Against Homeownership* in 2010:

- For the better part of a century, politics, industry and culture aligned to create a fetish of the idea of buying a house. Homeownership has done plenty of good over the decades; it has provided stability to tens of millions of families and anchored a labor-intensive sector of the economy. Yet by idealizing the

> We see people being very sensitive to the cost of money; they're very concerned about the debt crisis, they're very concerned about all these rumors that the U.S. could have a money supply problem, so we think that interest rates are the real X factor to watch.
>
> **Glenn Kelman**
> CEO Redfin

act of buying a home, we have ignored the downsides. In the bubble years, lending standards slipped dramatically, allowing many Americans to put far too much of their income into paying for their housing. And we ignored longer-term phenomena too. Homeownership contributed to the hollowing out of cities and kept renters out of the best neighborhoods. It fed America's overuse of energy and oil. It made it more difficult for those who had lost a job to find another. Perhaps worst of all, it helped us become casually self-deceiving: by telling ourselves that homeownership was a pathway to wealth and stable communities and better test scores, we avoided dealing with these formidable issues head-on.

It is small wonder, then, with the elites having lost faith in the idea of federal support for homeownership that the policymakers have also soured on homeownership. Even the CAP proposal, which is the most supportive of government action, wants to rebalance homeownership and rental housing.

In 2011, Treasury and HUD (hud.gov) released a joint report to congress entitled *Reforming America's Housing Finance Market*. Several quotes from the introduction are an eerie echo of the positions of the think tanks and academics:

- Our plan champions the belief that Americans should have choices in housing that make sense for them and for their families. This means rental options near good schools and good jobs. It means access to credit for those Americans who want to own their own home, which has helped millions of middle class families build wealth and achieve the American Dream. And it means a helping hand for lower-income Americans, who are burdened by the strain of high housing costs.

- But our plan also dramatically transforms the role of government in the housing market. In the past, the government's financial and tax policies encouraged housing purchases and real estate investment over other sectors of our economy, and ultimately left taxpayers responsible for much of the risk incurred by a poorly supervised housing finance market.

- Going forward, the government's primary role should be limited to robust oversight and consumer protection, targeted assistance for low- and moderate-income homeowners and renters, and carefully designed support for market stability and crisis response. Our plan helps ensure that our nation's economic health will not be jeopardized again by the fundamental flaws in the housing market that existed before the financial crisis. At the same time, this plan recognizes the fragile state of our housing market and is designed to ensure that reforms are implemented at a stable and measured pace to support economic recovery over the next several years.

- Under our plan, private markets—subject to strong oversight and standards for consumer and investor protection—will be the primary source of mortgage credit and bear the burden for losses. Banks and other financial institutions will be required to hold more capital to withstand future recessions or significant declines in home prices, and adhere to more conservative underwriting standards that require homeowners to hold

> **Would Congress and the second-term President really agree to slash spending on education, the military, the federal workforce and so on while maintaining federal support for housing? Time will tell, but the trends are not good.**
>
> **Rob Hahn**
> Notorious Rob

more equity in their homes.

And we know that as far back as 2008 Bernanke advocated for something called "sustainable homeownership." It isn't precisely clear what that phrase means, but it is safe to say that whatever it means it's something different than the "unsustainable homeownership" of the variety that policies of the past pursued.

One hint of where the policymakers are is the Qualified Residential Mortgage (QRM) rule, required by the Dodd-Frank Wall Street Reform and Consumer Protection Act of 2011. As is somewhat typical for regulations, the details of just how this rule would work are complex. But the bottom line is that QRM would significantly raise the down-payment requirement for mortgages to between 10 and 20 percent.

The National Association of REALTORS® has made broadening the QRM as much as possible one of its legislative priorities. NAR suggests that QRM, as currently written, tightens lending standards that are already too tight:

NAR has taken issue with Qualified Mortgage (QM) and QRM as proposed, because they would lock in rigid and overly tight down payments and debt-to-income ratios, and limit lenders' flexibility in providing reasonably priced loans to borrowers with less-than-stellar credit profiles. QM sets underwriting standards to ensure lenders only make loans to borrowers who have the ability to repay them, and QRM sets additional standards for loans that are securitized for sale to investors. For securitized loans that don't meet QRM, lenders have to hold back 5 percent of the value of the loans on their books, making them prohibitively expensive for borrowers.

Another hint is contained in the report of the National Commission on Fiscal Responsibility and Reform (Simpson-Bowles Commission). While the report's recommendations were ultimately rejected during the 2012 campaigns, both candidates picked elements of the plan during the recent election cycle. The Plan recommended that the mortgage interest deduction (MID) be sharply limited. First, it would only apply to the principal residence. Second, it would be capped at $500,000.

NAR went to war to defend the MID and when the Plan was shelved it was seen as a victory. But, while the Plan itself never went anywhere, the fact that the members of the Commission actually put the proposal forward is significant in and of itself as an indicator of elite sentiment about housing and housing support.

Yet another important sign comes from the Fair Housing Administration (FHA; fha.gov). FHA loans, with their low 3.5 percent down payment and lower credit rating requirements, have soared in popularity since 2008. FHA loans make up 30 percent of all originations, in some markets going as high as 50 percent of all mortgages. But, the FHA has been wanting out of the game and has tightened its requirements as well as lowering its loan limits.

And so we come to where the rubber meets the road.

Taken all together these reports, rules, proposed regulations and promulgated regulations suggest that it is a matter of time and necessity that government support of housing must be sharply curtailed. What it all adds up to is the fact that:

- Elite sentiment has turned against government support of housing.
- The fiscal situation appears insoluble, given the level of mandatory spending and interest payments.

The Cliff

TAX INCREASES
ELIMINATE 2001 AND 2003 TAX CUTS FOR AMERICANS WITH INCOMES BELOW $250,000
COST TO ECONOMY
$174 BILLION

ALTERNATIVE MINIMUM TAX IS NOT ADJUSTED FOR INFLATION
COST TO ECONOMY
$59 BILLION

SOCIAL SECURITY TAX CUT ENDS
COST TO ECONOMY
$100 BILLION

ELIMINATE 2001 AND 2003 TAX CUTS FOR AMERICANS WITH INCOMES OVER $250,000
COST $40 BILLION

SPENDING CUTS
ACROSS-THE-BOARD CUTS TAKE EFFECT
COST TO ECONOMY
$105 BILLION

EMERGENCY UNEMPLOYMENT BENEFITS
COST TO ECONOMY
$58 BILLION

WE ARE HERE

HOW OUR ECONOMY COULD END UP DOWN THERE
Each tax increase or spending cut in the fiscal cliff will take money out of the U.S. economy. Here's how they are estimated to reduce GDP in 2013:

- AFFORDABLE CARE ACT TAXES TAKE EFFECT $9 BILLION
- ELIMINATE VARIOUS TAX CREDITS $4 BILLION
- BUSINESSES LOSE BONUS DEPRECIATION $2 BILLION
- MEDICARE PAYMENTS TO DOCTORS REDUCED $9 BILLION

3.6% DECLINE IN GDP OR $560 BILLION

SOURCE © USATODAY
Courtesy of USATODAY

- There is very little sign of political compromise.
- Monetary policy is reaching the end of the road of what it can do.

The so-called fiscal cliff of 2012, along with the inevitable debate about raising the debt ceiling sometime in 2013, will put the federal government's commitment to support housing and homeownership to the test.

Since entitlement reform appears to be off the table, especially after the 2012 elections, there will be a struggle over discretionary spending. Funding the GSEs (Fannie Mae and Freddie Mac) is a discretionary spending item. Funding the FHA is a discretionary spending item. The MID is discretionary as well.

Would Congress and the second-term President really agree to slash spending on education, the military, the federal workforce and so on while maintaining federal support for housing? Time will tell, but the trends are not good.

SUMMARY

There are, then, three major implications for real estate:

1. There is a rising risk that monetary policy will be unable to keep interest rates down. There will come a point, absent significant fiscal reforms which are simply not on the horizon today, that the Fed will find itself unable to flood the markets with as much money as it would like to at the prevailing interest rates. Since mortgage rates and yields tend to move in tandem with 10-year Treasury bonds, a rise in the 10-year note would likely mean a rise in the mortgage rate.

2. In the fiscal arena, given the disposition of academics, journalists, think tanks, policymakers and the overall policy elite towards housing—and given how broad-based those views are across the political spectrum—there is a significant likelihood that housing subsidies will not be prioritized over other kinds of spending. Any serious conflict between allocating budget between housing and Medicare, for example, will be resolved in favor of the latter. And the size of the national debt and the historically high rate of deficit spending ensure that this conflict will happen sooner rather than later.

3. Given the changes in elite opinion towards government support of housing, future reforms are likely to focus not on encouraging homeownership but on encouraging access to housing—affordable rentals. Policy proposals such as capping the QRM or eliminating the MID, lower FHA loan limits further, etc. are likely to be more prevalent than less in future years.

All of these trends point to a fall in buyer demand coupled with a rise in rental demand. Even if everyone *wants* to buy a home, their *ability* to do so will be curtailed. The federal government appears likely to want to steer policy in this direction. Even "if" it wanted to stay the course, the mathematics of $16 trillion in debt makes that a dubious proposition.

This all has game-changing implications for residential real estate today.

Swanepoel TRENDS Report 2013

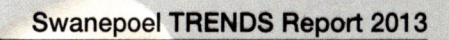

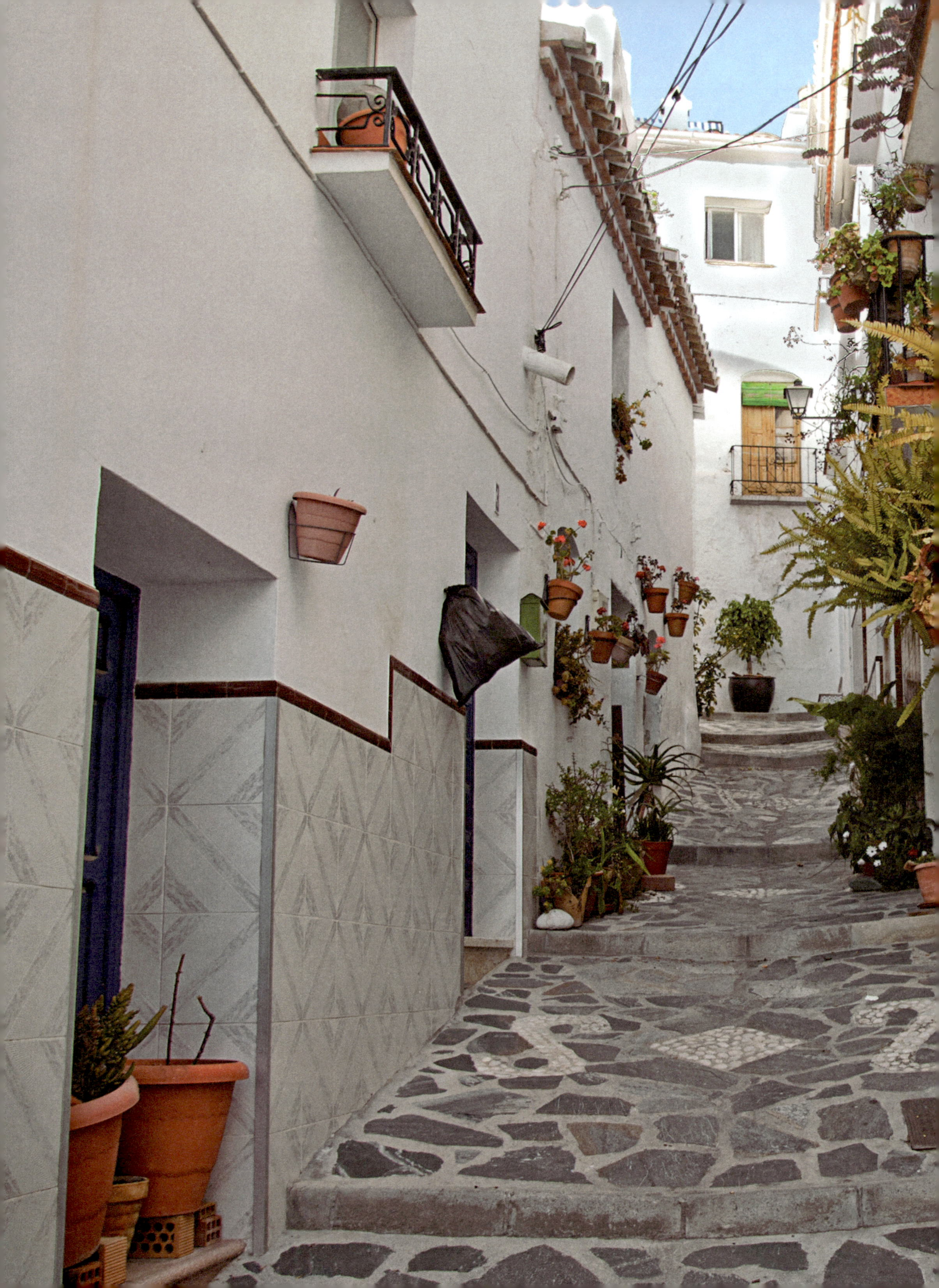

8 Rescuing Homeownership
Is the Government for or Against It?

Rescuing Homeownership

In this Chapter we explore the government's historic role in growing homeownership, look at those policies that brought us to this point and consider what's next on the government's agenda for the real estate industry and what that means.

In the 1980s a great deal of capital was being utilized in financing housing as many Americans no longer primarily viewed housing as shelter but rather as an instrument to accumulate capital and protect themselves against inflation, making housing the portfolio of choice. But when the market collapsed the results of that investment philosophy rippled back down *to impact the basic concept of homeownership.*

Since 2006 housing prices have fallen with some 40 percent in most areas (CoreLogic; corelogic.com) and millions of homeowners are now faced with substantial negative equity; estimated at 30 percent. According to the latest Census Bureau data (census.gov), homeownership in the United States of America in 2012 dropped to 65.4 percent, the lowest level in 15 years. Back in the 1990s residential mortgage debt was around 40 percent of gross domestic product (GDP). With the housing bubble it ballooned to 75 percent in 2007, and although it has subsided the last few years it is still at a high 60 percent.

So, as we delve into this issue we first need to take a brief look at the government policies that played a huge role in bringing us to this point.

SLIPPERY SLOPE
The "affordable housing" (AH) goals imposed on Fannie Mae (fanniemae.com) and Freddie Mac (freddiemac.com) in 1992 were major contributors to both the decline of underwriting standards and the resulting ten-year housing bubble that covered up delinquencies and stimulated the growth of a private securitization market for subprime loans.

Homeowners, like financial institutions, became highly leveraged. Government policies encouraged equity stripping through refinancing without prepayment penalty and low interest rates that, when fed by a hot market, encouraged cash-out refinancing and flipping. For example, in the three years between 2003 and 2005 the total withdrawal of equity was $1.1 billion. And when the market slowed and prices dipped, homeowners went under water and the debt burden crippled the housing market.

In a little over 20 years these faulty housing policies have been disastrous and the exploding federal debt (see Trend #9 – The Fiscal Cliff) has now forced tax reform to center stage with real estate industry clearly in the cross hairs of government taxation policies.

GOVERNMENT POLICIES
There is a long history of federal involvement in homeownership. In fact, a report by the American Enterprise Institute (aei.org) notes that the U.S. is the only large developed county in the world in which the government plays a significant role in housing. Therefore it's important to note several key policies that were

instituted that set the stage for the increase in U.S. homeownership and the bubble.

The GSE Act

The GSE Act (Government Sponsored Enterprises) of 1992 resulted in a number of changes that contributed to the degradation of the underwriting standards for the traditional mortgage. Through this act Fannie and Freddie were given specific affordable housing quotas. The initial goal was for 30 percent of their mortgage purchases to be loans made to low and middle-income families. During the Clinton administration that goal was increased to 50 percent and in 2008 the Bush administration further raised it to 56 percent. But the unintended consequence was that in order to achieve the increasing quotas they had to continually seek loans of less than prime quality.

By 2000 they were acquiring loans that had no down payment requirement at all; effectively opening the door to low credit scores, high debt and unverified income. In point of fact, it resulted in there effectively being no difference between prime and non-prime mortgages. The goal of using non-prime mortgages to increase the level of homeownership was achieved but the cost came in major losses in the ensuing years. By 2008 the government held or insured 74 percent of the non-prime mortgagees that defaulted in huge numbers, giving rise to the mortgage meltdown. And because government policy enabled the GSEs to dominate the market they became the standard setters, effectively lowering the standards for the industry.

Relaxed Standards

In 1997 the government changed the tax code to allow a married couple to live in a home for two years and then sell it without paying tax on the first $500,000 of capital gain, ushering in increased speculation in the housing market. At the same time the government's social policy ignored the risk—it's not afraid of losses—and advanced the bubble by relaxing its underwriting standards; homeownership rose to a high of 69 percent in 2004.

By 2006, 20 percent of all mortgages were subprime and investors were growing fond of the high yields offered by private mortgage-backed securities (PMBS). But by 2007 credit standards could not be degraded further and the market dried up, delinquencies rose, default rates increased and the inevitable collapse of market followed. It was the government's investment in over 20 million subprime loans that fed the bubble and its policies that drew in the private sector.

Appraisals and Automated Underwriting

Another change brought about by the GSEs, in an effort to achieve the government's mandate of increased homeownership, was the relaxation of appraisal standards. No longer were "replacement cost" and "rental value" a part of the appraisal process; only "comparable value" was used. As they dominated the market this change also became the accepted market standard. Therefore, if originators wanted to sell to Fannie and Freddie they no longer needed to use their costly appraisal process. In a rising market those appraisal errors were hidden, but when the market declined those errors were highlighted and homeowners wound up with the negative equity.

A further area in which their domination brought about change was automated underwriting. This change reduced underwriting standards and it had a wide impact as originators followed suit—why waste money on more stringent standards if Fannie and Freddie didn't use

> There is a longstanding American emphasis on home ownership that has gone to extremes. It is something that encourages people to take on a lot of mortgage debt. To be frank, mortgage debt isn't as popular as it used to be.
>
> Donald B. Marron
> Director, Urban-Brookings Tax Policy Center

them. This change also fed the GSEs' requirement to meet their affordable housing goals and therefore their automated systems were adjusted to incorporate more mortgages that met those goals. Originators followed suit and identified those loans that would meet the GSEs' requirements—enter "robo signing."

These are excellent examples of housing policies instituted by the government to affect their stated affordable housing goals, which did so by increasing the number of subprime mortgages to feed the growing PMBS market. In addition, as the market went up many Americans jumped on the "flipping" bandwagon while others took advantage of the rising market and withdrew home equity. In the process Americans incurred massive debt that would come back in the form of today's negative equity nightmare and a distressed property market with a huge shadow inventory that has yet to be effectively dealt with; all as the ultimate result of the government's drive to expand homeownership to "all" Americans.

WHAT'S AT STAKE TODAY?
In an effort to generate the funds required to meet America's increasing debt the Obama administration established the National Commission on Fiscal Responsibility and Reform (Simpson/Bowles) in 2010 to "identify policies to improve the fiscal situation in the medium term and achieve fiscal sustainability over the long run." The commission proposed five steps in addressing its recommendations:

1. Reduce discretionary spending
2. Increase tax revenues
3. Control healthcare
4. Reduce entitlements
5. Modify Social Security.

What's at stake for the real estate industry falls under category 2.

The government's proposed 2013 fiscal budget reflects the emphasis on tax reform in the context of "deficit reduction" by increasing taxes. On the table are a range of options including the expiration of the Bush-era tax cuts and the elimination or modification of a number of tax breaks such as the exclusion for employer-provided health insurance, the deduction for charitable contributions and benefits for low and middle income families and children like the earned income tax credit (EITC) and child tax credit. And high on the list are a number of changes that will have a direct impact on homeownership and the real estate industry. Here are the government's plans that will affect homeownership.

Itemized Deductions
Itemized deductions allow the reduction of taxable income by deducting amounts greater than the standard deduction. This includes things such as charitable deductions, mortgage interest (detailed below), state income taxes, property taxes, medical expenses, etc. These deductions are generally more valuable to upper income taxpayers—as defined by government—because the effect on tax liability is greater the higher the tax bracket. In the 2013 budget proposal the value of itemized deductions for those upper income taxpayers—single taxpayers with an adjusted gross income (AGI) of $200,000 and couples with an AGI of $250,000—would be capped at 28 percent.

Long Term Capital Gains
As of 2003 the long-term capital gains tax has been 15 percent for those in the 15 percent and above brackets and 10 percent for those in the 10 percent bracket. However, since 2008 taxpayers in the 10 and 15 percent brackets have paid no capital gains tax, but in 2013 those rates are scheduled to revert to their pre-2003

> The mortgage interest deduction is one of the pillars of our national housing policy, and limiting its use will have negative repercussions for consumers and home values up and down the housing chain.
>
> Chairman, Mortgage Bankers Association

levels. This means for all taxpayers in the 15 percent bracket and below those long-term gains would be taxed at 10 percent. For single taxpayers with an AGI below $200,000, head of households below $225,000 and joint couples below $250,000 the rate would remain at 15 percent. The taxpayers above these amounts would incur a 20 percent rate.

Carried Interest

Currently a partner in a real estate partnership may receive an interest in future profits of the partnership (carried profits or interest) as compensation for performing services for the partnership. If the partnership earns a capital gain then the partner reports his share—the carried interest—as capital gain and is taxed accordingly. Under the proposed budget a partner's share of income would be taxed as ordinary income, regardless of the character of the income at the partnership level.

Investment Income Tax

Beginning January 1, 2013 a new Medicare Tax of 3.8 percent on some investment income will take place to fund the healthcare and Medicare overhaul plans. While its effect on home sales won't be as big as some think, it could have a big impact on investors. The tax will be applied on some (not all) income from interest, dividends, net rents and net capital gains. It will fall only on individuals with an AGI of $200,000 and couples with $250,000. However, these thresholds are not indexed for inflation so more taxpayers will be affected over time.

But certainly the most visible and highly contested of the proposed changes are those relating to the mortgage interest deduction.

Mortgage Interest Deduction

In 1913, to fuel postwar home buying, as part of the federal income tax Congress made all interest tax-deductible, including mortgage interest (MID). The MID subsequently became a home buying incentive and was until recently widely regarded as the cornerstone of U.S. housing policy. The Institute on Taxation and Economic Policy (itepnet.org) reported that in 2007 the use of the MID peaked with a total deduction of $491 billion. The estimate for 2012 is $131 billion; the decrease being attributed to the effects of high unemployment and foreclosure rates resulting in fewer homeowners taking the deduction. According to estimates by the Congressional Joint Committee on Taxation (JCT; jct.gov) it will total $464 billion from 2011 to 2015.

Over the years the MID has been seen as the third-largest tax break for those who itemize their deductions. It has also been singled out by politicians, economists and two presidential commissions as a huge source of potential revenue for the government. There have been a number of failed attempts in the past to have the MID limited or eliminated and once again the government is focused on it in the proposed 2013 budget as part of the president's deficit reduction plan.

Currently the deduction allows taxpayers to deduct interest paid on mortgages up to $1 million for first and second homes and up to $100,000 in home-equity loans. The proposal on the table at the moment to limit the value of itemized deductions to 28 percent for families determined to be "high-income" tax-payers hits directly at the MID.

THE DEBATE

The Arguments Against MID

The primary arguments for eliminating the MID are:

It Inflates Demand: Housing demand has been artificially inflated by years of policy favoritism. The MID gets capitalized into the price of the house, which benefits the Realtors® and home builders but not

---

From the Vault: Real Estate Confronts Reality (1997)

Will the real estate brokerage industry itself yield its longstanding position as the hub of the wheel for property transactions to other contenders.

the owner. It does more harm than good because this misallocation of capital is at the expense of other industries that create more national wealth.

It Bids Up Prices: The MID, along with other government housing subsidies, causes buyers to bid up home prices. Elimination of those benefits would make home ownership less attractive, therefore allowing home prices to decline.

It Only Benefits Upper Income Families: The MID only benefits those in the upper income brackets and has little value for lower and middle income families, those most likely to be on the borderline between rental and ownership. And because it is a tax deduction and not a tax credit it only benefits those who itemize deductions. The majority of lower income homeowners do not itemize deductions and therefore get hit the hardest.

It Does Not Benefit Renters: Renters and lower-income homeowners that do not itemize their deductions don't get the deduction. A more appropriate approach would be to cap the MID and distribute the savings in the form of credits for first-time homebuyers and renters, making housing affordable for a majority of American families.

It Negatively Impacts Investing: There should be equal tax treatment of housing and other forms of investment. Unequal tax treatment of housing encourages speculative behavior; increasing price volatility and negatively impacting productive forms of investment to the detriment of economic growth and stability.

It Has Associated Economic Costs: High homeownership rates impose economic costs. They lock workers into houses that can be tough to sell, especially in recessions, making it harder for them to move to find new jobs. Cities with high homeownership rates tend to lag behind other cities in job creation and earnings. Removal of the MID and other housing subsidies will help to lower the homeownership rate to a more reasonable level of 55 percent.

It Limits the Private Market: Without government interference the private market would offer homeowners the features they would find desirable: interest rate reductions for substantial down payments, limited refinancing and shorter amortization. The result would be more home equity, lower leverage, lower interest rates and greater stability in downturns.

It Encourages Refinancing: The MID encourages refinancing without penalty, enabling borrowers to restart another thirty-year fixed-rate mortgage term with low principal amortization in the early years. This is yet another contributor to high leverage and low equity in U.S. homes. At the same time it forces lenders to adjust their interest rates to all borrowers to reflect the volatility.

The Global Argument: The U.S. has one of the most subsidized housing finance systems in the world and yet in a 2010 comparison by the American Enterprise Institute it only ranked 17th in homeownership (67 percent). Twelve countries have achieved 70 percent or higher rates without government subsidies, thereby drawing into question the necessity for the deduction. Many other countries also allow banks to go after a borrower's personal assets in the event of foreclosure thereby encouraging higher home ownership rates.

These arguments are varied but underlying all of them is the issue of the inequality. The belief is that the MID disproportionally benefits the wealthy at the expense of lower income families, those who don't itemize deductions on their tax returns and those who rent. They contend that the MID only provides an incentive to live in more expensive homes.

The Arguments For MID
Homeownership has always been a foundational goal of America and

> **People view this as part of the social contract, as something that represents the American dream, Therefore any changes are changes to the property rights of homeowners.**
>
> Lawrence Yun
> Chief Economist, National

studies have consistently reported that the private and social benefits of homeownership have included: improved education for children, better neighborhoods, reduced crime and better health. It has also been an excellent path to wealth accumulation as the average net worth of a homeowner is more than 45 times that of the average renter.

The primary arguments in favor the MID include:

Homeowners Will Lose: NAR has gone on record estimating that if the MID is eliminated, all at once or over time, the result would be a reduction in home values of 15 percent with local property tax revenues following suit. The after-tax cost of housing would increase and there would be an accompanying decrease in the demand for housing. The lower demand would put pressure on housing prices and the consequential decline would result in losses for existing homeowners.

Renters Will Lose: The MID incentive has long been known as one of the most important benefits encouraging renters to become homeowners. Given the high share of interest payments these buyers will make in terms of their total monthly mortgage payment it follows that two-thirds of renters feel that the MID is very important. A further impact on renters will result from the loss of tax revenues for local governments, leaving them with two alternatives: raise taxes or cut services. The impact on renters will come in the form of increased rents as landlords will be forced to raise rents to cover the additional tax burden.

The Middle Class Will Lose: Trulia (trulia.com) reported that there are 75 million homeowners in the U.S. and 38.5 million of them (51 percent) take the deductions for mortgage interest and real estate taxes. The primarily benefit goes to middle class taxpayers with incomes between $50,000 and $200,000 according to a study by the National Association of Home Builders (nahb.com). Those earning less than $200,000 pay 43 percent of all income taxes but they receive 68 percent of the total benefit of the MID and 77 percent of the total benefit of the real estate tax deduction.

The MID is also often criticized for being regressive but the NAHB's information source (housingeconomics.com) reports that data from the Congressional JCT reveals just over 65 percent of families who use it earn less than $100,000 and 91 percent earn less than $200,000. With over 86 percent of all mortgage interest paid over the past decade being claimed as an itemized deduction the belief that few homeowners benefit from the MID because they take the standard deduction is invalid.

Household Net Worth Will Lose: According to HousingEconomics.com, federal data from the JCT indicate that every one percent decline in housing values reduces household net worth by $164 billion. A six percent decline in value would wipe out $1 trillion in household net worth. If valuation declined by the estimated eight percent resulting from the elimination of the MID, net worth would decline by more than $1.32 trillion; NAR's estimate of 15 percent would approach $2.5 trillion.

	Country	Rate
	Homeownership	
1	Singapore	89%
2	Spain	85%
3	Iceland	83%
4	Belgium	78%
5	Norway	77%
6	Portugal	76%
7	Luxembourg	75%
8	Ireland	75%
9	Chile	73%
10	Italy	72%
11	Israel	71%
12	Australia	70%
13	UK	68%
14	Canada	68%
15	Sweden	68%
16	New Zealand	68%
17	United States	67%
18	Japan	61%
19	Finland	59%
20	Czech Republic	59%
21	France	57%
22	Netherlands	57%
23	Austria	56%
24	Denmark	54%
25	Germany	46%

SOURCE ALEX POLLOCK, AMERICAN ENTERPRISE INSTITUTE 2010

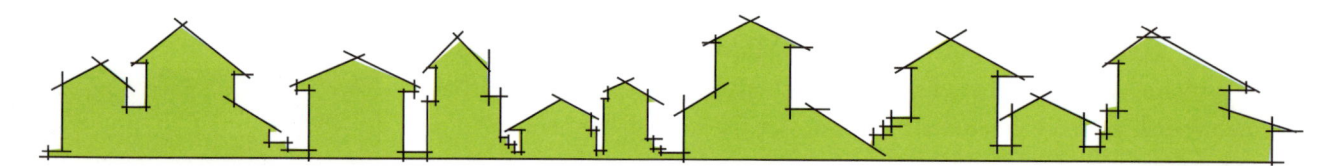

> Repeal (of the MID) would mostly pinch households with incomes between $75,000 and $200,000. It would put buyers at a disadvantage and create a new bias in the tax code that favors renting rather than owning your own home.
>
> John Weicher
> Director, Hudson Institute Center
> for Housing and Financial Markets

The Economy Will Lose: The loss of the MID will make it more difficult for families to obtain mortgages and will result in delaying their purchase. Since homeownership is a significant contributor to the national economy and generates millions of jobs, the loss of the deduction will further hinder recovery of the economy.

Americans Will Lose: A 2012 survey by Public Opinion Strategies (pos. org) and Lake Research Partners (lakeresearch.com) clearly revealed the voting public's opinion regarding the elimination of the MID.

Three out of four voters—owners and renters—believe that it is appropriate and reasonable for the federal government to provide tax incentives to promote homeownership; 84 percent of democrats, 71 percent of republicans and 71 percent of independents.

- Two-thirds say that the federal government should help homebuyers afford a long-term or 30-year fixed rate mortgage.

- Eliminating the MID was opposed by 73 percent of respondents and lowering the MID was opposed by 62 percent.

- 68 percent would be less likely to vote for a congressional candidate who proposed to abolish the MID.

- 78 percent said that owning a home is very important to them and 68 percent that do not own a home said their goal was to own a home.

The survey concluded in its bottom line: "There is little appetite for change to policies related to mortgage interest deductions."

The Global Argument: The premise that other countries whose governments don't subsidize homeownership have higher homeownership rates than the U.S. is misleading. Numerous conditions in foreign countries apply and it is the combination of the factors in play that create each respective country's unique circumstance, not just the MID:

- U.S. banks provide only about 20 to 25 percent of the credit for home purchases while in Europe it is closer to 75 to 80 percent.

- European mortgage markets generally have lower interest rates without government intervention, but they also have recourse to borrowers' assets in the event of foreclosure.

- Most other countries only offer adjustable rate mortgages (ARM) and rates are adjusted annually. The risk is with the borrower, not the bank.

- The majority of mortgages outside the U.S. have significant prepayment penalties.

- International underwriting standards tend to be much stricter than in the U.S., including higher required down payments (deposits).

Implementation of many of these conditions in the U.S. would disqualify or disenfranchise many homebuyers trying to purchase a home or homeowners trying to keep a mortgage.

However, these differences are not the only reason for the variance in homeownership levels. Germany, for example, is one of the richest countries and yet its homeownership rate is 42 percent. Bulgaria is one of the poorest and it has a homeownership rate of 98 percent. This is representative of those countries of the former Soviet Union, which have the highest rates of homeownership. These countries handed over ownership of public housing to those who were in occupancy when they instituted their economic reforms in the 90s.

On the other hand, it is generally the rule that the lowest rates are found in those countries with stronger economies. For example, the wealthier European countries tend to be highly urbanized, which means lower rates of homeownership. Large, dense cities generally have a much higher percentage of rentals.

So Whither MID?
What effect changing the MID would have on the housing market is the question at hand. It's hard to imagine that getting rid of it would be a net positive for housing. Certainly in the near term it would be negative and the impact would be severe in the midst of a depressed housing market and a stalled economy. In the broader sense it would mean less demand for the goods and services that support homeownership, thus rippling through the economy.

Eliminating or changing the MID would impact those who own homes to a greater extent than those who are new to the market. On average homeowners would get less for their house because prospective buyers would have to consider a higher down payment and how much of a mortgage payment they could afford; ultimately affecting what they could afford to pay—pushing down the purchase price.

The bottom line from our perspective: The MID, along with the other tax deductions, while perhaps being too politically sensitive

> If the deduction disappears, (home) values will go down. People who currently own houses will take a hit. They will not be worth as much as they are today, there's no way around it.
>
> Roberton Williams
> Tax Policy Center

to touch at the moment, will be revisited as part of any serious tax reform. With the arrival of the fiscal cliff along with the New Year that may be sooner rather than later. By the time you read this the answer may already be on the table.

SO IS THE GOVERNMENT IN FAVOR OF HOMEOWNERSHIP?
Historically government policies have been implemented with the sole purpose of increasing homeownership. As noted previously this is nowhere better reflected than in the guidelines given to Fannie Mae and Freddie Mac to lower their lending standards to accommodate the government's mandated goal of increasing homeownership among lower-income families; affordable housing. Unfortunately these lower standards, coupled with reduced appraisal requirements and automated underwriting, culminated in the huge number of subprime mortgages that were needed to feed the growing PMBS market, which was a major contributing cause of the bubble. Compounding the problem, Americans were encouraged to reduce the equity in their homes by taking advantage of low interest rates and lower lending standards; standards generally adopted by lenders to conform to Fannie and Freddie requirements. These policies led to borrowing on an unprecedented scale and what started as a government effort to improve the prospects for homeownership through a policy of "easy money" wound up with consequences that will leave many Americans economically strapped for years to come.

Based on the policies it has established one would have to conclude that the federal government was in favor of homeownership but approached it from a typical government perspective; they did not consider the consequences of their action on the market itself. Now it finds itself on the horns a dilemma. It desperately needs the real estate market to turn around as part of any meaningful recovery of the overall economy, but the action they are taking in the form of numerous government programs is stifling the market. The pendulum for underwriting standards has swung in the opposite direction and, coupled with the country's high unemployment rate, it has become almost impossible for existing homeowners to move up/out and new ones to move in.

One wonders why many of these policies that were instituted to prop up the market and the homeowner are still being maintained when results indicate that they have for the most part been a failure. Questions regarding their future and that of Fannie and Freddie, along with dealing with the shadow inventory, loom large. The Federal Housing Administration (FHA; fha.com)—the government's mortgage insurer—has also come under fire over its poor financial condition, having incurred billions of dollars in losses. Those losses forced Congress to pass the FHA Emergency Fiscal Solvency Act last September, which attempts to protect the FHA's cash reserves by creating minimum mortgage insurance premiums. But like many of the government's reactions it may be too little too late. If the housing market doesn't recover the FHA could be forced "over the cliff" as well.

There is also considerable discussion regarding moving the government's REOs into the rental market. If the government's goal of affordable housing was lost in the bubble and is now being abandoned, does that mean the emphasis is now focused on renters? In light of the current market conditions—a hot rental market—has the goal been shifted to deal with the REO issue by shifting the focus on the investor and the renter by changing the rules?

The November elections would seem to indicate that there will be no major change in the direction the government has taken. However, if there is an increased emphasis on turning to real estate for additional tax revenue—justified by balancing support for renters—then we can expect the move to reduce or eliminate real estate's tax advantages

Is the Government With Us or Against Us?

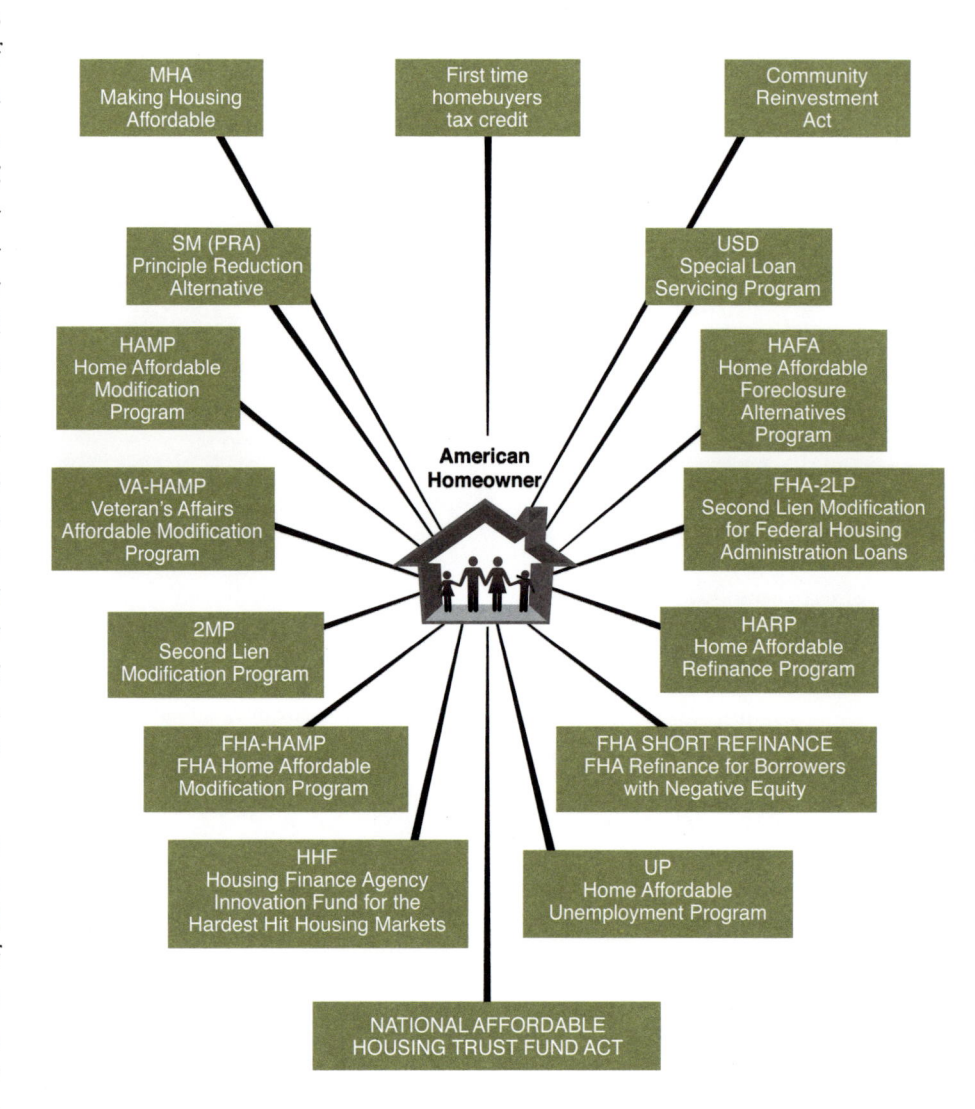

- MHA — Making Housing Affordable
- First time homebuyers tax credit
- Community Reinvestment Act
- SM (PRA) — Principle Reduction Alternative
- USD — Special Loan Servicing Program
- HAMP — Home Affordable Modification Program
- HAFA — Home Affordable Foreclosure Alternatives Program
- VA-HAMP — Veteran's Affairs Affordable Modification Program
- FHA-2LP — Second Lien Modification for Federal Housing Administration Loans
- 2MP — Second Lien Modification Program
- HARP — Home Affordable Refinance Program
- FHA-HAMP — FHA Home Affordable Modification Program
- FHA SHORT REFINANCE — FHA Refinance for Borrowers with Negative Equity
- HHF — Housing Finance Agency Innovation Fund for the Hardest Hit Housing Markets
- UP — Home Affordable Unemployment Program
- NATIONAL AFFORDABLE HOUSING TRUST FUND ACT

(American Homeowner)

to generate momentum in that direction.

But the fundamental challenge remains. There can be no real recovery of the housing market until the government recognizes that interfering with the "free market" has a cause and effect. Continued injections of government policy and tax dollars—or the withdrawal of tax dollars—in an attempt to change or prop up one section of the market will impact another. Eliminating real estate's tax incentives will not be a good first step to take.

The elections are over and President Obama was returned to office but we will however have to wait for 2013 to see what the country's position with regard to housing is going to be.

IMPACT ON REALTORS®

While many believe these deductions are "too important to die" it is more widely expected that at some point the government will reach into the subsidies that benefit homeownership and remove them. That means the real estate market will at some stage be impacted and if that should occur in 2013 the impact will be felt well outside the real estate industry.

According to the American Enterprise Institute, while those affected by these changes represent only 30 to 35 percent of all taxpayers, it's critical to remember homeowners are the heart and soul of residential real estate and they tend to spend considerably higher than the average American; the impact on the fragile economy will be significant.

What lies ahead when these changes are made is not possible to accurately determine, but here are some things to consider in planning for the change we believe is coming, affecting homeowners, renters and those who serve them:

- The Brookings Institution Tax Policy Center considered the effects of limiting the MID and property tax deductions to 28 percent along with raising the highest tax brackets to the pre 2001 level. They estimate it would result in housing values dropping between 6.9 and 15 percent. The largest impact is expected to be in areas of the country where there are high local taxes and the cost of renting compares favorably with owning.

- The loss of home value and the further slowing of the market—new buyers delaying their purchase because of the associated increase in costs and resellers finding no buyers—will have a direct fiscal impact on local communities as property tax revenue decreases, especially those with high property and sales tax rates.

- The growing rental market will be further impacted as more potential homebuyers become renters, competing with those already renting, resulting in even lower vacancy and higher rental rates.

- With the government supporting (subsidizing) renters this part of the real estate market will continue to expand. With the limitation or ultimate elimination of the MID the "all cash" purchase becomes more of an option and that would seem to play into hands of the investor. Add to that the current lag in construction of multi-family projects and the interest in the single-family market by the investment community will likely expand in the years to come as the shadow inventory continues to decline.

- With an increase in investor capital in the residential sector, and with a shortage of inventory in many areas, this may be the time the banking community (and Freddie and Fannie) begin taking serious action to unload outstanding REO inventories, further impacting home value.

- Lower home values and a slowing market will also impact the recovery of negative equity, which showed improvement during the last half of 2012.

SUMMARY

At this point there appears to be two most likely scenarios:

1. As part of the solution to the debt crisis the tax considerations discussed above will all be enacted and the impact on real estate will be significant. Not likely.

2. The political environment will make it too difficult to implement all of the changes and Congress and the Administration will compromise on a portion of the changes to avoid the fiscal cliff and it will be the beginning of change. Highly likely.

We cannot afford to assume that because the MID and property tax deductions are the cornerstone of U.S. tax policy that they are therefore too politically sensitive to be touched.

In our opinion removal of the MID will not come all at once, but phased in over several years. Because of that there is unfortunately no escaping the consequences as outlined in this Trend. The best action is to be prepared, position yourself accordingly, understand the changes and find the opportunities.

7 REVISITING ORGANIZED REAL ESTATE
Love me, Leave me, or Sue Me?

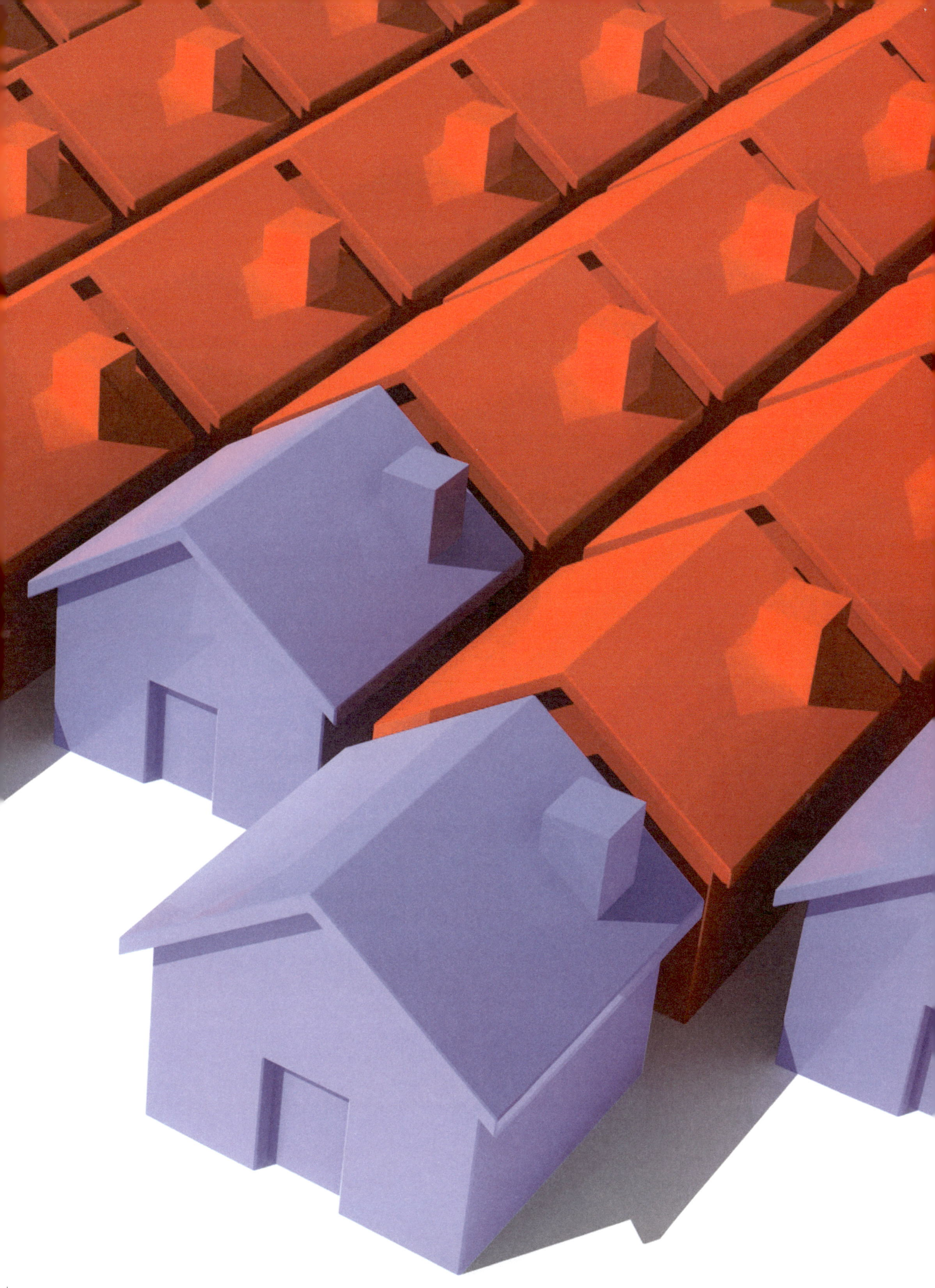

Revisiting Organized Real Estate

It has been a year since Inna Hardison posted an opinion online, one that sums up a feeling of a growing number of homebuyers and sellers, indicating that the consumer is blissfully unaware that there is any difference between a licensee and a Realtor®. And this seems to stem from growing disenfranchised movement from an "allegedly" growing number of real estate professionals debating whether they should, or should not, belong to "Organized Real Estate" (ORE).

Throughout 2012 we saw the question of value proposition break into the open. What has been whispered in conference hallways for years was finally acknowledged and officially reacted to. (Read Trend #1 in the *2012 Swanepoel TRENDS Report* titled On the Brink of Irrelevancy; free PDF copy can be downloaded at RETrends.com).

In last year's Report we took a hard look at some of the reasons the complex three-tier REALTOR® structure has struggled to remain relevant and we detailed how associations at all levels have resisted adapting to the new environment in which they find themselves. The core insight of that report was twofold:

1. Many membership services have become non-essential; and
2. Many leaders has become more disconnected with the needs of their membership.

In the 2013 edition of the our report we continue the journey with Realtor® associations and explore what has transpired during the year. Were it not so significant we would have covered it in a paragraph in another chapter, however, 2012 was a watershed year for associations—probably one of the top three most significant years of the last two decades.

With that in mind, we update and supplement the previous core insights with the activities and trends that developed over the past year:

- Disturbing Events in the U.S. and in Canada
- Contemplating Future Scenarios
- Constructive Action Being Taken

DISTURBING EVENTS IN THE U.S. – THE LAWYERS ARE COMING

Kevin Child vs. Greater Las Vegas Association of REALTORS®
On June 1, 2012, three members of the Greater Las Vegas Association of REALTORS® (GLVAR; lasvegasrealtor.com) sued the association, its board of directors and CEO Irene Vogel, alleging misappropriation of funds. Their claim is that membership dues (about $1,700 per year) have been misused and that Vogel, over many years as the association's leader has:

- Improperly distributed funds without approval from the board of directors.
- Paid out unauthorized cash bonuses.
- Selected her husband's insurance agency for the association's insurance without bidding out the contract.
- Purchased tables at political and charitable events with GLVAR funds without board approval.
- Allowed pirated DVDs to be sold out of the GLVAR office.
- Acted as a one-person pawnshop by "brokering" membership jewelry sales.

would amount to damages in excess of $60 million if the plaintiffs prevail. Furthermore, if the plaintiffs are successful in proving that the board violated its fiduciary duty of "care," then every single person who has ever served on the GLVAR board for the last ten years could be subject to personal liability; that may open a much wider door.

Of particular importance here is the identity of the attorney for the plaintiffs: Callister & Associates. They are currently involved in a class action lawsuit against Bank of America and LPS and have made a practice of seeking class action status in many of their other lawsuits.

to press it is our understanding that the judge ratified to move forward with the case.

Chicago Association of REALTORS® vs. Andrea Geller

A few months after news of the GLVAR lawsuit, on September 5, 2012, the Chicago Association of REALTORS® (CAR; chicagorealtor.com) filed a defamation lawsuit against one of its members, Andrea Geller, a broker/agent with Coldwell Banker. The lawsuit followed the impeachment of the Bob Floss, the 2012 CAR President, in June 2012, a few months before the end of his one-year term. Apparently an

> **The game changers and disrupters will be somebody you never thought about—who just came in.**
>
> Bob Hale CEO, HAR

The plaintiffs allege that requests made to GLVAR to see the financial records and audits have been refused. In addition, they contend that the board of director's election process has been tampered with for five to seven years. In response GLVAR filed a notice that it is unable to comment on pending legal matters.

In filing their lawsuit, the three plaintiffs are seeking damages in excess of $10,000. But more importantly they are seeking "class action status" on behalf of the association's nearly 11,000 members. And by going back 10 years that

We have all come to understand that this is a fairly standard strategy for any plaintiff's law firm working on a contingency fee basis. Large class action status can result in enormous judgments or settlements with the attorneys taking up to 40 percent of the award. However, once a plaintiff's attorney accepts the case the defendant has no choice but to settle or win at trial because the attorney is accepting the cost of litigation in exchange for contingency fees. The client is not paying the bills and the attorney makes the decision to press the case to trial or settle. As of going

internal audit of the associations' finances to resolve previous concerns raised did not take place. In essence the $50,000+ lawsuit alleges that comments posted on the Internet by Geller concerning the associations finances defamed the association and its CEO, Ginger Downs. Geller, in turn, has retained counsel and vowed to fight the lawsuit.

This is the first time in 129 years that CAR had sued one of its members for defamation and it has stirred up quite a public following. While some in the industry applaud the action taken by CAR, others

7 | Revisiting Organized Real Estate

consider it an unprofessional way to deal with a member and have turned the focus to Down's steep $327,000 salary. A few have even called for the removal of the CAR leadership and the starting of a new association. The situation is further complicated by the fact that Geller is not only a member of the association but a donor to the Realtor® Political Action Committee (RPAC) and has served with the association as committee chair and a member of its board of directors.

From the perspective of this Report, the critical issue is that the suit is one for defamation. Truth is a complete defense to the allegation blown discovery request as these firms typically do. One of the most important strategies for plaintiff's lawyers is to sue, and then get into discovery to see what else they might be able to dig up. If they find anything problematic while digging through the records of the defendant, emails, board minutes, depositions of witnesses and so on, they can always amend the complaint to claim additional wrongdoing and more damages.

A key sentence in the article above for me from this standpoint is this: 'GLVAR has denied the plaintiffs' requests to see financial development would provide a devastating blow to Organized Real Estate as we know it, on all levels. Think about it: if you have ever served on any association board you might find yourself party to a lawsuit claiming violation of fiduciary duties, and your personal liability could reach millions of dollars. Even if there were an association still left solvent after the lawyers get through with them, who would ever want to serve on an association board after that?

As a side note, CAR has a Legal Action Fund Assistance program for members. Ironically Geller, the member being sued, will most likely

---

"Given future consumer expectations, what is the role of the Realtor® in five to ten years, and what will the implications be for Organized Real Estate?"

---

of defamation or libel and, therefore, Geller and her attorneys would be entitled to prove that her allegedly defamatory comments about the financial operations of the CAR are in fact true. That, of course, requires discovery into the financial reports, board minutes and communications of the staff and leadership at CAR.

Commentator and blogger Robert Hahn (notoriousrob.com) wrote in regards to the CAR lawsuit, connecting it to the GLVAR lawsuit:

"A second fear, however, was that in the GLVAR lawsuit, Callister & Associates [legal team representing the plaintiffs] would bring a full- records and audits.' Well, now that there's a lawsuit in place I'm fairly certain that the plaintiffs will seek to have the court issue a subpoena for those records, as well as all emails, communications, minutes of board meetings, etc. etc.

Where things get awfully funky here is that if the plaintiffs and their very savvy class-action lawyers find evidence of board inaction or board malfeasance, each and every board member who has ever served on the GLVAR board for the last ten years is facing the possibility of personal liability."

We believe that such a qualify for legal assistance from that fund and be able to use funds she obtains form her association to fight the case against the same association.

Atlanta and Seattle – Agents Walking Away

Historically MLS services have been exclusively offered only to members of the local association/board. As all agents use the MLS, all agents therefore have been members of the local association/board, and therefore are Realtors®.

As MLS makes up the entire Trend #4: Big Data – The Next Frontier. Who Do Really Want a

National MLS?, we are not going to elaborate too much here other than to tie in the dilemma and opportunity as far as it relates to the Realtor® association. For example, due to legal rulings in the Thompson case and the Realtist case, California, Alabama, Georgia and Florida no longer require Realtor® association membership to gain access to the MLS. These four states probably represent about 20 percent of total number of Realtors®. NAR has also subsequently changed their rules so the decision to grant access to non-members is left up to each MLS.

In two boards, namely the Atlanta Board of REALTORS® and the Seattle-King County Association of REALTORS®, this has led to devastating consequences. In a very condensed period of time their Realtor® membership has been cut by nearly half, with an expected ripple throughout the finances of the organization.

Peculiarly it also creates a strange ambiguity in real estate companies where agents work side-by-side; some being Realtors® and some not. For example, one of the largest real estate brokerage companies in Atlanta, Better Homes and Gardens Metro Brokers, is now comprised of approximately the same large number of both Realtors® and non-Realtors®. Talk about potential confusion in the market place.

This new "duel" membership condition produces the unique situation in which for the first time there is apparently no longer a stigma attached to being a non-Realtor®. Yet, oddly enough, it also creates a magnificent opportunity for the Realtor® organization to redefine and reposition what is means to be a Realtor®.

CANADA – A MIXED BAG

Canadian Competition Bureau
The Canadian Real Estate Association (CREA; crea.ca) continues to deal with the effects of the ongoing legal action filed against it by the Canadian Competition Bureau for "abuse of dominance," which is Canadian for "antitrust." According to the Bureau, CREA used rules, under which it licenses its MLS trademark and related marks to member real estate boards, to maintain control of the market for residential real estate brokerage services in Canada. More specifically, the Bureau has articulated the position that CREA's MLS rules inhibit or prevent non-traditional business models, including fee-for-service and flat fee models, from effectively completing in the residential real estate services market.

In mid-September representatives of the Toronto Real Estate Board (TREB; torontorealestateboard.com) leadership team appeared before a Competition Bureau Tribunal to respond to allegations that the trade association is abusing its "substantial market power" and hurting consumers. Antitrust expert Gregory Vistnes claims, "TREB has abused, and continues to abuse, its substantial market power and control of relevant markets to reduce competition and protect its member brokers' interests at the expense of consumers." Sources indicate that Bureau of Competition sanctions, beside their contentious nature, could run into several hundred million dollars.

Quebec Pulling Out
In August the Quebec Federation of Real Estate Boards (FCIQ; fciq.ca) advised CREA that it plans to withdraw from the national association. This is unheard of in either the U.S. or Canadian REALTOR® Associations' century-old histories, and it is raising more than a few eyebrows.

The Federation, a group of twelve local boards, says that real estate brokers in the province are angered over CREA's decision to hike fees on agents and brokers rather than trimming national expenses. It's reported that CREA's fees are slated to increase to $310 per year starting in January 2013, following a $50 increase in 2011 and $40 in 2012. It would appear that members are fed up with the increases, but some say there is more to it than that and refer to the disagreement over certain elements of a new CREA direction (more following).

CONTEMPLATING THE SCENARIOS FOR CHANGE

Canada – CREA Futures Project
CREA decided that as a collective of national, provincial and local

Revisiting Organized Real Estate

Realtor® associations they needed to address the question:

"Given future consumer expectations, what is the role of the Realtor® in five to ten years, and what will the implications be for ORE?"

It's a big question and a huge undertaking if you really seriously want to try and resolve it—in our opinion it would appear that CREA is very serious indeed. Therefore, the planning scenarios and results make for very interesting reading, and furthermore they are very meaningful and significant to the entirety of ORE.

The CREA Futures Project started in 2010 with extensive interviewing of the leaders of national and regional real estate boards, along with select staff, industry consultants and others. This led to their Drivers of Change, Expert Interviews Report, Scenario Planning Workshop in Montebello, possible scenarios for the future of ORE through 2021 and various additional meetings and discussions.

Ultimately, in March 2012 at their annual general meeting the CREA membership approved the "Organized Real Estate Collaborative Strategy—A Map to the Future." This 17-page strategic plan, as well as other key documents associated with this process, can be downloaded at RETrends.com.

In summary, the mission for ORE was defined as helping Realtors® meet consumer needs: "The ORE value proposition is therefore to empower Realtors® to be the choice of consumers, to add value to their real estate decisions by fostering an environment of innovation and collaboration in the development and delivery of premium tools, insight and knowledge." Their proposed "23 Initiatives" form the basis of all their new plans:

Consumer Insight

> Like many things in life, some things have to get worse before they can get better.

- Develop an integrated national consumer engagement strategy.
- Build requirements for a "Rate Your Real Estate Experience" tool, including "Rate Your Realtor®."

Technology and Data

- Connect, share and evolve MLS Systems into a national, provincial or regional structure—a single national data feed with multiple inputs (individual Realtors®, regional, large boards and national) and outputs to be used in different ways that can be accessed regionally.
- Adopt, enhance and enforce uniform standards for data, security and operations.
- Create a business plan for an independent organization to run realtor.ca and CREA's technology services.
- Evaluate if and how best we can make FSBO and non-MLS® data available on realtor.ca.
- Brand all MLS® content as Realtor® verified.
- Facilitate sharing of app development, data sharing and technology advancements through partnerships within and external to ORE.

Professional Development

- Establish national competency standards, including apprenticeship and mentorship programs.
- Establish a national virtual college.
- Establish national post-licensing certification and education programs.
- Establish an enforcement process for the REALTOR® Code that is acceptable in all jurisdictions.

Member Services

- Develop a strategy to enhance member services and benefits.
- Develop a national Realtor® engagement strategy and research panel.
- Develop a mechanism to facilitate the incubation of new ideas—"greenhouse."
- Investigate the feasibility of making à la carte services available to members.

Operating Structure

- Optimize the structure of ORE

From the Vault: Real Estate Confronts Reality (1997)

Competition for the consumer — external or internal — will severely alter the form and structure of "organized real estate." The NAR of the future will not be the same as it is now, but it "will be.

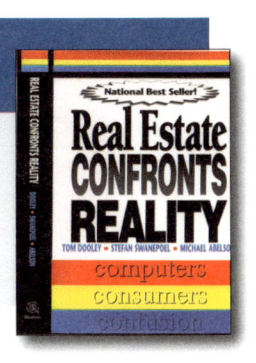

and establish very clear roles and responsibilities at each level to avoid duplication.

- Support changes with a Futures Fund.
- Review membership eligibility and create a partnership strategy to be inclusive of industry, franchisors, appraisers, etc.

Governance

- Identify opportunities that can be implemented today to optimize the number and/or the type of councils, committees, task forces and working groups; e.g. eliminate AGMs for CREA's Councils.
- Ensure succession plans are in place for informed and knowledgeable volunteer leadership at all levels with appropriate terms based on best practices.
- Align governance with ORE structure and the operating model as outlined in the operating structure.
- Share board practices across ORE to establish and compare against benchmarks.

At a 30,000-foot level all these initiatives are excellent and one should applaud the efforts of all those who participated, especially those of Gary Simonsen, CREA's CEO, who championed this process. But as we all know, the devil is in the details and successful implementation requires detailed action plans and mapping out the specifics; it's here where the differences in understanding and interpretation are usually highlighted. While these are all practical and tactical issues that can be worked through, it seems that in this instance the implementation has surprisingly been met with very mixed results; suddenly, previously agreed upon concepts have become very contentious.

One of the prickly issues includes adding FSBO properties to realtor.ca; the equivalent of our realtor.com, but wholly owned and operated by CREA. This quickly became a non-starter with most members arguing that the business reasons raised for including these properties were not significant enough to change the existing paradigm.

Most industry prognosticators and consultants would strongly argue that this shouldn't be a major stumbling block and should be permitted in order to effectively compete against "outside" forces that "do include" FSBOs. However, resistance is widely found where entrepreneurs and/or associations get very emotionally wed to the "babies" they created and find it almost impossible to change the status quo.

Furthermore, CREA has started creating a separate technology company, stronger brand awareness, a richer online experience for consumers and so on, only to further a growing uproar of resistance by leading brokers that are claiming that CREA is becoming too consumer-centric and beginning to compete with brokerage companies. Subsequently, in provinces like Quebec where a concentration of big brokers dominate the market share, the associations have advised CREA that they are pulling out of the national three tier structure—national, provincial and local. Discussions are of course being held at the highest level, but at the time of going to print they were heated and no finality had been reached.

U.S. – The NAR "Rethink" Initiative

The first initiative was the launch of NAR's "Rethink the Future of Real Estate" program (rethinkfuture.com). Billed as a scenario planning exercise

7 | Revisiting Organized Real Estate

designed to gather feedback from various parts of the entire real estate industry—agents, brokers, vendors, consultants and thought leaders—Rethink is actually attempting to address three key challenges of today:

1. What is the value of the Association?
2. What will be the value of the Association?
3. What should be the value of the Association?

From the "About Us" section of Rethink's website:

The Strategic Planning Committee is taking a fresh, new approach to how we are developing our strategic plan. It is specifically designed to encourage dialogue and to open minds about thinking big for our future. We will begin by exploring and discussing different versions of what the future holds for our association and our industry. We believe that learning and engagement are strategic and we need to create the space where they can happen. We believe this is the best way to determine what the future holds for us, and, more importantly, how we would like to shape the future we think is most likely to occur and the one we'd like to help create for our industry. We will be holding workshops that will be followed by round table discussions where we discuss several different possible examples of the future for our industry. In addition to these workshops, we will have a website where people can comment and share their ideas. If you have ever heard of crowd sourcing, which is a term for gathering ideas and opinions from a wide-variety of sources, we are applying it to our strategic planning.

This is first time that NAR has officially undertaken a public conversation about this controversial topic. Rethink conducts a scenario-planning exercise in which a series of possible future scenarios are presented and the participants are asked to discuss them; considering what the local, state and national association ought to do in response. One interesting fact is that when one examines the actual scenarios presented they "all" assume that the association as currently organized is deeply troubled.

Rethink presents three short-term scenarios (Ostrich, Beauty and the Beast and Jungle) and two long-term scenarios (The New American Dream and the American Dream Recaptured). Here are the relevant assumptions of the three short-term scenarios taken from the Scenario Report (a complete narrative of the Rethink program can be downloaded from RETrends.com).

Ostrich
- Slower incremental changes, especially at the association level.
- Driven by institutional inertia, political gridlock, industry fragmentation and the slower pace of the housing market recovery.

The assumption is that associations bury their collective heads in the sand, ignoring the real problems with the end result being the end of the association:

Like many things in life, sometimes things have to get worse before they can get better. In the end, there was a silver lining. All those frustrated agents, young and old, leaving the association started to create innovative solutions on their own, triggering a great deal of entrepreneurial activity that would benefit the industry's renewal as a whole down the road. The lost opportunity, of course, was that much of this was happening outside, not inside, the boundaries of traditional ORE.

> Rethink conducts a scenario-planning exercise in which a series of possible future scenarios.
>
> This is first time that NAR has officially undertaken a public conversation about this controversial topic.

The hopeful note is that organized real estate will continue, but it probably won't through the existing local and state association structure as we know it.

Beauty and the Beast
- Big shifts in the real estate value proposition, led by select industry players.
- Collaborative effort driven by the big data opportunity, external threats and the need for more future-facing consumer-centric models.

The assumption of the Beauty and the Beast scenario is that some association leaders stop being an ostrich and take bold steps to reform organized real estate in order to bring it into the 21st century. The end result is a new compact that endures:

Most people didn't think it was possible. Getting key players to collaboratively re-shape the real estate industry was just too difficult. Too many barriers were in the way, from divergent interests to legal, institutional and political issues. And, as many argued, this had been tried before with unclear or unsuccessful results.

However, this time was different. Defying conventional wisdom, this was a future where the real estate industry was successful in a path-breaking effort that redefined the industry's value proposition.

But buried in how the scenario plays itself out is this nugget:
- The MLS is taken over by dominant tech players: Zillow, Trulia, Facebook and some completely new organizations.
- Big data is the key differentiator, driving a new value proposition.
- But human judgment from the agent is still important to effectively manage the complexity and information overload associated with the transaction.

Given that most associations recognize that the only reason why licensees join is to gain access to the MLS, the Beauty and the Beast scenario is silent on the question of why organized real estate would survive once the MLS is taken over by technology companies.

Jungle
- Rapid, game changing shifts to the industry and business environment.
- Driven by new entrants, new politics, shifting values and external forces like rising energy prices.

The assumption of the Jungle scenario is that changes in technology and the entrance of major non-real estate technology players, such as Amazon. com—"after acquiring Zillow"—take the real estate industry completely by storm. Furthermore, classic political advocacy (i.e., lobbying) is overtaken by "swarm advocacy."

The end result is that organized real estate is, once again, no more.

Meanwhile, many existing industry organizations were blindsided by the scale and speed of these changes, or were simply out resourced by the new entrants. Of the industry leaders who did see these changes coming, they discounted these new fangled innovations as a passing fad. Indeed, by 2015 we see many brokerage houses imploding, industry associations shuttering their offices and once mighty franchises going under. The few franchises that survived were the ones that partnered early on with new entrants and technology firms or became highly specialized.

CONSTRUCTIVE ACTION BEING TAKEN

Canada – Alberta, BC and Ontario Creating Momentum

The new CREA direction has also stimulated some other Canadian local and provincial associations into realizing that ORE is not structured as efficiently as it should be.

A good example is the province of Alberta. The Calgary Real Estate Board (CREB; creb.com), under the leadership of Alan Tennant, former President of the International Real Estate Consortium (ICREA) and now CEO of CREB, is a professional body of over 5,000 licensed brokers and registered associates in over 240 member offices. The organization is strongly proposing the appointment of a task force to investigate the potential of creating a unification of all of Alberta's real estate boards and associations with CREA into a new organization.

The new organization would have some 10,500 individual members with a centralized governance and administration. The local service provision would be in the form of

First Group of 40 Associations to Take On the Challenge with the Pinnacle Program

- Anne Arundle County Association of Realtors®
- Berkshire County Board of Realtors®
- Burlington Camden County Association of Realtors®
- Chicago Association of Realtors®
- Coastal Association of Realtors® of MD
- Columbus Board of Realtors®
- Duluth Area Association of Realtors®
- Eastern Connecticut Association of Realtors®
- Fredericksburg Area Association of Realtors®
- Gallatin Association of Realtors®
- Georgia Association of Realtors®
- Greater Chattanooga Association of Realtors®
- Greater Rochester Association of Realtors®
- Greater Tampa Association of Realtors®
- Greensboro Regional REALTOR® Association
- Harford County Association of Realtors®
- Houston Association of Realtors®
- Jackson Association of Realtors® (MS)
- Lexington-Bluegrass Association of Realtors®
- Mainstreet Organization of Realtors® (IL)
- Metropolitan Indianapolis Board of Realtors®
- MetroTex Association of Realtors®
- Miami Association of Realtors®
- Minneapolis Area Association of Realtors®
- Minnesota Association of Realtors®
- Missoula Organization of Realtors®
- North San Diego County Association of Realtors®
- North Shore - Barrington Association of Realtors®
- North Shore Association of Realtors®
- Orlando Regional Realtor® Association
- Passaic County Board of Realtors® (NJ)
- Peoria Area Association of Realtors®
- Pinellas Realtors®
- Realtors® Association of the Palm Beaches
- Rockford Area Association of Realtors®
- San Francisco Association of Realtors®
- Southeast Minnesota Association of Realtors®
- Southwestern Michigan Association of Realtors®
- St. Paul Association of Realtors®
- Toledo Board of Realtors®

local chapters and the ultimate goal would be greater efficiencies, a more even distribution of resources and overall a better value proposition for Alberta Realtors®.

The current structure of ORE in Alberta is very typical of most civic governance models of the U.S. and Canada; each community has a mayor and council and they focus on "local" issues while the provincial and federal governments have their own areas of responsibility. When most real estate boards were formed in Canada in the first third of the last century it made sense to emulate the traditional municipal/province/federal model, in part because it was familiar and also because it made efficient use of limited travel and communication options.

The problem, which is glaringly obvious to members and staff, is that there is significant overlap and waste in product and service delivery. A favorable future state would see the unification of all of Alberta's real estate boards and associations into a new organization.

Personally we support such a step, but once again we will have to see if whether or not all the parties involved can put the interests of the collective ahead of the individual. All indications are that this is a huge hurdle to get over, but with good leadership anything is possible.

U.S. – The Pinnacle Program

To significantly move the dial in any organization, especially in large ones as well as non-profit entities, is very difficult indeed. It requires outside the box thinking, a willingness to explore the unchartered waters, talent and resources to address the challenge and the commitment to see it though.

Understanding this huge mountain to climb, NAR's CEO, Dale Stinton, made known his personal desire to "change the game," and working with industry strategists Jeremy Conaway, Jim Sherry and Stefan Swanepoel, he birthed the Pinnacle Program. This two-year program provides Realtor® association leaders (elected as well as appointed) with two foundational elements:

1. A current and relevant flow of knowledge, strategies and tactics that associations can customize and reengineer to meet their respective needs; and

2. A think-tank through which associations can discuss current challenges and collectively explore "best practices" for associations.

The program, which is a two-year, hands-on intensive leadership and management course, incorporates eight modules, six onsite sessions and 16 coaching calls/webinars. The first group consists of 40 associations that have agreed to take on the challenge to change the game (see table above).

This is the first time a multiple module program by NAR is being delivered with newly developed material, created just 60 to 90 days ahead of delivery of each module. As such the courseware, challenges and solutions are dynamically adapted by the Pinnacle Group Coaches and participating associations. The following are modules currently envisioned by the Program.

1. Building the Consumer/Realtor® Relationship.

2. Creating an All-inclusive Wide-Ranging Strategic Mindset.

3. Building Leadership Excellence on Every Level.

4. Fully Integrating Mobile and Social Media Effectively.

5. Creating Superb and Relevant Products and Services.

6. Succeeding in the New Big Data World.

It remains to be seen which associations can and will follow through with implementation and execution of the program. However, the positive step from our perspective is that the very creation of the Pinnacle Program is significant in and of itself.

SUMMARY

So at the very moment in time when the Chicago Association of REALTORS® should be focusing on becoming more relevant and redefining its value proposition to its members, it has elected to immerse itself in a lawsuit with one of its members. We do not seek to judge whether this suit was meritorious or not, but we do believe that it will create an environment of discontent and disharmony that will linger within CAR for many years to come—a very peculiar decision.

Should any of these lawsuits mentioned go against the associations involved—whether that is a loss at trial or a settlement large enough to whet the appetites of class action attorneys everywhere—then we must add to strategic leadership, tech-savvy innovation and increased diversity the further requirement of accepting the risk of personal liability suits. And NAR itself is likely to come under attack if either the GLVAR or CAR cases result in a payday for plaintiff's lawyers. With a board of directors that is larger than the U.S. Congress, NAR and its numerous directors will clearly be a target. Although there have been doomsday predictions and threatening court cases before, and most did not materialize, the possibility of serious consequences this time is very real. (Scuttlebutt is also that there are other class action suits in the works, the next possibly being in the northeast).

On a different note, the fact that association leaders on all three levels are openly discussing doomsday scenarios and predictions (refer to NAR and CREA scenario planning documents) is both very interesting and impressive. However, discussion is not enough and the industry needs more association executives and leaders, especially on a state and local level, that are willing to actually take the necessary bold steps to affect change. Success in the new environment will require a new brand of leadership design and function that emphasizes strategic and tactical leadership, tech-savvy innovation and "hands on" interactivity.

ORE is clearly at a critical crossing, one that has taken all of a century to reach. On the one side are strategies and actions that protect the status quo and on the other side are unchartered waters, restructuring and the search for relevancy. So, from the perspective of both survival and opportunity, the next few years are going to be pivotal. Consolidation is inevitable and restructuring will be critical.

6 REDEFINING REAL ESTATE PROFESSIONALISM

Hello, Capital. Are You Coming In?

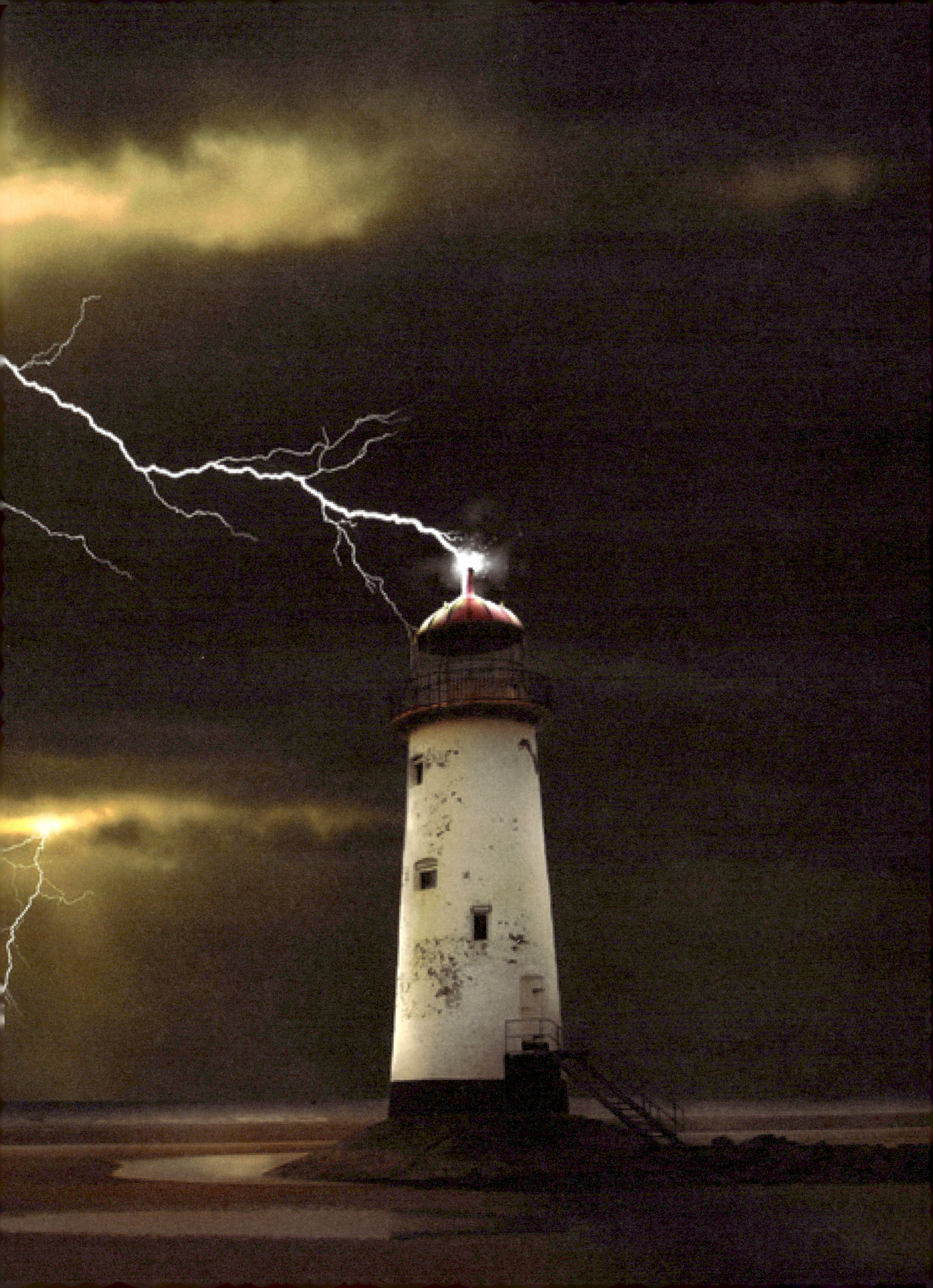

Redefining Real Estate Professionalism

The rise of professionalism and the American "professional" from 1947 to the early 1980s and its subsequent decline to the present day has had a major impact upon both American society and business culture and bares close examination by anyone connected to the near-term future of the real estate industry. It's noteworthy that the very same trends and dynamics that accompanied the fall from influence and power of virtually every other profession over the past twenty years are currently occurring within the real estate industry.

The ability to understand the current status of this dynamic and the remaining stages through which it will pass on its way to ending the reign of the traditional agent role and the classic brokerage business model is critical. It holds significant information and insight for those who are charged with designing, developing and implementing the real estate service models that will respond to the transitioning industry marketplace.

The saga of the American professional from 1947 through the present includes a cast of millions. The main characters were the many fine individuals who, since the Second World War, invested their lives, educations and fortunes into the experience of becoming and living the life of a professional. And they have done it within one of the many professional spheres of influence that have heavily impacted and influenced our lifestyle and culture

The supporting actors are the hundreds of millions of consumers who both trusted and relied on various professions and professionals to protect, serve and care for them over the last 65 years. Recognition must also be given to the role played by the tens of thousands of regulators, managers and executives who, over the past twenty years, have inherited and assumed the tasks and responsibilities of reforming the systems and processes. The very systems and processes that ensure that we receive the benefit of accessible, affordable, dependable and accountable professional services across the entire spectrum of providers, businesses and vendors who undertake their provision.

In today's integrated and sophisticated economy few businesses don't in one way or another incorporate professional services in one or more aspects of their business. Because of this the circumstances impacting the transitioning professional segment have impacted virtually every sector of the economy.

From the very beginning of the post WWII economic boom the same dreams, philosophies and compulsions that drove the 1947 real estate agent to seek out the professional designation (characteristics, status and standing) also motivated individuals seeking professional status in almost every other sector of the business economy. In fact, the historic and almost irrational need to define oneself as a professional has ultimately led to the current situation. Today almost every individual employed within a common classification, such as flight attendants, mechanics, mail order preachers, cooks, housekeepers and child care givers, clings to the notion that with even a wisp of training and commitment that they too can be a professional. As a result, many perpetuate the ultimate obscurity of adding the term "professional" to their labor organization.

Over the past twenty-five years the debate has raged on: Professions, Professionals or simply being Professional. Is there a difference, does it matter and how could this shape our industry in the years ahead? To answer these questions we first need to glance back before taking a leap forward and examining 2013's answer to this question.

1945 – WWII ENDS AND THE YANKS RETURN

The men and women who joined the military during WWII left home as teenagers, and when the war was over they came back as adults. Many had been places and seen things beyond anything they could ever have imagined. The nation wanted to thank them for their service and jump-start the economy so Congress decided to accomplish both of these objectives through what would be popularly known as the GI Bill of Rights. The official title was the "Servicemen's Readjustment Act" that President Franklin D. Roosevelt signed in 1944, even before the war ended, providing the following benefits:

- Education and training opportunities.
- Loan guarantees for a home, farm or business.
- Job-finding assistance.
- Unemployment pay of $20 per week for up to 52 weeks.

The GIs (Government Issue) had a lot of time to think about what direction their lives should take after the war. Interestingly enough, many who had never even talked to a college graduate before going into the military, other than perhaps a schoolteacher or minister, found a chance to discuss and observe first-hand the benefits of a college education in the officers they served and fought with. As a result, for the majority of them the educational opportunities were the most important part of the law. Veterans were entitled to one year of full-time training plus time equal to their military service, up to 48 months. The Veterans Administration paid the university, trade school or employer up to $500 per year for tuition, books,

> Professions, Professionals or simply being Professional. Is there a difference?

fees and other training costs. They also received a small living allowance while they were in school. This changed the landscape overnight.

By 1947 veterans comprised 49 percent of U.S. college enrollment. Over 7.8 million veterans trained at colleges, trade schools and in business and agriculture training programs, most completing their education and never returning to the farm. The law was changed in 1952 to help veterans of the Korean War and, in 1966, veterans of the Vietnam War. Although the program ended in 1989 there are similar government programs to help today's military personnel pay for educational expenses and buy a home. Many of those who graduated from college before accepting a commission used their benefits to secure professional degrees.

The ramifications of becoming a college graduate in the early 50s were astounding. By way of example, during the 40s only 4.5 percent of 25-year-olds in the U.S. held college degrees compared with 30 percent in 2011.

With the G.I. Bill leading the way the country moved from its agricultural base to manufacturing and ultimately into a service oriented society. At the same time the millions of new family units that were created resulted in a growing need for professionals of all types, especially in the fields of health care, law, accounting and engineering.

WHAT WAS COOL ABOUT BEING A PROFESSIONAL?

While a wide variety of personal and philosophical factors were in play at that time, research shows that the GIs' military experience might have had a significant impact.

- Even for field grade officers the military experience offered little in the way of respect and dignity; combat is a very basic level experience.

- The military caveat of "need to know" made being part of a profession that gave access to all of the available information very attractive.

- It isn't hard to believe that the superman image and control that professionals had over their patients and clients at that time were attractive, especially after several years of military service where everyone was or wasn't a superman depending upon the day.

- While the level of greed and financial focus of the Civic Generation never approached that of the Boomers it was still a factor. Those were the days before anti-trust regulators and third-party reimbursement entities controlled fees; "charge whatever they will pay" mentality was alive and well.

- There can be little doubt that, after years of dealing with superiors that were often less than competent, the fact that professionals didn't have to tolerate a "stinking boss" was also an attractive feature.

If some of these aspirational considerations might seem a bit harsh one must remember that in 1947 they were only considerations, later they would become doctrines. However, by the time the Boomer professionals entered the marketplace in substantial numbers in the mid 60s these very considerations had become mandates for a way of life that was to dominate professionalism for the next forty years.

REAL ESTATE'S PROFESSIONAL EXPERIENCE

Over the years many have questioned who or what made real estate a "profession?" The answer is simple: real estate agents did. At the onset of the post WWII economic boom the real estate industry, as it is known

> Over the years many have questioned who or what made real estate a "profession?" The answer is simple: real estate agents did.

today, almost completely reinvented itself. The "dirt peddler" that had gone off to war returned to a nation that was about to recreate its entire housing inventory and marketing process to facilitate the greatest economic and demographic boom in world history.

In 1947 the institutions, entities and individuals responsible for innovating and developing this new real estate industry had a number of choices relative to how to design, develop and present the new Realtor®. Some direction was provided by the previous establishment of the REALTOR® Code of Ethics (COE) in 1913, but for a number of reasons, driven by the very factors set forth here, they decided to pursue a "professional-based" model. This decision was to become an enduring mainstay within the Realtor® movement. It was further cemented when the movement added to its COE culture by creating an innovative professional standards process that served the Realtor® space until into the early 2000s when Generations X and Y deemed it largely irrelevant.

THE THREE MYTHS OF PROFESSIONALISM

Over the 60 years of its post WWII existence the professional sector evolved a vision of its role that incorporated three concepts. By the 90s the failure of these concepts to a great extent doomed professionalism's long-term success. Understanding how this vision failed and its impact on professionalism provides a key part of the answer to understanding the probable future of all "professional-centered" industries, including real estate.

Tracking these myths is made easier by referencing the medical profession. This approach is not undertaken to focus on the medical profession but rather arises from the fact that most professions, including Realtors®, did not invest in chronicling their history as well as the medical profession, which is obsessed with the need to document its history. It has, however, provided the classic example against which other professions can be observed, and it can best be seen through the experience of the American Medical Association (AMA). The AMA enjoyed a meteoric rise in prominence, power and membership beginning in 1947 and continuing through the 80s, when medicine became one of the first professions to implode with the advent of peer review, institutional dominance and managed care. Today the AMA membership is well below 30 percent of all physicians, a trend that is reflected in most professions.

Myth #1 – Professional Ethics Survived the Boomer Generation

The first and arguably most important element of the original vision of professionalism was that professionals were guided, governed and influenced by professional ethics. Professionally trained individuals and those working in acknowledged professions were assumed to exercise specialist knowledge and skill. Society deemed professionals capable of making judgments, applying their skills and reaching informed decisions in situations that the general public couldn't because they hadn't received the relevant training. One of the earliest examples of professional ethics is probably the Hippocratic Oath, which medical doctors still adhere to today.

Professional ethics traditionally consisted of a set of general and often ill-defined standards that were adopted by each professional community. Their purpose was two-fold: they first served to set a general boundary of conduct and second to provide a basis of action against individuals within a profession whose behaviors outraged a critical mass within the profession. But with the beginning of the post WWII economic boom, ethics were considered to be a matter of individual consciousness and self-enforcement. This status quo remained in effect from the late 40s through the 60s, but it rather quickly ceased to be the case as the Boomer Generation began to assume control of the professional dynamic in the mid 70s. As increased competition, advertising, lucrative incomes, multiple divorces without stigma and luxurious lifestyles became increasingly available the ethical imperative of the professional began to shift across the board. Its destination became what many commentators and former spouses came to refer to as "situation ethics."

By the mid 70s inappropriate and actionable behaviors had fallen under the purview of the plaintiff's bar, itself engorged by tens of thousands of Boomer attorneys struggling with their own ethics, as they chased their own 5 series BMW. By the mid 90s ethics in almost all professions had become tired and ignored, reduced from relevant influences to worn-out and generally ignored references.

> Real estate is the last "profession" impacted and incorporated into the corporate practice.

Myth #2 – High Standards are an Inherent Part of Professionalism

The second professional myth relates to the idea that professionals were guided and influenced by high standards. In the 60s and 70s the American cultures at both the

27

From the Vault: Real Estate Confronts Reality (1997)

The real estate industry has been in awe for a long time with the desire to be a profession. If your perception of a profession is the same as lawyers' and doctors', the real estate industry will never be a profession. If your definition is that of licensing, education and ethical standards, then real estate industry is already a profession. I believe it is immaterial in any event.

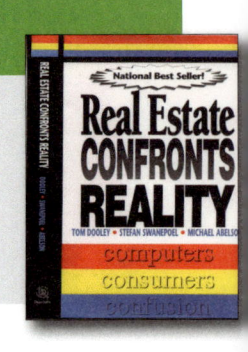

consumer and judiciary levels were unable to articulate or imagine a consumer with the sophistication necessary to set, monitor or enforce standards. Accordingly, it was during this period that ethics moved from being an individual responsibility to an institutional task. During the first phase of this new era the culture decided that the professions could police themselves if they had the benefit of institutional oversight. The result was the emergence of "peer-based standards," backed up by government or association mandated entities that were used to judge and regulate professions. This was the golden age of what became known as "professional standards."

There is no doubt that the Civic Generation professional started out impressed by the power of his or her peers to render judgment on professional performance. Unfortunately history now reveals that, at least in the U.S., this concept was to be doomed by the egos and material needs of individuals in all professions. The "peer review" boom, inspired by the writings of Ishap bin Ali al-Rahaw (Ethics of the Physician) who described the first medical peer review process, peaked during the 70s with the Federal government's establishment of a national Peer Review Organization (PRO). It began its downfall with the Health Care Quality Improvement Act of 1987, which generally discounted internal professional standards in favor of those established by legislative and regulatory entities.

In the final analysis the myth of peer review as a process to maintain the quality and consistency of professional services failed. In the end it was perceived as being uninformed, not feasible and generally ill advised. By the mid-90s America had discovered that the vast majority of professionals were incapable of self-monitoring and self-enforcing standards and quality assurance.

Myth #3 – That Charity and Selflessness are Primary Professional Motivators

The third professional myth was founded in the early societal impression that charity and selflessness were primary motivators for all true professionals. Certainly this was the image portrayed on TV by Marcus Welby MD (1968 – 1976) and Perry Mason Esq. (1957 – 1966), neither of whom was ever caught denying services for lack of resources, arguing with an insurance carrier or negotiating a retainer. Media representations such as these, coupled with the last days of professional "sainthood," were responsible for the image of the professional who wasn't in it for the money.

By the late 80s, for a hundred individually based reasons, thousands of malpractice suits and millions of dollars in judgments, the myth of the charitable or "honorable" concept had also been discovered and America's love affair with the professional began its decline.

THE TRADITIONAL PROFESSIONAL BUSINESS MODEL

Before our discussion leaves the world of the "profession-centric" era it is important to examine the business model that this group developed and used to deliver professional services. While many, if not most service-based businesses have long since been forced by the realities of modern economics and enlightened management to abandon this model, the real estate industry continues to cling to its dying form.

The real issue here is why a professional business model even existed that long, especially given the fact that over the years it failed to incorporate any of the hard lessons learned through experience and those perpetuated by the nation's business schools:

1. **Generate Revenue:** The first and foremost function of the classic professional business model was to provide a mechanism through which professionals could generate revenues to support their life style. This objective never evolved into profitability or generated a market level return on investment. Neither of these two concepts were ever to be a part of the classic professional business model. Some might suggest that this point is too subtle to raise, but to the contrary it will end up being the very point on which the demise of the professional model will be finally sealed as an investor-centric industry has moved to institutionalize profitability.

2. **Feed the Professional Ego:** It was personal aggrandizement rather than economic feasibility and common sense that guided the classic model. Nowhere was this more obvious than in the "bricks and mortar" architecture of professionalism. During most of the period in question professional success was marketed by both the life style and the grandeur of the offices occupied by these individuals. A strong argument can be made to support the contention that the overhead expenses created by these spaces contributed greatly to the ultimate downfall of professionalism as practitioners were forced to cut corners to pay the bills.

3. **Venue to Deliver Services:** The most stable rational for the traditional business model was to provide a venue from which to deliver professional services. The idea of "build it and they will come" did not originate with a movie about baseball in a cornfield.

The order of these three factors is important because they also represented the three top priorities of the professional during the last years of the professional-centric era. Whatever positive contributions professionalism might have made to the American culture were largely diminished by the spectacular divorces that emerged from their efforts to foster the emotional support of nurses, secretaries and associates who "understood" their unique situation. In large and small communities across the country these doomed affairs and legal clashes may well have marked the beginning of "reality-based" entertainment. The halls of justice were filled with the cries of wronged spouses and their anguished announcements that it was they who had put the professional through school, early practice and helped them build their business.

The classic professional business

The Evolution of Business

Professionals

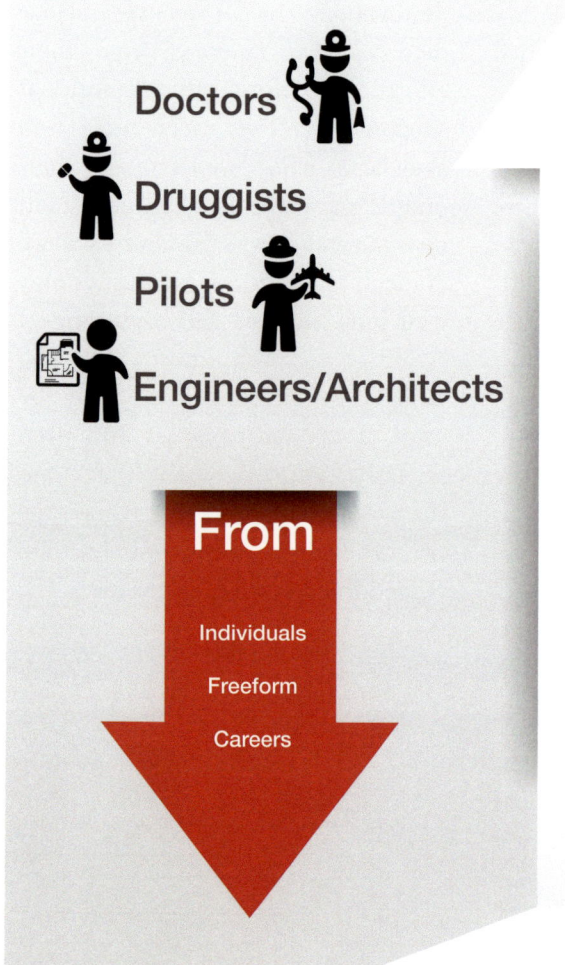

- Doctors
- Druggists
- Pilots
- Engineers/Architects

From
Individuals
Freeform
Careers

Businesses

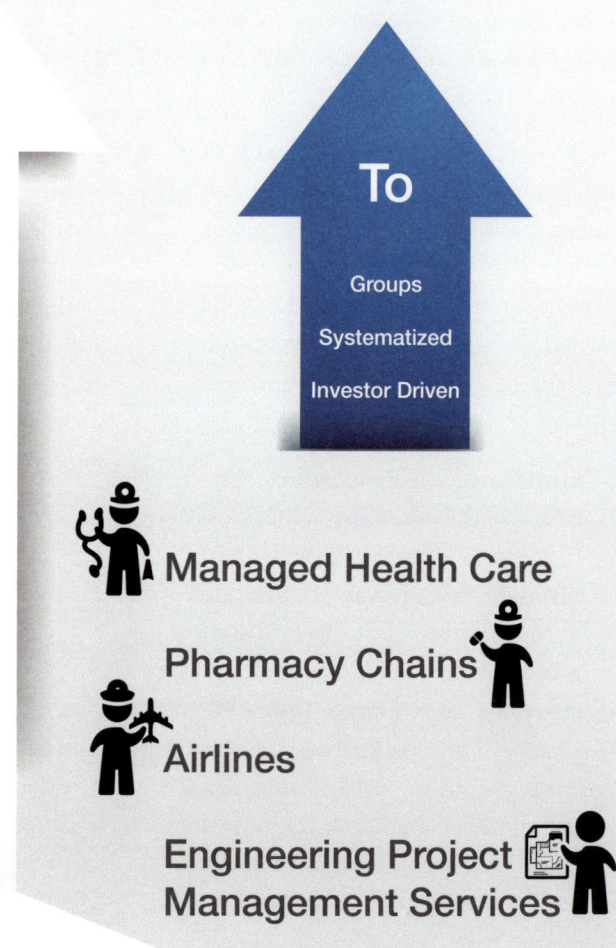

To
Groups
Systematized
Investor Driven

- Managed Health Care
- Pharmacy Chains
- Airlines
- Engineering Project Management Services

Underpinning Foundation

- Career
- Respect / Status
- Independance / Freeform
- Generalist
- Name Your Price
- Local / Neighborhood

- Data Driven
- Corporate / Investor Driven
- Very Specialized
- Lower Pricing
- Economies of Scale
- Automatic / Systematized

©2012 RealSure, Inc.

(aka firm, practice or group) was hyper-local with competing professionals often locating themselves in the same neighborhoods and buildings, further spreading the self and consumer perception that they were just one big happy family. As it turned out, not only did each of the professional communities engage in brutal political battles and territorial wars, there was also a great deal of inter-migration as professionals flitted in and out of various firms and groups, desperately seeking the perfect combination of increasingly illusive financial success and collegial respect. Some will argue that this activity the consumer playing but a supporting role.

- There was an absolute assumption of value. A true professional never questioned that they were the ultimate gift to the culture. Of course of equal importance was the fact that it would never have occurred to them to ask anyone else; self-confidence was considered the consummate virtue.

- There was little or no perception of competition. Professionals were often friends, fraternity brothers, sorority sisters or propensity for shifting practice settings on the slightest whim.

- Differentiation was never a positive factor. In fact, great efforts were taken to be sure that everyone appeared to be similar in dress, procedure and policy.

- Consumers were generally not seen as individuals nor were their needs and expectations considered unless they just happened to parallel those of the traditional professional. "You need services and I need compensation."

> And it carries with it the distinction of being the last "profession" impacted and incorporated into the corporate practice.

was just competition in action. Unfortunately this observation fails to note that several generations later these behaviors failed to evolve a better or more competitive product

However, when all was said and done, what ultimately led to the decline of classic professionalism in the American economy were the following traits that marked the very essence of the professional business model:

- The model was extremely "provider-centric." Each and every aspect of the enterprise revolved around the professional with staff, assets and indeed neighbors, but never were they seen as forces to be overcome or outsmarted. This is not to suggest that one in fifty professionals didn't act out an aggressive competitive strategy, but those who did were generally soundly ostracized by their professional community.

- While traditional professionals might have practiced their calling with groups and firms, the emphasis was always on the individual and almost never on the collective being. This of course was a handy perception given traditional professionals'

- Efficiency of practice or operation was only considered if it might make more resources available for the professional's life style. Lifestyle needs always outranked profitability and tax deductibility was a gift from the heavens.

- Benchmarking and metrics were considered the devils handiwork. Save us from the accountant who dared to suggest that the elimination of those personal expenses being carried as business write-offs might lead to profitability or company equity.

- Decisions were usually made based upon experience and opinion: "I don't need more information to make this decision" was a widely held belief. Unfortunately this approach was too often used to make decisions regarding professional services. Personal and professional infallibility became the mark of the true professional.

- There were absolutely no business strategies, generic or otherwise, incorporated into the business of being a professional. Instead of strategic goals the next level was defined by moving from a BMW to a Mercedes Benz, building a new house at the "club" or picking up one of those condos at the beach. The value of the business element was ignored and its future success assumed.

- Neither sustainable business nor professional standards were enforced. Why would a professional who was working 80 hours a week need something as limiting as standards?

- Accountability and transparency were rejected as making one more vulnerable to the spouse's divorce counsel.

- Finally, as generations of legal secretaries, nurses and receptionists were to learn, there was unilateral loyalty. The test of loyalty for all concerned was obedience to the professional master. As legions of con men were able to demonstrate, this was an ego of Olympian proportions.

THE DECLINE OF PROFESSIONALS

The Lawyers
By the early 80s the sheer number of Boomer Generation lawyers seeking to live the good life assured America of a highly litigious environment with lawyers taking aim at any likely defendant group or plaintiff's cause. The plaintiff's bar, temporarily stymied by increased automobile safety, better drivers and no-fault insurance, began to explore far and wide for new causes of action. The medical malpractice crisis of the late 70s and early 80s set the tone and the prospects for a bright and prosperous future for legal professionals while at the same time laying the seeds of destruction for many others.

At the root of every lawsuit for professional negligence is the assertion of professional standards and an allegation that the defendant professional failed to meet them. Slowly but surely this avalanche of litigation forced industries and professions to develop and adopt clear and compelling standards for virtually every aspect of manufacture and service delivery. The choice was simple, either the industry adopted its own standards or the judiciary would do it for them.

Within a very few years the frequency and size of judgments against professionals forced most to carry some form of malpractice insurance, the cost of which began to rise adding more nails in the professional coffin. While not all professions were equally attractive to either plaintiffs or their counsels the overall impact was intense enough to force all professions to begin to limit the length and breadth of professional discretion.

It is interesting to note that the level of litigation involving real estate professionals, even at its hiatus in the late 80s, while troubling, never reached a point where judicially established standards became the norm within the industry. Most litigation was directed at issues of representation or misrepresentation. No, it wasn't the courts that would ultimately bring standards to the real estate industry, it was the consumer.

The Emergence of the New Consumer
While such matters are sometimes difficult to establish, many experts suggest that the most important impact of the litigation era was the ubiquitous publicity that rained down on all professions. Consumers, long protected from the reality by the veil of professional secrecy, suddenly

> With each new "alternative" model the real estate practice is forced to evolve to the next level.

found themselves awash in stories about professionals who had not acted or performed appropriately.

Another factor that contributed to the decline of the professional era was the slow but steady transition of the consumer from an individual living in the darkness of informational deficiency to the status of a fully informed Social Media activist and engaged consumer. While some would suggest that this transition started with the emergence of the Internet, this is probably not true. However, the Internet did exponentially expedite this evolution and finally provide the why, where and how of the solution.

The consumers' early education came from the consumer advocates of the late 60s and early 70s; the Ralph Nader era. In almost every professional arena there emerged unique and articulate individuals who took it upon themselves to bring transparency to the world of the traditional professional. As was always the case the inherent attractiveness and impact of some industries and professions led to an earlier disclosure for others. The real estate industry is an excellent example of a "profession" that was able to avoid the dynamics set forth above until nearly the last moment. But ultimately all professions, including real estate, have found themselves the subject of the process.

The Arrival of Professional Women
Through much of its history the American professional community was an almost total male experience. Of course there has always been what might be described as a "token" presence of women in all professions, but by 1980 Boomer Generation women were beginning to filter into the professions. Most of them initially found work in institutional settings outside the influence of the "good old boys" and their professional business models that continued to dominate both the practice and professional organizations. But by the late 80s woman professionals began to transition into a fully accepted option for practices, firms, clients, patients and consumers. By the early 90s they were almost ubiquitous in the

Examples of the Consolidation of Industries and/or Professions into Conglomerates

HEALTHCARE	LAW	ACCOUNTING	PHARMACY	ENGINEERING	TRUCKING	FOOD SERVICE
Kaiser Permanente	Baker & McKenzie	Price Waterhouse Coopers	Walgreens	Fluor Corporation	Fedex	SYSCO
UnitedHealth	DLA Piper	Ernst & Young	Rite Aid	URS	Con-way	US Foods
Well Point	Jones Day	Deloitte	CVS Pharmacy	Jacobs Engineering Group	YRC Worldwide	Services Group of America

marketplace. And as women gained influence within the professional realm so to serious changes began to occur. Consider the following:

- The priorities of female professionals were in sharp contrast to those of their male counterparts; the original "quality of life" movement. While women professionals certainly wanted to make a "good" living they equated that status with much more than income. In the beginning these women practiced the "Superwoman" model that required them to match the professional energies of men while at the same time bearing responsibility for raising the family and administering the home. Later on the women of Generation X evolved a saner and more balanced model in which, and perhaps driven by the fact that their income options might have been less than for males, the ability to both work and raise a family were expressed as equal priorities. All too many males on the other hand continued to equate 80-hour weeks to the good life.

- Women, being willing to work for less compensation in exchange for reasonable hours and more dependable schedules, gave rise to their attractiveness as "employees." The initial beneficiaries of this arrangement were male professionals but this potential economic benefit was quickly perceived by corporate America and the subsequent development of the professional practice.

- While their male counterparts were busy learning about "situational ethics," women professionals were asking pointed questions about this or that practice, especially about those that seemed to violate more classic ethics. Suddenly there were two standards with women professionals representing the higher bar.

- As technology began to appear in the professions many men rejected it as invasive except for those that allowed their assistants, secretaries and clerks to be more productive; i.e. cheaper. Women professionals almost immediately embraced technology for its ability to make them better professionals. This fact was also to provide the corporate practice with a leg up in the following years.

- While male professionals chased up and down their industries and professions looking for a "better deal" and a quicker route to the top, their female counterparts demonstrated a higher level of loyalty and patience in favor of more settled and dependable lives. This trait offered yet another opportunity for those in the corporate sector who were sensitive enough to play on this expectation.

- Women in the professions demonstrated both an ability and willingness to develop stronger and more supportive relationships with customers, clients and patients.

THE ECONOMIES OF PROFESSIONALISM

The entire country, not just the professional sector, profited greatly from the post WWII economic boom. But by the mid 90s the national economy was experiencing serious repercussions from its unfettered growth and expansion. It seemed as if everyone was getting hooked on the good times and their expectations regarding what factors constituted a "quality life" were expanding wildly, which some suggested were getting out of control like the healthcare system.

For the past 50 years the U.S. has had the highest absolute medical expenditures and highest per capita medical expenditures of any nation. According to Schieber, Poullier and

> Capital comes at a price…to create value for all involved, especially its shareholders.

Greenwald, the U.S. has also had the fastest growing percentage of Gross National Product (GNP) devoted to the health sector. The rate of medical utilization and expenditure growth began its greatest level of acceleration over the period of 1970 to 1990 as articulated by Jencks and Schieber: "After 1970 U.S. health care expenditures grew at an annual rate of 11.6 percent, 2.9 percentage points faster than the U.S. GNP." According to the Health Care Financing Administration, the U.S. spent approximately 13 percent of its GNP on medical care in 1991 and 13.5 percent in 1992. These expenditures rose to 18 to 20 percent of GNP by 2000. But healthcare costs cannot be viewed in isolation.

Consumer demand for increased health care services doesn't suggest that the consumer was getting sick more often. Rather it reflects the fact that the consumers' expectations regarding a quality life included accessing health care professionals more frequently than in previous times. This growing demand for services could be seen across the entire range of professional services from heart surgery to dance instructions and from estate and financial planning services to trainers and dieticians. The professional was redefining life style and the professional community was a prime beneficiary of the process.

By 2000, 53 years after the start of the post WWII economic boom, the share of the U.S. GNP being generated by the professional segment had reached the point to where it had come to the attention of the investment and corporate sectors. The gross numbers being generated and the expanded markets that were being served impressed these financially motivated experts. They were also knowledgeable with respect to the total lack of management, efficiency and marketing skills being applied.

Put in other terms, there came a time as the 20th century drew to a close that the professional segment of the economy was simply controlling and consuming too much of the GNP. America is a free enterprise society and in such an environment money, not professionalism, is the controlling force. It was time for the national economic forces to align the economy with reality and classic roles.

Accordingly, by the onset of the new millennium, a whole new business model emerged in which professionals were increasingly being cast in the role of employees working within highly structured environments. In this new environment they were stripped of their independence, the ability to set their own incomes, control of the information pertaining to their profession, professional centricity and, perhaps most painful of all, much of whatever respect remained in the eyes of the consumer.

What they gained was the ability to focus on their profession while corporate America worried about management, logistics, competitiveness, finances, marketing, communications, standards and profitability. One-by-one virtually every profession was swept into the world of corporate practice and all that it has come to represent. Healthcare professionals first went to work for entities delivering prepaid health care, then for managed care and now for large regional health care systems. Legal, accounting and engineering professionals found themselves working for larger and larger regional firms. The great reputations of these professionals evolved into the brands and publically recognized names of the corporate entities that employed them.

On the other side of the ledger there appeared a new requirement that had not previously been incorporated into the professional model; the ideal consumer experience.

The immediate impact of these steps on the various professions came from the absolute influence of the cost accountants, risk managers, actuaries and strategic managers. The priorities of the professional that started in 1947 with a focus on client, customer and patient care, which had lost out to supporting the professional lifestyle during the 70s, 80s and 90s, were now being set by managers who were focused on the investment and return of the investment potentials for delivering professional services. Decisions that initially had been made based upon the best interest of those in need were now being made by automated management systems that used management technologies driven by the standards, metrics, facts and figures oriented to maximize production and profitability. The names of these corporate practices have become legions in the history of American business (see table).

Virtually all of these entities have the following characteristics in common:

- Automated management systems.
- Standards of practice.
- Verified universal accountability.
- Defined customer experiences.
- Utilization of metrics and benchmarking.
- Competitive and differentiation strategies.

WHAT ABOUT THE REAL ESTATE INDUSTRY EXPERIENCE?

Why wasn't the real estate industry caught in this downward spiral… or was it?

For a wide variety of reasons the real estate "profession" has been able to withstand the pressures and forces that caused others to collapse. But now, based upon the events of the past seven years, it appears destined to join the ranks of the reengineered professional. And it carries with it the distinction of being the last "profession" impacted and incorporated into the corporate practice.

The local nature of the real estate industry and market place, the fiercely independent status of its participants and its less than stellar image have contributed greatly to this situation. Even the largest and most sophisticated brokerages and brokers were hyper-local in the 70s and are still today very much focused on local market conditions and issues, with most agents operating so independently that change, be it positive or negative, often takes decades to filter through.

> The real estate industry, just like the others previously discussed, is in the final stages of its initial consolidation down to a handful of dominant players.

Despite the fact that some 40 percent of brokerages are party to a franchise agreement, franchisors have for the most part shied away from exploring, developing and/or promoting alternative brokerage business models that compete with their franchisees' existing business model. This reticence stems from decades of broker and agent responses: "Well, we aren't seeing that in our market." Another contributing factor here is the fact that while many brokers are college graduates very few have industry specific or business related studies.

Regrettably, the real estate industry has also seen itself, not in terms of its efficiency, cost effectiveness or profitability, but rather as a "people" business. Agents pride themselves in their ability to "control" their customers and brokers pride themselves in their ability to "satisfy" their agents.

Another factor is time. During the great boom of 1992 to 2005 there was no apparent need to be concerned. Driven by both demographic and economic stimulus those years saw greater levels of sales until 2005 peaked with levels 50 percent higher in volume than a decade earlier. And these are homes we're talking about, not consumer retail products. But the population didn't increase 50 percent during the same time period. 2005 was followed by a period of seven disastrous years that caused a significant number of brokerages to either fail or become engaged in "shotgun mergers." Once again there was neither the time nor the resources needed for updating the industry. Taken together these circumstances caused the industry to squeak through two decades without taking a critical look at its practices and procedures. But time has caught up and change has apparently become critically necessary.

As is the case in all industries, there is always one company that begins the process of re-engineering the traditional model of the day. In the early 1970s the industry was thriving as local independent brokerages when Century 21 and ERA came along and went the opposite way by creating a national franchise organization. Then in the 70s and 80s, when normal 50-50 commission splits were the order of the day for the majority of real estate companies, along came RE/MAX that went the opposite way with the 100 percent concept and shifted an entire industry. In the 90s and 2000s, when the industry stood strong on a broker-centric model, along came Keller Williams Realty with the opposite view by building an agent-centric model.

With each new "alternative" model the real estate practice is forced to evolve to the next level. In the current shift taking place the KW model is driving the industry to better profitability and productivity, more transparency, metrics and benchmarking and increased universal accountability.

Now a new model is evolving that again builds on the former, but it is driving in a totally new direction. This time, unburdened by the realities of the traditional brokerage model, the new third-party aggregators such as Zillow, Trulia, Move Inc. and possibly Market Leader's recent acquisition of RealEstate.com, have focused on creating a more technology-driven and more consumer-centric model. In principle it uses a sophisticated lead generation system, automated property valuations, transaction management systems and an environment of universal accountability.

These changes are being driven by newly minted public entities that are better capitalized than the industry generally experiences and are implementing initiatives and changes that most likely are not going to be copied by the traditional establishment for many years as they continue to resist the shift. Very few 65 year-old business owners have the desire or willingness to invest a number of years into boot strapping the reinvention of their current businesses. They are merely supporting these new initiatives together with the younger generation entrants that find solace in the fact that at least someone is using technology they way they believe it should be used.

Meanwhile the real estate industry, just like the others previously discussed, is in the final stages of its initial consolidation down to a handful of dominant players. The "Fab Four" at this stage, with an estimated 40+ percent of the industry, are: Realogy (Coldwell Banker, Century 21, Sotheby's, BH&G Real Estate and ERA), Berkshire Hathaway (HomeServices of America, Prudential and Real Living), Keller Williams Realty and RE/MAX. (Read more about the latest consolidation move by Berkshire Hathaway in Trend #1).

SUMMARY

Consolidation is happening on two fronts simultaneously, and already new companies have emerged in each space. Approximately 80 percent of the major players are already public companies; remember that 20 years ago these companies were not in real estate, were not publically traded or didn't even exist. Today these major players have more capital and better access to capital than most, if not all, traditional companies have ever had. Capital has moved from tertiary resource to primary importance.

But capital comes at a price. The primary purpose of a company, and therefore the business model used, is to create value for all involved, especially its shareholders. This has not been the case in a previously mainly self employed, professional, independent contractor environment.

With the current real estate model widely acknowledge as not being profitable, especially for outside investors, change is imminent. Moving forward, investment capital will only be available to the real estate industry if significant changes are made in the traditional brokerage business model, thereby allowing the investors to generate appropriate profits. Critical mass has in most cases now almost been reached; technology is in place to provide the scalability and capital is ready to flow. These circumstances affirm change is imminent.

In turn this means the environment in which successful brokerages work with agents will also significantly change. Once again we return to the business model attributes that will mark a successful and profitable real estate industry:

- Automated transaction management systems.
- Standards of practice.
- Verified universal accountability.
- Defined customer experiences.
- Utilization of metrics and benchmarking.
- Competitive and differentiation — based strategic management.

Real estate brokerage is far from being dead, but the traditional real estate brokerage model has become dysfunctional. Being a real estate professional is not dead, but the real estate professional of the coming decade will do things differently— "significantly differently."

Professionals will be less self-centered and less independent and more consumer-focused and more investor-centric. The majority will, based on the current consolidation, work for or with one or more of the previously noted large corporations — most likely taking home less than before, whether though declining commission fees, increased referral or lead gen fees or settling for a fixed income.

So, is capital redefining being a professional in real estate? Absolutely!

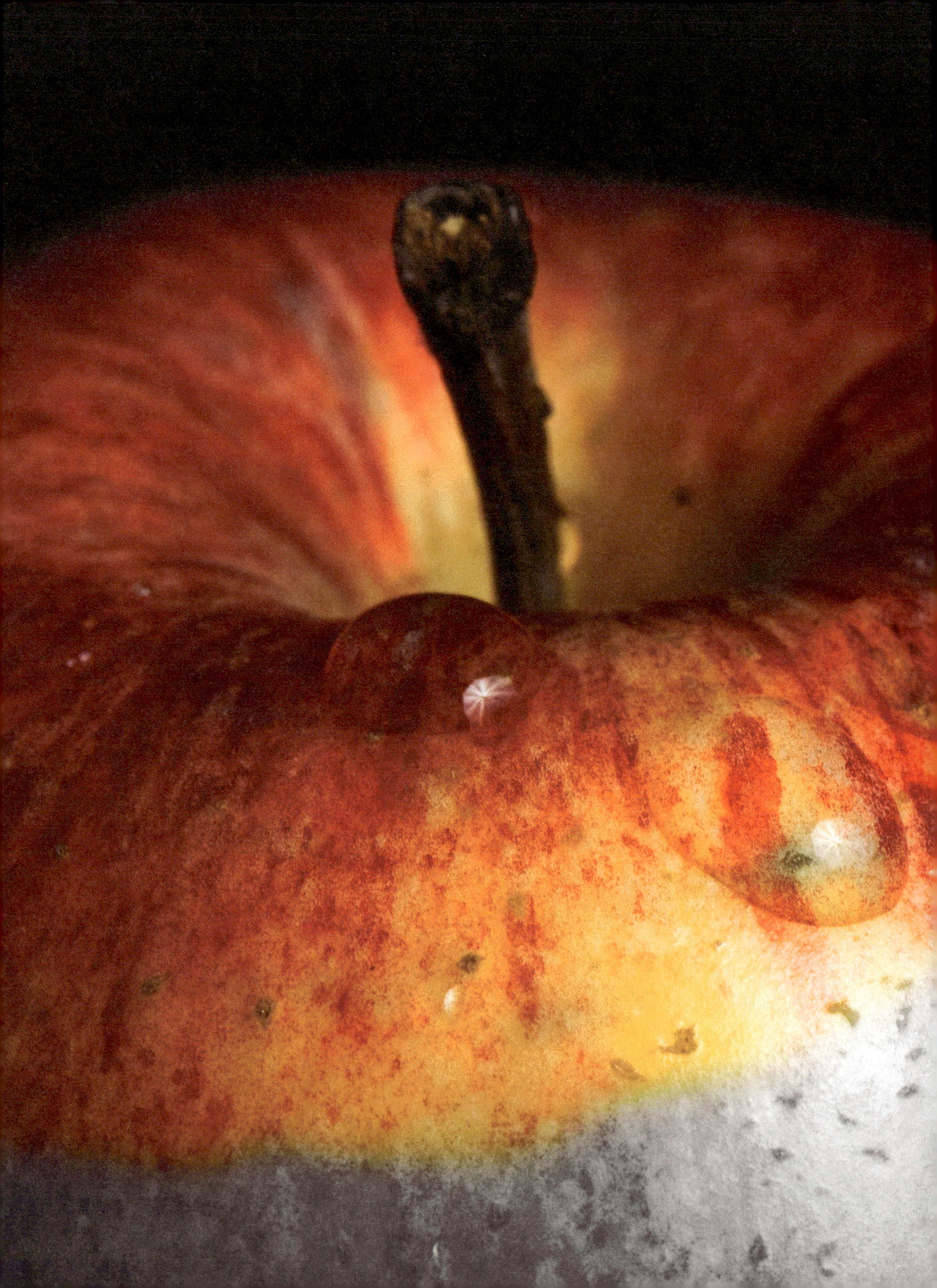

5 THE VALUE PROPOSITION OF BRANDS

Do Brands Matter in Real Estate?

The Value Proposition of Brands

This year, in light of the birthing of a new brand in our industry (see Trend #1; Berkshire Hathaway Takes Another Huge Step into Real Estate: Merely a Big Investment or is This a Game Changer?), we believe its an appropriate time to revisit branding and to provide an in depth discussion on the value proposition of brands, specifically as it relates to the residential real estate brokerage industry.

In the powerful world of consumerism, brands absolutely do matter. Imagining a world without "brands" is like imagining life without oxygen. If brands didn't matter 100 million people wouldn't be buying iPhones, 300 million people wouldn't be standing in long lines for a cup of Starbucks coffee or buying 1.7 billion Coca Colas every day to quench their thirst.

But to conduct a frank discussion about brands we must first shelve certain beliefs or restrictions we have that explain what we believe constitutes a "brand." We all have our own personal brand affinities and preferences, whether it's a particular clothing designer, sports team, appliance manufacturer or a hotel chain. Every time we interact with our brands of choice we do so because that interaction triggers a good feeling, and that feeling doesn't happen by accident. Emotion is truly a powerful activator.

Savvy organizations understand that emotion drives sales with a greater relative return on investment than traditional sales and marketing tactics can and often do. People aren't just buying Starbucks; they're buying a larger perceived lifestyle-like experience through their interaction with the brand, their fellow customers and everything else associated with Starbucks. Brands romance their customers to the extent that they become disciples and marketers of the brand (just think of Apple).

The question this Trend endeavors to address is, "Do Brands Matter in Real Estate?" And it's considerably more complicated than providing an immediate "yes of course brands have value" or "no brands are meaningless in real estate" answer. Why? Because residential real estate has more levels of branding types than are commonly found in other service industries or professions. So to address this question effectively means addressing branding on all these separate levels in order to meaningfully come to a conclusion.

Here is what we mean. Residential real estate is one of the few (some say the only) professions or services in which you not only deal with the company brand but also with the individual brand of the sales person.

Think about that for a few seconds. When interacting with Kaiser Permanente or Blue Cross you go to the company's website rather than the unqiue website of an individual doctor. The same applies to let's say a car dealership. You may go to LexusNewYork.com, but the individual sales agent would not have a separate website outside the company website.

So let's start from the outside and work ourselves inward.

FROM THE CONSUMERS' POINT OF VIEW

The residential real estate industry is blessed with many high profile brands. Some of those brands are almost as well known as the high profile consumer brands that enjoy multi million dollar-advertising campaigns. At the same time there are many well-established regional and local brands that have been serving the industry for many years.

Brands in residential real estate can primarily be divided into three different types:

- National brands (franchise groups)
- Local brands (agents and local brokerages)
- Online brands (media companies and aggregators; also a mixed bag of others)

Residential real estate sales is a fierce, competitive battleground in which there is an intense fight for the consumers' dollar, now reportedly exceeding $50 billion a year. The majority of brokerages compete for that dollar using the same three basic elements: listings, agents and ancillary services. From the consumers' perspective no specific brand consistently delivers any better or more unique client service than another as they tend to attach the quality of the service to an individual agent rather than a specific franchise or brokerage brand.

Within most brands you will find service that is exceptional, middle-of-the-road and bottom-of-the-barrel. Of course these extremes apply in some degree to any type of business but they are more prevalent in real estate than in most others.

Historically, unlike most other industries, real estate has generally not used large-scale, corporate advertising campaigns as a method of building a consistent, national brand identity. Notable exceptions are RE/MAX, Coldwell Banker and Century 21. It's difficult to build up a consistent brand image on a large scale without investing relatively heavily in mass marketing. The result is that branding messages have not been established in residential real estate through this method, they have only been effectively put out broker-by-broker and agent-by-agent.

Consumers have therefore not seen a consistent national brand identity. They have been continually exposed to brands at the local level, whether through the brokerage or the agent. In either case it has varied from market to market.

When asked to describe a real estate brand most consumers' response is: "They're a real estate company or they sell real estate but I can't describe any unique feature, market niche, position statement, etc. that relates to the brand." But this doesn't mean that there isn't opportunity for someone who's interested in creating a strong, uniquely identifiable real estate brand.

NATIONAL BRANDS (FRANCHISES)

Most other industry franchises have their own individual business system incorporating specific procedures by which their products and or services are to be delivered. For example, a Ruth's Chris Steakhouse experience is for all practical purposes identical at each location. But in residential real estate sales this is not even remotely so. The service delivered in almost every national real estate franchise office will differ

Brand Ranking

Top 20 most valuable brands based on criteria that includes financial performance and the role the brand plays in inlcuencing consumer choices.

Most Valuable Brand in:

'12		'11	'10
1	Coca-Cola	1	1
2	Apple	8	17
3	I.B.M	2	2
4	Google	4	4
5	Microsoft	3	3
6	General Electric	5	5
7	McDonald's	6	6
8	Intel	7	7
9	Samsung	17	19
10	Toyota	11	11
11	Mercedez Benz	12	12
12	BMW	15	15
13	Disney	9	9
14	Cisco	13	14
15	Hewlett-Packard	10	10
16	Gillette	16	13
17	Louis Vuitton	18	16
18	Oracle	20	22
19	Nokia	14	8
20	Amazon	26	36

SOURCE INTERBRAND

5 | The Value Proposition of Brands

The World of Real Estate Brands

- **Great Brand Awareness with consumers** — Century 21
- **Well Marketed and Promoted Brand** — RE/MAX
- **Great Online Brand** — Zillow
- **Great Century-Old Brand** — Coldwell Banker
- **Great Intuitive Brand** — REALTOR.com
- **Known Consumer Brand** — Better Homes and Gardens Real Estate
- **Great Financial Carryover** — Prudential
- **Strong Online Brand** — trulia real estate search
- **Great Brand Consistency** — Sotheby's International Realty
- **Great New Brand** — Berkshire Hathaway HomeServices
- **Interesting and Unique Brand** — EXIT
- **Acronym Brand** — ERA Real Estate
- **Powerful, yet Unmarketed Brand** — Keller Williams Realty

88 www.RETrends.com ©2012 RealSure, Inc.

significantly from office to office within the same stable, and even from agent to another agent within the same office.

The reason behind this is the fact that real estate franchisors themselves disagree as to who their client really is. Most agree that the ultimate consumer is the homebuyer. But the question is, who is the brand trying to build a relationship and/or awareness with; the home buyer/seller, the broker/owner, or the agent?

Companies like Coldwell Banker and Century 21 consider the consumer more the client while RE/MAX and Keller Williams consider the agent to be their client. Both these strategies work as these four companies are widely acknowledged as the top four in the nation (read more about the Fab Four in Trend #1).

In the case of a Ruth's Chris Steakhouse or a BMW dealership, the meal, the car and the total experience are the brand; it's the combination of product and service. Well, in real estate it's not the product (each house is different) and it's not the service (each agent delivers a different experience). In the case of BMW the sales person is selling the brand (the car) and the owner of the car (manufacturer or dealership) derives a profit from the sale of the car. The sales person derives a small commission from the sale and, as an employee and part of the overall BMW team, helps build the "Ultimate Driving Machine" experience.

Here again real estate is significantly different. The real estate sales person sells a different owner's house every time, derives no profit from the sale, receives a significant commission on the sale and builds his or her own brand experience; very seldom that of the franchise or brokerage brand.

You can see why franchisors are unclear as to who the client is.

One of the most popular "pop culture" books of 2011 was Simon Sinek's *Start with Why*. The central message of this book is that "People don't buy what you do; they buy why you do it" and that:

- There are only two ways to influence human behavior: you can manipulate it or you can inspire it.
- When companies or organizations do not have a clear sense of why their customers are their customers, they tend to rely on a disproportionate number of manipulations to get what they need.
- If there is hope for a loyal, lasting relationship, manipulations do not help.

So without a compelling "why" it's hard to build a strong national brand, and most real estate franchises have lost their big "why."

Lack of Direct Interaction with Consumers

Real estate franchise brands have little or no direct contact with the home buyer and/or seller, be it through a product (they don't really have one) or a service that no one directly responsible to the brand offers. Therefore any consumer interaction with the brand is indirect.

Allow us to be more specific:

- When agents perform their job perfectly it's the agent that is seen as delivering the service, not the brokerage or the brand.
- Barring some unusual circumstance—and those usually involve a negative scenario—when there is a problem with a transaction most clients never meet the broker/owner. Ergo, most clients' knowledge of "the brand" begins and ends with the agent. The actual broker/owner is almost never a part of the "client service experience."
- For the vast majority of agents, 95 percent of the job of selling real estate is conducted outside the walls of a typical brokerage.
- When working with sellers, the only time they typically set foot in a real estate office is at the closing. But generally closings take place at a title company so the majority of them never see the inside of a brokerage.
- When working with buyers, the only time they typically spend in an office is to sign an offer and that usually only happens once. The closing is generally held offsite so there is almost never a need for the buyer to visit the office again.

The end result of this is that the typical client never sees the franchisor and most likely never sees the franchisee, so there is little or no opportunity to attach brand value, good or bad, to the brokerage and by extension the national brand.

LOCAL BRANDS (BROKERS)

Most of the recognizable national brands like Century 21, RE/MAX, Coldwell Banker and Prudential Real Estate have a strong local presence in almost all major cities across the country. However, there are also cadres of local brokers that have over the years built up a strong awareness of their own local real estate brokerage brand.

Local brokerage brands have mattered and enjoyed a strong footing in local markets as far back as we could research. For example, a century ago it was Baird and Warner, eight decades ago it was John L. Scott Real Estate, six decades ago it was Ebby Halliday Realtors®, five decades ago it was Long and Foster, four decades ago it was Schlott Realtors® and so on. Today it's companies like Nest Realty, Good Life Team, Hawaii Life and Do Good Real Estate.

Locally owned and operated brokerages had a meaningful presence in the community because of the strength of broker or individual agent relationships, loyalties, commitments and contributions to and within his or her local community. Brokers and agents attended Rotary meetings, they were involved in local government, they supported charities, etc. They were part of their community before, during and after the real estate transaction and people knew them by name. They weren't just real estate companies, brokers or agents, they were neighbors—the brokerage and personal brand were one (read Redefining Real Estate Professionalism in Trend #6 for a detailed evolution of this changing relationship).

While many have passed these characteristics and practices down to second- and third-generation owners, a natural evolution has afflicted the industry. The emergence of franchising intensified competition and catastrophic market downturns, unbalanced splits and a host of other factors dramatically affected profit margins for many brokerages and brands. All of these things drastically impacted the frequency and quality of many local brokerage brands and their profit margins declined.

Local brokers have realized that the power and potential of being something more than a name on a nationally recognized yard sign has real cache. In every town brokers still lure agents by offering them proprietary tools or cutting deals with the best vendors in pursuit of quality solutions. But to be a brand that truly matters, brokerages must provide both their agents and consumers with those special things that are unique to them, matter enough and allow them to recognize the brand for being something other than what every other brand is.

One way of doing so is to find a niche that you can capitalize on such as the luxury market. For example, in this end of the market brand matters more than in the remainder of the price spectrum. Selling a multi-million-dollar home requires more advanced skills because these customers are generally more demanding as they're paying more. This created an opportunity for differentiation and international brands such as Sotheby's and Engel & Völkers, as well as highly respected local brands such as Houlihan Lawrence in New York and Michael Saunders in Florida, discovered how

> **Consistency is a backbone in building a quality brand.**

to position their brands as experts in this niche.

Standing for something such as quality and innovation meant they had to invest big in building more robust and attractive websites, licensing new tools for their agents and roll out newer and better services that are consistent with business franchises outside real estate. At the same time they neeeded to be different than most existing residential real estate franchises. They had to do this during good and bad times, irrespective of the economy and they had to implement this across the board on a uniform manner.

Consistency is a backbone in building a quality brand.

LOCAL BRANDS (AGENTS)

Consider your insurance provider, whether it's Allstate, State Farm, Geico, Progressive or any of the other household brands. Each has spent years branding themselves through assorted campaigns, slogans and characters, and most of us recognize all of them. But do any of the brands really connect with you emotionally to the extent that you feel one is significantly different than another?

Now ask yourself whether or not the brand played a factor in the insurance company you ultimately chose. Probably, because the one you chose had successfully drummed up enough top of mind awareness to create a sense of comfort. At least enough comfort to enable you to choose them over the many lesser-known local companies, most of which you probably never heard of. In this case, decades of corporate branding paid off.

Why this matters is because the comparisons from insurance to real estate are very striking. In your database or on the calendar on your wall there is most likely a company to which you have been sending money for a long time. But other than perhaps that new calendar you get every year from their agent, during all that time the brand probably never once made an effort to connect with you on any meaningful level. At the end of the day your decision on insurance most likely came down to two things: price and the local agent.

So how do we choose a real estate agent?

Is it the local agent's name you have on the calendar, the for sale sign you saw in your neighbor's front lawn or the one that returned your phone call or email first? Many of the agents that got into the game of building strong personal or local brands have many things in common: they were progressive thinkers, early adopters, bold branders and tech savvy. They were not a lot different from their broker counterparts that had the same mindset when building their companies.

These agents strived to be different. For them the brand actually became the differentiation—not the franchise or brokerage brand but their own brand. During the last 20 years of the previous century, the top-producing agents became the rainmakers as opposed to the brokerage companies. Agents increasingly focused on finding buyers and sellers wherever they were, whether with designed market materials, by saturating a given neighborhood, using mailing campaigns, writing well crafted blogs, driving traffic to their websites to generate their own leads, teaming up with lead generators or becoming active proponents of Social Media. And increasingly they became the face of the real estate transaction and often the only person consumers would see face-to-face. And the brokers just stood by as agents gradually diluted their brands.

So, today's reality is that most real estate business is obtained through the efforts of the agent. And the proof can be observed in the many markets where no brand truly dominates market share. It's also in understanding why so many agents hop from one brokerage to the next, often several times throughout their careers and in some instances literally year in and year out. Proof might also be in explaining why only 11 percent of consumers hire their last agent to represent them in their next transaction. Such a sorry statistic would certainly seem to suggest that neither the broker nor agent brand

YouTube

We found two informal researches online regarding the views of consumers concerning real estate brands (both released in 2010).

Professional One Franchising published a video called "Does Brand Matter to the Consumer?" (http://youtu.be/Ka8GaXU2t2w). They randomly interviewed people on the street in suburban Detroit and asked them for their opinions regarding real estate brands and the differences between them. The bottom line is that literally no one could explain the difference between the top five brands in real estate, and the few that had specific guesses were wrong in terms of what they understood.

Keller Williams Realty published a video called "Does Brand Matter?" (http://youtu.be/iT9zzA0biic) that performed very similar random person-on-the-street interviews with people in Austin, Texas. The most compelling statement that came out of that video was this: "4 out of 5 consumers said the brand did not matter."

5 | The Value Proposition of Brands

matters.

Many agents would argue that we have just proved their point that brand doesn't matter. But it does matter because although the consumer selects you—the agent and not the national franchise or local broker brand—they still selected a brand. It was your brand, your image, your credentials and your quality of services, branding and advertising.

Yes, branding does matter. It's merely a question of whose brand we're talking about and who did the better job of branding. In many cases agents have an equal or stronger brand footing than their brokerage or national franchise.

Within the industry, national brands have a "pecking" order in which the industry itself ranks the perceived "value" of each respective brand. That order is largely fueled by industry buzz, the profile of key individuals within the brand, industry related press releases and of course the 40-year feud over which real estate company is #1. However, local opinion and perceptions vary so significantly from zip code to zip code that hardly any consistency can be found. Throw local brands into the mix and it seems that agents tend to follow the credibility and awareness established by a dynamic local broker. It would appear that brand has very little impact.

So at different levels, at different times and in different circumstances, brand impact provides a different result. The best would be a combination of all three levels of branding: a great national brand, a strong local progressive and technology savvy brokerage image and a honest and trustworthy agent reputation.

More tangible and credible proof that brands are very personal in the real estate industry comes from the 2012 National Association of REALTORS® Profile of Home Buyers and Sellers, in which the "most important factors" consumers use "when choosing an agent" are listed (see table).

So what is brand again?

If it's measured by how often an agent is selected by a consumer by virtue of being associated with a specific company, then it's a low three percent. If brand means the image you portray—your reputation, honesty, your knowledge—then it's three of the top four items representing more than 50 percent.

BRAND FRAGMENTATION BY AGENTS

Most major real estate brands have minimal, if any, restrictions on their agents in terms of how they market themselves. As a result, if a brand has 50,000 agents nationally that means the public is very likely encountering 50,000 adapted marketing and branding messages from the same brand. And while it's true that individual agents don't advertise nationally but rather within a small geographic range, even on that smaller scale a given consumer is likely to encounter a number of unique marketing messages within a given brand, and those messages are almost never consistent. Some agents leverage their 25 years of experience as their personal brand differentiator, others market themselves as a first-time buyer specialist and still others feature funny pictures of themselves with their dog.

Most Important Factors When Choosing an Agent

Factor	%
Agent is honest and trustworthy	24%
Reputation of agent	21%
Agent is friend or family member	15%
Agent's knowledge of the neighborhood	12%
Agent has caring personality/good listener	9%
Agent is timely with response	6%
Agent seems 100% accessible	3%
Agent's association with a particular firm	3%
Professional designations held by agent	2%
Other	4%

SOURCE NATIONAL ASSOCIATION OF REALTORS®

The end result of these "mixed brand messages" is a significant dilution of the overall branding message. In the long run, when people are exposed to these local, mixed, all-over-the-board branding messages, the result is that the larger branding message is simply lost. Contrast this with how tightly controlled the marketing messages are from the most recognizable brands in the world: Disney, BMW, Apple, etc.

Now, think about this. Can you imagine how differently we'd feel about those brands if every Disney store was allowed to create its own marketing? What if each Apple store was allowed to create its own unique store atmosphere? What if BMW dealerships weren't 100 percent consistent in their use of "The Ultimate Driving Machine" as their slogan? We'd think very differently about those brands if they were absent those tightly controlled marketing messages and branding cues, wouldn't we?

ONLINE BRANDS

Because brokers didn't protect their brand from being diluted by the growing agent-centric branding invasion of the 70s and 80s, they also didn't at first notice or consider the further loss of brand awareness significant enough to respond when the online world erupted and posed a new threat.

These new online brands were very fortunate that national franchises and Realtor® associations were generally slow to respond, and as such the newcomers were given a very friendly environment in which to establish and grow their new brands. Individual real estate agents—being local and not national—were not serious competition and within a matter of a few years these new online media brands, also referred to as "aggregators," became some the most recognizable names in residential real estate.

Great marketing strategies played out well when companies like Zillow (zillow.com) began creating brand awareness months before their launch, which built up so much interest that it crashed their site the first day it went live. Trulia (trulia.com) had launched the year before with the same thirst for brand awareness with consumers and, like Zillow, it followed the classic branding playbook.

Trulia promised consumers a delightful search experience and they delivered. Zillow promised to give consumers a home value with no strings attached and they also delivered. Whether Zillow's notorious "Zestimate" was right or wrong didn't matter. Consumers were given what they were promised; a number. This appealed to the masses who wanted information they previously couldn't obtain without falling into the clutches of a sales person. Now they could get it quickly with no strings attached. Incorrect answers may have irritated an industry of agents, but from a branding perspective it worked fantastically well.

These new brands have very successfully seduced home buying consumers, providing them with the experiences they want, ones they seemingly are not getting often enough from the industry brands; national franchises, local brokerages or agents.

Today much of traditional real estate off line marketing and advertising has already migrated online and brand interaction has moved from terrestrial encounters to digital ones. This could have created a branding bonanza of opportunity for brokerages had so many not been so dreadfully slow to migrate to the web. In fact, some of their efforts of the early years may even have damaged the real estate franchise brands more than they helped. Shallow content, poor technology, lead generation trap doors and tortuous email marketing left consumers painfully unfulfilled.

Entrepreneurial agents grasped the opportunity to seize new local market share by capitalizing on "sexy" new brands that grabbed the consumers' attention and fueled their growth. These platforms provided many new mediums where agents could showcase their local market knowledge and personal brands and cultivate new business—business which was less and less being generated by franchises and local brokerage companies.

Trulia Voices and Zillow Zip Codes are both examples of interesting and meaningful user-generated content where consumers can view agents in action and see for themselves which agents provide useful information and which ones don't. These sites provide the context needed to help consumers decide which local agent to work with because they provide more depth and dimension than the typical agent roster page on a broker website that just displays a face, name and contact

5 | The Value Proposition of Brands

Real Estate Wheel of Fortune
The Key Players 2012

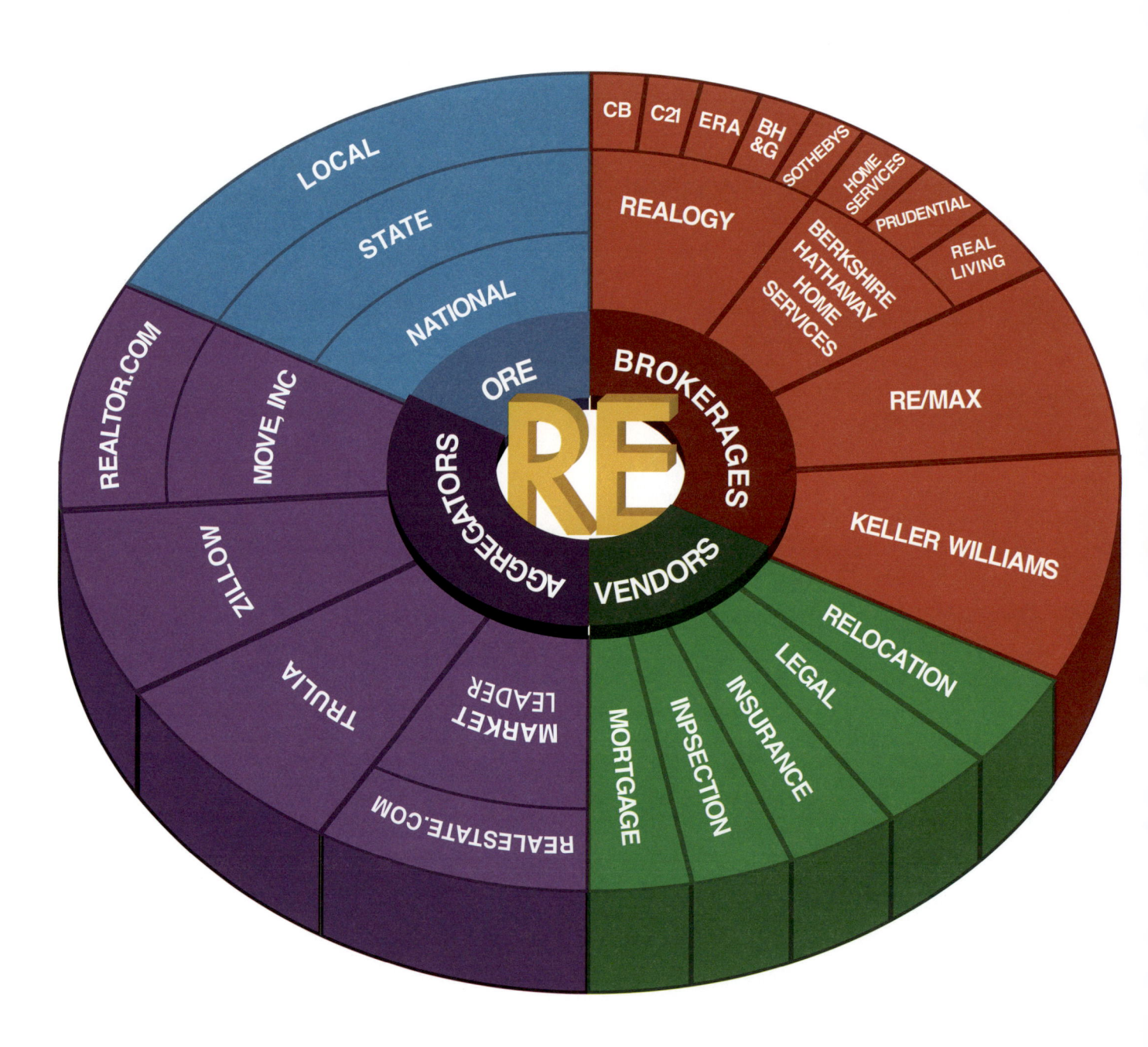

94 www.RETrends.com ©2012 RealSure, Inc.

information.

So, with each new press release and iteration of the aggregators' websites, these new media brands entice more consumers further and further away from the brokerage and the agent.

EYEBALLS OR HEARTS AND MINDS?

In today's reality the majority of homebuyers get most of their online real estate information from sources other than a national real estate franchise or local real estate brokerage. But large real estate brands are fighting back and some have created a large online presence with significant content. They have, however, lost the top rankings to the "aggregators" and it seems unlikely that they will be able to regain that position.

Building a brand is more complicated than just advertising, franchising or capturing online eyeballs. Consumers aren't just buying Starbucks, they're buying a larger experience through their interaction with the brand, their fellow customers and everything else associated with Starbucks.

Will the newly minted real estate brand, Berkshire Hathaway Home Services, be any different? Time will tell. They still have some baggage in the existing HomeServices of America, Prudential Real Estate Affiliates and Real Living brands, but they also have somewhat of a clean new slate in which to establish a new consumer experience. Let's see what happens over the next few years.

SUMMARY

The *Swanepoel TRENDS Report* has been researching and analyzing brands and the most popular vehicle for branding in the real estate industry, namely franchising, for 15 years. Recent editions have included The Franchising Mix Modifies (Trend #3 in 2010), The Tug of War (Trend #7 in 2008), The Race is On (Trend #7 in 2007) and The Franchising Revival (Trend #10 in 2006).

Branding is a very complex, highly sensitive and very customized endeavor. It is made even more complicated in real estate by the fact that consumers basically only deal with an agent when they sell their house, an average once every seven years. As a result, it's hard for people to attach significant brand value to any process they encounter so infrequently.

A real estate brand is a multi-tiered business that represents potential value to the franchises and brokers desiring to grow their company and the agents hoping to distinguish themselves from their competitors and sell more homes. It's also important for the home sellers in determining their perception and selection of the best agent/brand in town.

What is very evident from our research and discussions with many brand experts, brand builders and brand users in our industry is that franchises, companies and agents can and need to do a far better job of branding than they are today.

So lets return to the question we started with: "Do Brands Matter in Real Estate?"

Yes! In the end, the overall arguments in favor of brands having value, considering all levels and types, significantly outweigh those from the opposite point of view. Real estate brands may never be featured on the top of the list of most the valuable brands in the country but they are here to stay. With the competition for the Office of Tomorrow (Trend #2) and Berkshire Hathaway bringing a powerful new brand into our industry (Trend #1), real estate brands are destined to become even more important.

Hiring someone in real estate is based on the promise of integrity, trust, knowledge and excellence. Therefore anyone—franchises, local brokerage companies or agents—that can consistently fulfill those promises with relentless conviction and passion will develop a very profitable business.

4 BIG DATA: THE NEXT FRONTIER

Do We Really Want a National MLS?

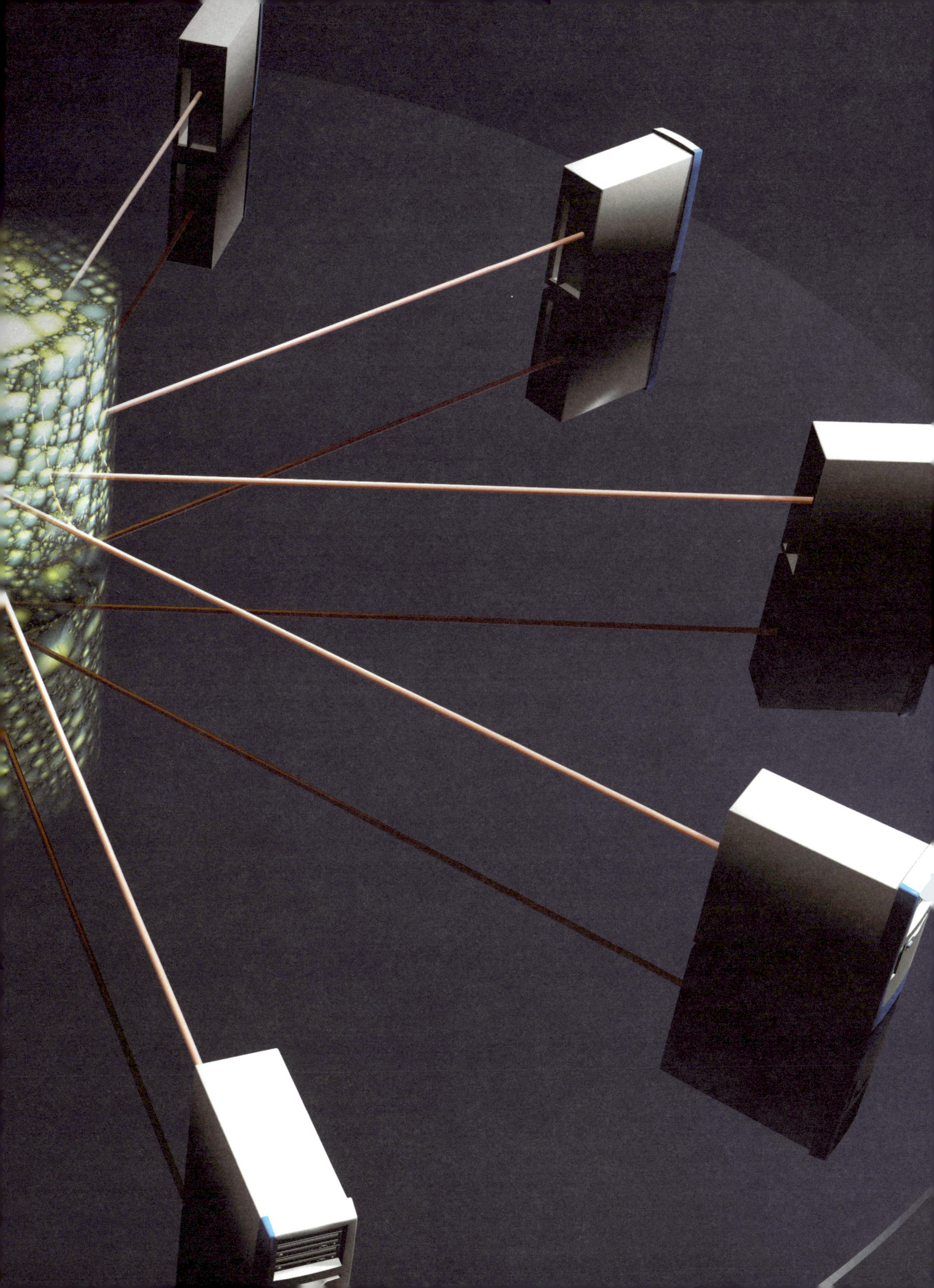

Big Data: The Next Frontier

For many years, industry pundits have speculated about who would be the first to try to create a national Multiple Listing Service (MLS). Such speculation has swirled around nearly every roll out of a national website, portal, database, service or virtual office website (VOW), even when the service being introduced has adamantly stated it has no interest in such a venture. The questions that are often asked include:

- Would a national MLS be possible?
- Would it make the business and the industry any more efficient, more transparent or more streamlined?
- Would such a service be a public utility or a private province of the practitioners?
- Who would such a national MLS service really serve—the broker/agent or the consumer?

In this Trend chapter we try to wrap our arms around all these issues and answer the big question: "Do we really want a national MLS?"

As far back as 1887 estate agents in San Diego, California set up what today would be called a multiple listing service (MLS). Brokers would gather and exchange information about their listings and frequently carried out an auction as they came to these meetings prepared to purchase certain properties desired by a client they were representing. However, it wasn't until 1907 that the term multi listing was first used.

By the 1920s multiple listing had become widely accepted and by the mid 60s MLS books with photographs of the exterior of the property became available. In 1968 one of the first attempts at computerizing MLS failed at the Long Island Board of REALTORS® due to equipment being both cumbersome and expensive. By 1972 the Baltimore Board of REALTORS® had instituted a centralized, computerized system to compile information. In 1975 the National Association of REALTORS® (NAR) published their "*Handbook on Multiple Listing Policy.*"

In 1982 the first cooperative regional MLS, formed by multiple associations of Realtors® was created in Phoenix; the Arizona Regional MLS. Between the years 1983 – 1987 more than 20 percent of all local boards of NAR had started their journey in making computerized MLS mandatory and laying the foundation for the basic system in use today.

Oddly, the U.S. is still one of the very few countries in the world that universally uses the MLS concept. This practice, that significantly benefits homeowners in selling their homes quickly and for more money, is one that is not used elsewhere in the world as "exclusive mandates" and "pocket listings" are generally the order of the day.

MLS EXPLAINED

In order to clearly understand the discussion about the feasibility of a national MLS it's important to clearly define the terms that are used. NAR defines MLS as follows:

- A facility for the orderly correlation and dissemination of listing information so participants may better serve their clients and customers and the public.

Conversely, a service that meets the test imposed by one or two, or even three of these definitions may not qualify as an MLS. National home search portals like Zillow (zillow.com) correlate and disseminate listing information, serve clients and the public, perform analysis on market trends, offer automated valuations of property and allow contributions to the common database, but they are not MLSs. It is singularly the universal offer of compensation between participants that differentiates an MLS from any other data service. It is the contractually codified requirement that one broker pays another for bringing forth a ready willing and able buyer who completes a sale transaction that makes an MLS an MLS.

the highest price they are willing to pay for a house, while making a lower offer in writing, the agent had the legal responsibility under sub-agency to tell the listing agent that information.

Our industry has come far since

> **MLS is no longer just a business cooperative operated by competing brokers to exchange listing information for the mutual benefit of all.**

- A means by which authorized participants make blanket unilateral offers of compensation to other participants (acting as subagents, buyer agents or in other agency or non-agency capacities defined by law).

- A means of enhancing cooperation among participants.

- A means by which information is accumulated and disseminated to enable authorized participants to prepare appraisals, analyses and other valuations of real property for bona fide clients and customers.

- A means by which participants engaging in real estate appraisal contribute to common databases.

These terms are important when testing whether a particular service qualifies to be called an MLS. In the Internet world many online services embody one or more of them but do not rise to the level of being an MLS.

The practice of sharing commissions dates back decades and is tied to the earlier practice of sub-agency, where the broker represents the seller and cooperating brokers working with buyers were actually sub-agents of the listing broker, also working beneficially for the seller while treating the buyer fairly. It was common practice as recently as 1990 for pre-license instructors to explain to students that if a buyer tells you

then. The advent of buyer brokerage made the offer of sub-agency not only unnecessary but in some cases dangerous because of the liability involved. Fortunately, while some MLS systems still provide a field through which to offer sub-agency, most brokers forbid their agents from accepting such an offer.

Yet because of the lending practices of mortgage loan originators, which allow only the commission paid by the seller to be rolled up into the sale price and thus the mortgage loan, direct compensation paid by the buyer to the buyer's agent has not become the norm. Sharing of commissions without the practice of sub-agency is still the most common practice for paying buyers' agents.

It has often been remarked that a national aggregator like Zillow is only one field away from being a national MLS. Well that field actually already exists. It's called "Make Me Move" on Zillow.com, where a homeowner names a price for which he would sell the house even while not actively listing the house with a broker. But even with a "For Sale=Yes" field Zillow would still not be a MLS as they would still have to actually facilitate the compensation arrangement between the participating brokers as well as a whole host of other functions (see below for more details).

THE ROLE OF MLS
While we have addressed the factual side of the question—is a national MLS possible or feasible—we have not considered the broader question of whether or not a national broker-to-broker business process platform could be created that performs all the other functions of the MLS.

The role of the MLS has evolved over time to include a diverse selection of activities such as:

- Marketing and advertising of the listings through syndication.

- Provisioning of agent and broker process management tools: CRM, showing appointment scheduling, lock box security systems, market analysis and home valuation, integrated additional databases like public records and school data, transaction automation and management.

- Common rules, policies and practices, compliance and the arbitration of disputes between participants.

- Data distribution and data standards.

- Broad technical support for both the MLS service as well as general technology issues.

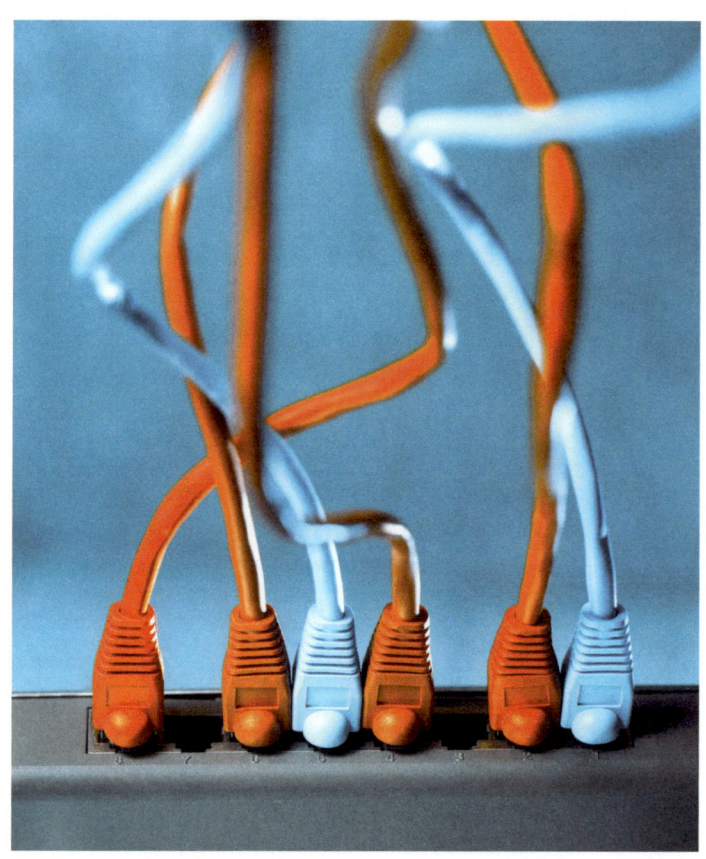

Setting the Rules
Where the going gets tough in discussing a move to a national system is when the discussion turns to the rules, the compliance enforcement of those rules and the arbitration of disputes that arise when brokers differ over the interpretation of the rules or their applicability to a given transaction. History did not record who first said, "All real estate is local." But that is never truer than when trying to get two or more MLSs to discuss a common set of rules and business practices in anticipation of a data sharing or merger activity. Every player at the table will insist that their local rule or practice is the best for all practitioners, and few are willing to compromise on those beliefs.

Successes in rules mergers are few and far between; California Real Estate Technology Services (CARETS; ca-rets.com) being the biggest example. Success often depends on the strength of the chairperson leading the charge and CARETS success can be attributed directly to Russ Bergeron and Art Carter, two MLS CEOs who have the "team vision," that together everyone accomplishes more.

However, more often than not, such discussions break down as the players become more intransigent in defending their home turf. Many industry consultants have been paid big dollars to advise MLSs on merger activity only to walk away in frustration that they were unable to get the participants to discuss common interests rather than debate uncommon rule sets. It seems that while they recognize that all real estate is local they forget that "all searches are national."

Enforcing the Rules
The role of the MLS as the creator and enforcer of the rules governing

behavior of participants is probably the biggest hurdle to the creation of a national business platform for brokers and agents that includes true MLS service requirements. Even ignoring the differences in state laws governing the licensure of agents and the practice of real estate by those licensees, resolving the differences between rules of various MLSs within a state is difficult and between MLSs in different states is nearly impossible.

Many state level merger and data sharing initiatives have failed because the local practitioners were unable to agree on such mundane things as how to count bathrooms, how long a listing could remain active after a contact was signed or even how many pictures would be either mandatory or allowed. Given the opportunity these discussions will degenerate into minutia and trivia at the expense of debate on more serious topics like governance structure, financial stability and agent practices.

Fees
A common set of rules is not the only impediment to creating a national MLS. Most MLSs, particularly those that operate as a wholly owned subsidiary of a Realtor® board or as a committee of the board, funnel some portion of the subscriber's monthly fee back to the board or association. Boards use this income to support non-MLS programs. Often a board seeking to increase revenues will raise the MLS fee rather than the board subscription dues, thinking that agents will object less to an MLS increase because MLS service is core to their practice, whereas they may see Realtor® membership as a necessary evil to be tolerated in order to get MLS service. If an association were to give up its MLS by merger or regionalization the lost revenue from that MLS operation could not be quickly replaced without a dues increase. Most association leaders are loathe to increase dues at any time and particularly in the face of the real estate collapse we have been working through for the past five years.

Economies of Scale
One of the benefits of regionalization or even nationalization is economy of scale. More people can be served with fewer employees. But that presents another hurdle to the regionalization process in dealing with the personnel toll exacted on the merging organizations. When smaller MLSs roll up into a larger entity or bigger ones roll up to mega-size, some jobs are duplicated, others overlap and the end result is dismissals or layoffs. Considering how painful job loss can be, many Realtor® leaders are disinclined to merge during a down economy when those affected would have a difficult time finding other employment. This can be a particularly sticky challenge when there are two CEOs of the merging organizations and only one spot open at the top of the org chart.

Service Providers
The brokers who operate the businesses that the MLSs serve make the decision about how they want to cooperate among themselves. If a mega-regional or national MLS cannot make a solid case for a business model that will serve the brokers better than they're being served now, there would be no support for such an initiative and no hope for its success. The brokers have the final say, and if they don't like the way the ball game is being played they could just pick up their ball, bat and glove and head home.

Marketing
Over the years the role of the MLS changed from B2B (business-to-business in the broader context and broker-to-broker in this specific instance) to B2C (business to consumer). MLS is no longer just a business cooperative operated by competing brokers to exchange listing information for the mutual benefit of all. As we noted earlier, MLSs have ventured into many other service areas. But one area stands out as the most successful endeavor any MLS has undertaken beyond its core purpose of facilitating cooperation and compensation between participants.

The MLS is still the most cost effective real estate marketing machine ever created. For a monthly fee that is less than a classified advertisement would cost in a local newspaper a broker can use the data feed from the MLS to create a publicly viewable website. That website will contain not only all of that broker's listings but through the NAR sanctioned IDX program it can also display any or all of the listings of every other broker in that MLS.

Consumers no longer need to buy the Sunday paper to search for information on properties for sale. Now the Internet offers one stop

From the Vault: Swanepoel TRENDS Report (2007)

Listing and property information access and delivery methods have changed. The gate is open and the option to keep the information is slipping away. The opportunity is here and now for the industry, brokers and agents to filter, process, deliver and interpret the information for the consumer; or someone else will.

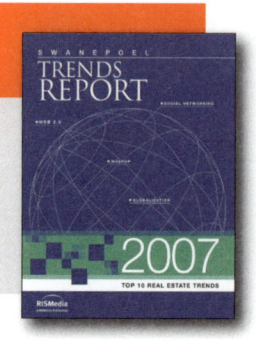

comprehensive shopping, and if local exposure on other broker sites is not sufficient the MLS, at the brokers' election, can send those listings to multiple national websites where consumers worldwide can view and consider properties in the comfort of their own home, constrained only by the speed of their Internet connection.

Outside Help

But brokers are not always allowed to use their MLS to their best marketing advantage. Instead, MLSs often create rules to protect the existing businesses rather than policies to promote new, innovative and expanding business services. Some MLSs have come under fire in recent years for adopting restrictive trade practices that prevent innovation in brokerage models. With the advent of the Internet and the desire of some brokers to move their entire businesses online—a proposition that threatened many traditional bricks-and-mortar brokers—NAR and the U.S. Justice Department (justice.gov) became entangled in a multi-year legal action that cost millions of dues dollars and delayed technical development of virtual offices by years. In the end, the new brokers won and NAR established policies governing virtual offices that all NAR sanctioned MLSs were required to adopt.

Faced with accepting the Internet as an integral part of real estate life (Read the new 160+ page *2013 Swanepoel TECHNOLOGY Report*), MLSs have started to embrace their new role and are assisting brokers in the distribution of listings beyond the sites operated under IDX and VOW rules. Most have contracted with one of the larger syndication partners to handle distribution. Some have created compliance processes to monitor displays and insure conformity to the rules. Still others have taken possession of the syndication process themselves, operating data servers and integrating the process of publisher selection directly into the MLS system. Very few have held fast to the traditional thinking that MLS data should be private, shared only between participants and never shown to consumers except in the presence of a Realtor®. The day of the closed MLS system is gone forever.

Finally, the MLS has often been seen as the equalizer between real estate brokers. In many markets MLS provides services beyond just listing entry and maintenance. These services are often requested by smaller brokers to match similar services already offered by large brokers. In doing so, MLSs are often accused of "leveling the playing field" and high-volume agents and brokers resent the MLS using their subscription dollars to support smaller operations that cannot afford such development on their own. Such concerns would only increase if done at a national level.

ANSWERING THE BIG QUESTION

"Do we really want a National MLS?" Perhaps that's a question that should never be asked again.

The problem is that the question is awfully vague and can mean too many different things and not allow discussion to reach a meaningful conclusion. So we must first define which one of the three primary models we're talking about:

- Should there be one national MLS Software System?
- Should there be one national MLS Database?
- Should there be one national MLS Organization?

Although the first two may seem less central than the third, questions about the risks and benefits of a national organization depend, at least in part, on understanding the issues relating to possible consolidation of the core software and database. For that reason let's address them first.

Should There be One National MLS Software System?

In this scenario there could be one or many local MLS organizations and one or many databases, but there would be one national MLS software package.

Having one national MLS software system is usually compared only with the status quo: having one (occasionally two) MLS software package for the local market. But let's also compare it against a range of possible options, including one in which individual subscribers select their own MLS software inside each MLS organization, as well as hybrid approaches.

Having a single local system provides the local MLS organization the buying power needed to make extensive local software customization affordable, splitting the costs over many users over time. Also, while an MLS organization can advocate with a single MLS system vendor for local needs and changes, it may be less feasible to advocate with many system vendors. If the individual users contracted directly with system vendors it would be more difficult for the MLS to advocate with many system vendors if there weren't a direct financial and licensing connection as exists between the local MLS organization and the MLS vendor. How would changes in the many systems (and accompanying training) be communicated to subscribers?

In addition, as multiple systems

> Could a system be put in place that would encourage competition for the national MLS system contract? It is unclear that a company would want to spend three to six million dollars to create a competitive MLS system just for the chance to "win" the business from an incumbent national system.

change (at once or over time) the underlying local database changes would need to be managed. That could get expensive for the local MLS organization, especially if many MLS software vendors were constantly innovating. Providing support for mission-critical software—especially as it changes—is a complex process, and while it's difficult enough to support one software package at the local level, supporting software from multiple vendors could be untenable. Such concerns argue that limiting the core MLS software packages to only one or two is the better approach.

But individual subscriber choice also presents its own advantages. Anyone who has ever helped select (or support) MLS software can tell you that it is difficult for a single software interface to satisfy everyone in one local market. Some users prefer a very simple MLS system, others a more functionally robust system. Some users prefer the CMA of this system, others like the client collaboration tools in that system. Also, since people don't need local support for popular business applications like Microsoft Word, why would they need it for the MLS software? Finally, since technology may make local customization easier in the future, the "buying power" argument may lose ground to the individual choice option.

However, recently MLSs have begun fielding a single core MLS system but providing an "app store" where individuals can differentiate around that core by purchasing the apps and tools they want—like property reports, CRM, CMA, mobile apps and marketing software—and this new practice may reduce the attractiveness of fielding multiple core systems. This approach could help enable a single national "core" MLS system and a standard national interface to suffice for many users while simultaneously making additional innovative add-ons and interfaces available for agents or brokerages to purchase. The suppliers of these add-ons could compete for users at the national, state and local market levels.

Historically, in comparing the advantages of a national system with those of a single local or individually-purchased system, the biggest question has been whether a national system could be customized to handle all of the local requirements and business rules of all the local MLSs. Any vendor that has tried to service 100 or 200 or more MLS organizations can already tell you how difficult it is to balance those customers' needs and priorities, and serving the needs of some 800 would be far more difficult. With a national system, local customers waiting for a vendor to service the local requirements might experience a lot of frustration.

Finally, would a national software system best serve subscribers? Would competition among multiple MLS software companies spur innovation and lower cost, and how would these concerns balance against a national system's potential efficiency? Currently, the competitive, innovative software market serves local MLS organizations and their subscribers well. Could a system be put in place that would encourage competition for the national MLS system contract? It is unclear that a company would want to spend three to six million dollars to create a competitive MLS system just for the chance to "win" the business from an incumbent national system or, if a new system won the business, whether the industry would want to risk a whole-country cutover to an unproven system. But without this competition would subscribers truly be well served?

To summarize, it's difficult to argue the benefits of a single system and easy to raise concerns that are hard to address. The current model of one system per MLS organization works. But looking forward, if concerns could be addressed, it might be feasible to move toward a more consolidated "core" MLS system, mitigating some of the concerns about competition and innovation by allowing for individual subscriber-purchase of well-integrated ancillary software and user choice of "front-end" software that seamlessly works with the "core."

Should There be one National MLS Database?

Despite being told for years that size matters and only the large would survive, the efforts of MLSs to regionalize and to merge into fewer, larger systems have mostly been unsuccessful. Today there are some 800 individual MLSs, some serving fewer than 100 agents, and local parochial interests have prevailed with small systems holding out as long as possible, promising to keep their systems tailored to the "special, local system requirements" that made them unique.

The failure of MLSs to consolidate or cooperate on a national level has yielded larger, better-financed national web services catering to both agents and consumers. But their failure to combine at the organizational or governance level doesn't necessarily negate the need for or the possibility of MLSs combining resources to create a national resource.

NAR began a similar effort some years ago to give MLS participants a rich database of information on all properties. The RPR (REALTOR'S® Property Resource) is a closed system, not available to the consumer and was funded by NAR with the intention of being self-sufficient by selling derivative data products and services. To a large extent RPR was created to fend off the growing threats from national aggregators that are providing more and more free information to the consumer.

Many smaller boards welcomed RPR with open arms. But larger regionals resisted participating, fearing a loss of power on their side, yet more power consolidated in the hands of a national trade association with a poor track record of operating large technical initiatives. This caused dissention and unfortunately prevented RPR from gaining the much needed traction to achieve critical mass quickly. However, the product ideas behind RPR have merit.

This is a national service that produces good-looking marketing pieces, in depth market analytics and puts a wealth of knowledge gathered from databases of every kind at the agents' fingertips. The shortcoming is, however, in thinking that the public will ask the Realtor®

for this information when the Web has already shown that the consumer wants to find, read, digest and understand this information on their own, before reaching out to a Realtor®.

But the platform exists and if restructured could fairly easily be morphed into a powerful national marketing platform for industry brokers and agents to own and would compete commendably with various different national aggregators.

- *Would it be a national MLS?* No, not by the traditional definition.

- *Would it make the business and the industry any more efficient, more profitable, more transparent, or more streamlined?* Absolutely, and it would be a way for Realtors® to finally acknowledge that they too believe the consumer is #1.

- *Who would such a service serve—the broker/agent or the consumer?* All three.

- *Would such a service be nothing more than a public utility and no longer the private province of the practitioners?* The information would be public and the ownership and operation private/non-profit and the result would be a win for both. They would not fall into the same trap that NAR did in licensing Realtor.com while allowing its members think it was a member benefit when it was actually a commercial for-profit enterprise.

A Single Database and a Common Back End

It is possible to have multiple MLS systems that have a single national database or "back end" in common, including listing content and even other core types of data found in today's MLS systems; contacts, saved searches, financial worksheet data and associated documents and other media.

Technically a national database would consist of more than one physical set of database servers in multiple locations and might involve either of two processes. The MLS system's "front-end" interface uses the national database directly via an API or direct data access, or it uses a replicated copy of the data or only part of the larger data set as needed by that front-end.

The main benefit of a national database would be that those requiring datasets that cross MLS boundaries could more easily get that data from one place (with local MLS organizational approval for specific local data, of course). Because the hardest aspects of data aggregation are obtaining and managing that permission as well as adequately addressing the related legal agreements and compliance, a unified database technology would not provide that much benefit over what we have now. In addition, national aggregators are already addressing the technical aspects of aggregation and distribution. Syndication companies like ListHub (listhub.com) and Point2 (point2.com), and national efforts such as Corelogic's Data Co-op (corelogic.com) and RED's reDataVault (redatavault.com) have each invested several million dollars to aggregate, cleanse and enhance the local data on a national level, and they can each distribute the data based upon whatever directions and rules the content owners provide.

A national MLS database would certainly provide the benefit of making it easier to generate better real-time nationwide statistics.

Would such statistics be much better than those today, based on data that are sent to NAR to generate national statistics that lag the market?

agent, licensed at the state level and doing business locally. Although aggregating data in larger regional MLSs and having larger multi-MLS data aggregations would benefit large, multi-office regional brokerages, regional aggregation is a much easier endeavor than attempting to compile a national database. How much effort should the industry expend to create a national MLS database that doesn't provide much benefit to local practitioners, but mostly to national players?

Also, and perhaps most importantly, there are three additional risks posed by a national database. First, it constitutes a greater information security risk: it's a very big target. Second, if all systems depend on that database to be up and running it also introduces a single

for national real-time statistics and analytics, and the desires of those who might legitimately want nationwide listings data for other purposes, would outweigh those concerns. The creation of a national database only starts to make sense, as a matter of efficiency, if there is a national MLS organization.

Should There be One National MLS Organization?

Most people advocating for a national MLS are thinking about the advantages of a single system and database. Having a national MLS organization is seen only as an end to those objectives since it's seemingly impossible to get many MLS organizations to agree to a single system and database.

> The failure of MLSs to consolidate or cooperate on a national level has yielded larger, better-financed national web services catering to both agents and consumers.

Certainly, more accurate national real-time statistics and analytics would have immense value to investors, government organizations and the lending industry. This value would represent a substantial revenue stream to the source. This advantage of creating a national database is undeniable.

But, a national database would provide limited benefit to the average real estate broker and

point of failure. Third, a national database might also constitute an easier legal target for those seeking access to the mother lode of listing data.

To summarize, although creating a national database would offer limited benefits, especially for the local participants who make up the bulk of the stakeholders, a national database would raise a number of concerns. It is unclear that the need

The central reasoning against the formation of a national organization is that it fundamentally creates a monopoly, and monopolies rarely provide the best products and services at the lowest possible cost over the long term. Also, governance issues would likely make it more difficult for a national organization to service local market needs. Consider the challenges MLSs currently face getting things done at the NAR Multiple Listing Issues and Policies Committee, a group that has only a very limited non-operational scope. Furthermore, like a national database, a national MLS organization also would create a single legal target for those seeking MLS access or recompense for patent or other infringements.

Many local MLS organizations are currently hubs of software and service innovation, both internally and working with small software vendors. They provide an opportunity to experiment and fine-tune offerings on a small stage, out of the national spotlight. Would one large MLS become an impediment to that environment—even putting up financial roadblocks to smaller vendors getting access to subscribers, as some of the larger industry organizations already do?

On the other hand, a national MLS organization could provide significant benefits. First, there always seem to be well-funded efforts on the verge of disrupting the industry and a single MLS organization would be better positioned, in terms of both governance and funding, to take on those challenges. In addition, the arguments against the formation of a national MLS could be addressed. In terms of product competition, for example, the organization could field multiple MLS system options or choices of front-ends, which would generate daily competition among technology providers. The result would be a fight for market share among the subscribers and competition on price and quality. Further, although many large decisions would be made at the national level, there could still be local MLS service centers, which would be expected to meet regularly measured standards of service and potentially compete for subscribers on service and price as well. Although the governance and legal issues may be more difficult to address, those challenges and risks might be managed to some degree as could the potential risks of a single national MLS organization.

Finally, some might argue that if the present industry doesn't create a national MLS (software, database and organization) then another group might. If a well-funded company wanting first access to MLS data offered service to MLS subscribers nationwide for a large discount over what subscribers currently pay, could that company successfully host a national MLS? Assuming the value was there, many practitioners would move to the lowest priced system with little or no regard to who the existing MLS provider is, and obviously this could be very disruptive to the current structure of MLS. If structured properly, and care is taken to address the issues raised above, a national MLS organization should be able to deliver more cost-effective MLS service than the current model and reduce the risk of this type of potential disruption.

IS THERE A MIDDLE GROUND?

Having some 800 Multiple Listing Service organizations certainly has inherent problems. Many of the smaller organizations don't have the resources to provide a strong service or software package to subscribers, defend against better alternatives, implement a secure infrastructure, plan for disaster recovery or even to hire professional IT staff or management. Having more than one MLS in a property market area causes great inefficiency: brokers and agents must belong to multiple MLSs, which increases subscriber cost and data aggregation cost and effort. In addition, people need to learn multiple MLS software packages and manage multiple sets of login credentials—but still can't perform a unified MLS prospecting search to provide search results to their clients.

The answer to these problems is not necessarily to create a national MLS organization, system, or database. There may actually be a very viable middle ground. If the smaller MLSs were to merge into regional MLSs, ranging in size from multi-state MLSs (for example, a New England MLS, Mid-Atlantic MLS, or Dakota MLS) down to some states which might have two or three (such as Northern California and Southern California) we would be able to address basically most the frustrations but inherit few of the major challenges.

Many of the concerns surrounding a "national" MLS system, database and organization would of course still hold to some degree if one substitutes the terms "state-wide" or "regional" for "national" as many regional systems may still not have quite the buying power or governance advantage of a national model.

Nonetheless, a new modern network of fewer but larger MLSs could provide a practical middle ground between the current model and a national model. At the very least it would be a logical building block towards a future national model, if this were still deemed appropriate.

A THREATING DEVELOPMENT

In 2011 MarketLeader (housevalues.com) purchased RealEstate.com (REDC; realestate.com) from Lending Tree (lendingtree.com) as part of a package that included multiple patents, trademarks and 400 domain names. It also included a brokerage operation licensed in multiple states that was hemorrhaging money. They reemerged as a pure referral model and things started to get interesting.

REDC belongs to numerous MLSs by virtue of its licensure and Realtor® membership. REDC therefore obtains MLS-IDX data as part of their subscriber benefits from all the MLSs they join. They use this data on their national site to attract and interest consumers. Consumers who ask for more information about a property were referred to the local referral partner that purchased that territory. Referral agents' pay for the privilege of receiving these leads by buying exclusive territories from REDC for a flat price and then paying a portion of their commission to REDC for any closed transactions that result from REDC leads.

However, REDC makes no pretense of actually listing or selling houses, only that they are licensed and therefore could receive referral fees from agents/brokers to whom they send leads (both buyer and seller leads, one presumes). But a mere possession of a broker's license is not sufficient to qualify for MLS participation. Some argue that this is an unauthorized use of MLS data by a firm that did not qualify under MLS rules (adopted as part of the DOJ-VOW settlement) as a Participant. The NAR settlement and the policy that resulted from it, however, are silent on whether a referral model complies with the spirit and intent of the settlement.

> Having a national MLS organization is seen only as an end to those objectives since it's seemingly impossible to get many MLS organizations to agree to a single system and database.

Want to know more about the actual wording of the settlement document? Go to http://www.justice.gov/atr/cases/f239600/239655.htm.

So, for now the rules still remain basically untested and thereof things continue to evolve.

If an MLS does challenge REDC's position that it has a right to use the data in its business model by virtue of being a broker and MLS participant, the MLS that makes this challenge will be fundamentally changing the role and mission of the MLS. No longer will the MLS be the facilitator of business between participants but it will be deciding who those participants can or should be. If the MLS wins, it expands its charter from mere utility to guardian, something most believe it should not be. If the MLS loses, the gates will be thrown open for any company that wants to become brokers, join the MLS and use the data for any business purpose for which there is a demand and a profit potential.

Meanwhile, just as we end 2012, along comes HomeLight (homelight.com). They are licensed in over 20 states and belong to over 30 MLSs as real estate brokers. They use the MLS data not for listing or selling houses but for rating agents according to criteria entered by buyers. The criteria vary according to the desired geography, price range, type of property desired and what kind of service they're looking for; best price, toughest negotiator, quick sale, etc. The buyer picks an agent who gets the referral lead from HomeLight and if a sale results HomeLight is paid a fee by the agent.

If they are using MLS data, and one must presume they are or they wouldn't have gone to the trouble to get licensed and join 20+ MLSs, then this business model seems even more removed from the intent of the NAR-DOJ settlement and the resulting policies than is the case of REDC.

Something big is going to happen here, and when it does the *Swanepoel TRENDS Report* will once again be there to analyze the evolution and future of MLS.

SUMMARY

The future of MLS has never been murkier. Industry practices and consumers are evolving rapidly (Read Trend chapter #3 - The Gentle Revolution) and slow moving MLSs and their parent Realtor® organizations (Read Trend chapter #6 - Revisiting Organized Real Estate) will have to make big decisions much faster than their historic comfort level allows. For example, after three years of debate the NAR MLS Policy Committee, as of November 2012, has still not adopted rules or guidelines for local MLSs to regulate and oversee the use of MLS listing content in Social Media contexts. An earlier attempt to include national franchise organizations in the IDX policy was ill conceived, poorly executed and resulted in the policy being reversed within a year of adoption.

The regional MLS formations that have occurred in most large metro areas have, for the most part, removed the necessity to join multiple MLSs to get the market data. Large consolidations, like southern California, are further eliminating the need for duplicate fees and are reducing the cost of doing business for those brokers and agents who operate in more than one MLS territory. Although there are dollars to be saved in a national rollup of all MLS organizations, politics and territorialism make it difficult. Most consideration and conversation regarding a national MLS presupposes dragging along all the current rules, services and structures, and all of these are impediments.

The only opportunity that would threaten the existing MLS structure would be a national database of homes offered for sale by consumers with offers of compensation to someone who brings a buyer. This option would create a significant savings for the consumer and therefore could be a sufficient driving force for the creation of such an entity.

This would, however, not be an option popular with any of the current stakeholders (agents, brokers, franchises, associations, MLSs and MLS vendors). It would require a large well-financed non-Realtor® entity to approach this undertaking and this is not currently probable. One of the significant challenges to any non-Realtor® national database would be a methodology to insure accuracy and currency of the data. Consumers would have little incentive to insure quality of data and therefore the usefulness of such a database would be severely compromised. It would likely give rise to an organization to run and administer the database that might just look like what we have now.

Thus in conclusion, we find no compelling driver for the formation of a national MLS.

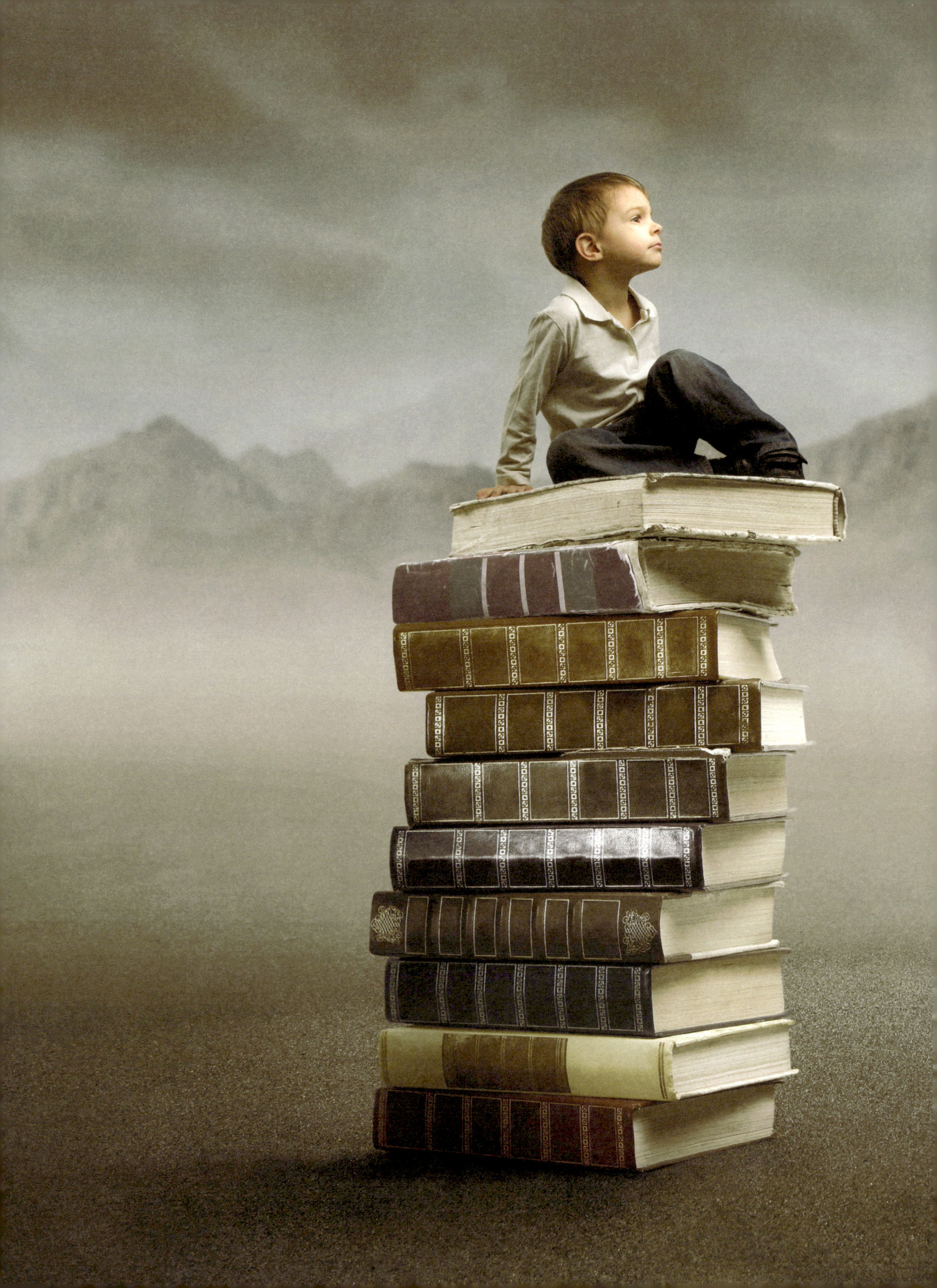

3 THE GENTLE REVOLUTION

Smart Young People
Connecting with Wise Old Realtors®

The Gentle Revolution

Over the past several years the *Swanepoel TRENDS Report* has researched, investigated and interacted with trends reflected in virtually every aspect of the real estate industry. During this period remarkable developments have been discovered and tracked in the areas of technology, innovation, strategy, business models, brokerage operations and agent practices. But what makes this year unique is that we are seeing the emergence of the American real estate consumer as a freestanding, self-protecting, relationship seeking, mega-force in the marketplace.

The vast majority of today's homebuyers are no longer vulnerable nor in need of third-party protection. Over the past few years a quiet transformation has taken, place and in today's marketplace consumers have become a force to be reckoned with, as their expectations and demands are setting new standards for industry operations, brokerage management and agent practice.

THE AMERICAN CONSUMER

The History of Consumerism

Like many of the forces that have shaped our contemporary lifestyle, the history of the current consumer movement traces its origins back to 1947, the date that marked the beginning of the post WWII economic boom. Then the businesses and professions that ruled the economy through much of the 20th century reigned supreme in the dissemination of information.

This left the consumer vulnerable to a wide range of scams and schemes because of their lack of knowledge and limited access to information. But the economic growth during the twenty years that followed the war was so robust that it overcame the downside of consumer vulnerability, the economy prospered and the civic-driven consumer remained active and passionate about consumption and participation.

Parenting

During this period the resident mindset generally held that someone or something had to "take care" of the consumer and when television went mainstream it assumed that role and became part of the protective process. By the mid-60s consumerism was in full force, being led by the likes of consumer advocate Ralph Nader. The Federal government, non-profits like Consumer Reports and academia were also busy initiating consumer advocacy programs. As more information regarding the dangers and flaws of consumer related programs, products and services became available consumers began accessing it.

By the early 70s the Boomer Generation had discovered law schools and very soon everyone had either a friend or family member who was a lawyer. By the next decade the courts became the center of consumer advocacy by adopting a preference for "taking care of the consumer."

In the light of contemporary history it should come as no surprise that the consumers' honeymoon with the legal community was relatively short lived, especially once they discovered the cost and probabilities of legal satisfaction. During this period our culture was forever stamped with the knowledge that legal remedies, if and when realized, were often greatly delayed with a cost that often exceeded the value of the remedy.

During the 80s Congress, state legislatures and local governments picked up the consumer cause and began to pass statutes designed to offer consumer protection. Warning labels, lemon laws and warranty requirements blossomed and the EPA took on the responsibility of saving us from ourselves. At the same time consumers were becoming more sophisticated and businesses were becoming more "consumer wise" and many of the more drastic anti-consumer scams were occurring less frequently.

Self-determination

It was at this point that, for the first time, the consumer theme began to shift from "parenting" to "self-their secret path to information; the foundation of the consumer revolution was laid. As the 20th century morphed into the 21st improved Internet service, broadband capability, unlimited access to data, refined search processes and wireless mobile access provided consumers the keys to knowledge and power; power that eventually found a conduit in a new and rapidly growing concept called Social Media. The ultimate revolutionary tool set was now in place; information, knowledge, communication, collaboration and transparency.

From an almost totally "ignorant and independent" consumer era emerged the single most powerful force in the marketplace, a force that them. For example, consumer-rating systems have widely become an accepted and even expected part of the consumer landscape.

The Rebirth of Consumerism

With all of this attention given to the consumer revolution it's interesting to note that another significant revolution has been occurring at the same time. It most likely started at some point in the 90s and, although birthed in information, historians will likely conclude that it was driven to its current levels by one of the more basic economic forces known to mankind.

Whether it's a matter of history, poetic justice or divine intervention, the business economy is being given

---

In some regards, today's consumers have become their own advocate, judge, jury and executioner. For better or worse they have acquired the most power and influence in the economy they have ever had, and there is no sign that this new standard has even come close to reaching its zenith.

---

determination." To a great extent this Trend can be traced to the fact that during the 90s the "information age" came into full swing and the current state of affairs relative to the consumer was birthed. This new age was first memorialized in the New York Times bestseller, *Megatrends*, by John Nesbitt, and from that moment on access to more and more information about everything began to shape the consumer experience.

By the late 90s the Internet had become a widely accepted and utilized tool as consumers discovered continues to revolutionize what it means to sell and serve the consumer; technology.

In some regards, today's consumers have become their own advocate, judge, jury and executioner. For better or worse they have acquired the most power and influence in the economy they have ever had, and there is no sign that this new standard has even come close to reaching its zenith. Ironically, Social Media is allowing consumers to regulate many of the very same businesses and professions that previously took advantage of a much need hiatus in between the consumer revolution and the consumers' discovery of their new powers. Regardless of its origins, the fact is that today's Internet and Social Media empowered consumers have yet to fully engage the awesome power they gained in recent years; communication, self determination and transparency.

This natural delay between power acquisition and implementation by the contemporary consumer isn't all bad for those corporations, businesses and entities that provide consumers

3 | The Gentle Revolution

with the items they seek to consume. Unfortunately, however, this group is also in the dark relative to the new powers and influence of this empowered consumer. In the spirit of a kinder and gentler society it might be said that, all-in-all, it would be best for all if the vendors and suppliers of the world were to come to grips with this new concentration of influence before the consumers do. If these merchants and peddlers of products, goods and service consumables can change their approach to today's consumers before they're forced to, they just may escape the consumers' wrath.

Modern Day Consumer Power

This revolution has netted today's consumer an unbelievable arsenal of new powers.

And interestingly enough, for the first time in recent history, these powers weren't gained as a result of turning to legal counsel and the judicial system.

According to marketing guru and author Seth Godin, this new consumer power is derived from something as old as the marketplace itself; competition. The Internet has opened up a whole new world of competitive behaviors and has given them more choices. In turn this several fold increase in choice has provided consumers increased leverage over the big corporations. But what makes this new consumer environment even more interesting is that those large corporations were given a gift during the revolution they are on the verge of exploiting on a large scale. Any number of services and websites (e.g., Yelp, Zillow and Trip Advisor) now exist for the primary purpose of providing both consumers and service providers with the ability to offer information that allows consumers to make more informed decisions.

Godin also suggests that this new power doesn't come from populist uprisings such as those recently encountered by the Bank of America and Netflix. Those were mere tantrums said Godin; "Such minor league activities are incapable of resolving really complicated issues in the long-term." Informational technologies have made it much easier for the companies with good products and appropriate marketing to become winners in the eyes of the consumer. According to Godin, "If you can make it clear to consumers that you have a better offer; it's infinitely easier to acquire a million consumers than ever before." The first rule of the consumer revolution is therefore relatively simple: Play fair, be transparent and be rewarded.

The Influence of Social Media

This new consumer power even goes beyond these achievements as the power and influence of Social Media rapidly spread into the business world. Aggrieved and concerned consumers are realizing that they can use Social Media to organize themselves around shared values and initiate effective movements. It gives them a sounding board to share ideas as well as a means to punish irresponsible corporate behavior.

The ability to use Social Media as a golden wand to reward companies and businesses that "get it" in terms of appropriate business practices or, in the alternative, use it as a weapon to punish those who question the consumers' new power. Consumers can now put pressure on businesses to be more socially responsible and re-engineer value creation as a long-term investment in society. Through these victories they have gained the power to ask corporate leaders to make a substantial shift in their thinking about accepted business models, and adopting just one of these consumer requests can alter

> During the post WWII economic boom real estate brokers were often some of the most powerful individuals in their respective communities, but this growth in consumer power is now leading to a decrease in Realtor® power.

114 www.RETrends.com ©2012 RealSure, Inc.

From the Vault: Real Estate Confronts Reality (1997)

Consumers will no longer be wedded to traditional approaches in either marketing or seeking property. Instead, many will explore the advantages of working with practitioners who have a different way of doing things and will reward those who succeed with more business for the innovators.

business structures and processes in profound ways. Social Media is also evolving way beyond just being another marketing and branding tool. Based upon its current dynamic and direction it has the potential of driving an increasingly focused pressure for large-scale global and political transformation.

Social Media has evolved into a robust mechanism for social transformation and the results are already evident. Those who continue to advocate that Facebook, Twitter, YouTube and the like are not serious tools of reinvention are not monitoring the facts closely enough. In the past two years the world has witnessed impressive examples of Social Media platforms being employed for important causes, including both meaningful political reform and desperately needed disaster relief.

There have been few, if any, periods during the past fifty years in which revolution has not been present somewhere in the world. The power of Social Media during the Arab Spring was an historic example of the power that today's world citizens are capable of and willing to unleash in search of remedies for the dissatisfaction caused by the economic, political and regulatory excesses practiced by individuals, groups and institutions in power.

The force behind this potential is a growing crusade of socially, ethically and environmentally conscious consumers who are seeking to use their voices and purchasing power to halt unsustainable business practices and temper reckless capitalism. Social Media is being used by consumers as a powerful tool they will strategically and tactically use to influence business attitudes, force companies into greater social responsibility and (imagine this) move society towards a more sustainable and probably more profitable brand of capitalism. So whether it's following Lady Gaga's every move, tweeting about your favorite Olympic athlete, announcing a new Football coach in Arizona, providing help after a devastating earthquake in Japan or toppling governments during the Arab Spring, Social Media is rising to the occasion.

THE REAL ESTATE CONSUMER

The real estate industry, marketplace and transaction have also started experiencing, and will continue to experience, the effects of this new consumer power and influence as early signs reveal that:

- Consumers enter the real estate space very knowledgeable and more prepared with a full array of information.

- Consumers—almost 75 percent—have already identified the neighborhood they want to live in, the properties they want to see and often even the home they want to purchase.

- Consumers have developed both financial and lifestyle knowledge relative to specific properties and neighborhoods.

- Consumers have even attempted to use some form of rating systems or consumer generated peer-to-peer communication to identify what agents they want to work with.

- Consumers are demonstrating little or no reticence to either praise their agent online or to communicate what they perceived as weaknesses in professional knowledge or responsive behaviors.

During the post WWII economic boom real estate brokers were often some of the most powerful individuals in their respective communities, but this growth in consumer power is now leading to a decrease in Realtor® power. Generally, as a collective, Realtors® have been very successful and prosperous by taking full advantage of the housing boom that was part of the post war economic boom. They have been indirectly responsible for the development, acquisition and investment of tens of millions of new housing units; single family homes, condominiums, collectives, apartments and subdivisions. And with their financial success many were afforded the opportunity to assume and shoulder powerful appointed positions as directors of banks, hospitals and other community and charitable positions, even elected political office.

But beginning with the rise of "agent-centricity" in the 80s, the gradual aging of the powerful WWII brokers in the 90s and the declining profitability of the brokerage business model by the turn of the century, this shift in power became more evident. It was fueled by the collapse of the mortgage market and the subsequent housing bubble half way into the first decade of this century. A time in which very few brokers—even fewer agents—were classified as powerful, highly respected and/or very influential in their state or local communities.

THE IMPACT OF HOUSING

The Incentive of Choice

Student loans, the real estate market, mortgage meltdowns and recession activated economic disasters have left a permanent financial stain on a huge number of American families as well as a debt-burden on the country as a whole. (Also read Trend #9 *On the Edge of a Fiscal Cliff: Is Real Estate on the Precipice Too?*). As a result it appears that the Millennial Generation is going to bear the lion's share of this financial burden in the coming decades. Couple that with the fact that at some point during this period this will be worsened when millions of Boomers whose resources and retirement plans will have failed and the effect will have a significant impact on housing and all those involved in the industry.

Housing, as both a consumer pursuit and a social issue, is ideally suited for the application of this new consumer power. The essence of the consumer housing experience is both to secure appropriate housing for the consumer and to afford brokerages and service providers the opportunity to make a contribution to the neighborhood the consumer is buying into as well as the larger community. But there is of course, as always, a choice.

Brokerages and agents can see this new consumer power as a threat to their continued practices, especially if they fall below what might be considered an appropriate standard of understanding and implementation. Or, in the alternative, they can view this new consumer sphere as an excellent opportunity to establish the kind of relationship and interaction being sought by the contemporary consumer with their real estate services provider.

Therefore, understanding that today these consumers come into the marketplace and transaction with a rather finely tuned set of powers that can either praise or punish should incentivize real estate agents and service providers to make a special effort to create a more advanced and personal kind of working relationship than ever before—one that today's consumer is "actually" interested in.

Today's Consumers Want to Know Who the Best Agents Are

"Agent rating" is a concept and practice that has been generally rejected by the majority of traditional brokerages and agents, and has become one of the most divisive issues in modern residential real estate.

The concept is unpretentious. Virtually every consumer is, or has been, a participant in a work environment or occupation that is comprised of multiple individuals performing similar functions where everyone knows whose work is good and whose isn't. So why can't a consumer know who is the most successful agent in a specific neighborhood and who isn't?

It's hard to fool the technically connected consumer. Google and other search engines make it too easy to validate information, compare services and contrast properties and functionality. Understand that Millennials will quickly reject those professionals or service providers who attempt to serve them without the appropriate connectivity, apps and immediate responsiveness. But having the latest technologies is not just a mark of commitment in the eyes of today's consumer; it's rapidly becoming the minimum standard of practice. They have a multitude of ways of communicating and they don't limit themselves to just one. They also don't like to spend a lot of time traveling around in their car to gather information so they use their technology to double check and validate what the agent has said, search for properties the agent has decided not to disclose and obtain information the agent may not know or disclose that he or she knows.

Consumers realize that the industry's failure to provide transparency and rating information is a direct insult to their intelligence and they're not alone; another group also recognizes that fact. Virtually every "alternative" brokerage model and/or third-party Internet-based portal is already offering or planning to offer an agent-rating program. And yet the industry as a whole continues to keep this information under lock and key. Very unwise indeed.

> **Consumers realize that the industry's failure to provide transparency and rating information is a direct insult to their intelligence and they're not alone...**

Growing Importance of Lifestyle

Recent surveys by the highly respected WAV Group (wavgroup.com) have disclosed that 92 percent of consumers they surveyed want access to a "home buying system" that can provide them with a real time and highly accurate status check of their transaction. But resistance to this consumer need is coming from many Boomer Generation agents who don't wish to disclose the reasons for the delays, errors and poor performance that are often a part of the transaction.

Consumers have met the basic challenge of identifying the inventory information attached to the bedrooms, baths, geographic location and price of their target properties. They are now desperately seeking more advanced information regarding what manner of lifestyle they can create for their families within the envelope of their target properties, and this information has not traditionally been forthcoming from their agents.

This matter raises two peripheral issues. The first has to do with the fact that traditional agents are declining to get involved in the lifestyle issues because "that isn't what we do." The second is that virtually every Internet-based entity currently competing for the consumer's attention is "offering lifestyle information." In either case, with respect to lifestyle information, agent rating, consumer relationships, rental lifestyles, expanded inventory information and transaction management, the industry must decide when and under what circumstances it is going to balance its products and services with consumer expectations rather than traditional agent values and superstitions.

Although long on promise and short on real delivery, "going green" has, over the past few years, gone mainstream. We have evolved from embracing a "chic idea"—or an obnoxious one, depending upon one's perspective—to the widely accepted mindset of "buy local," "eat organic" and "be sustainable."

Realtors® don't have to be selling environmentally engineered houses to appeal to the "green" shopper; there are many other things to do. It's most often the day-to-day interactions that consumers use to determine the attitude of their agent regarding issues of environmental sensitivity. Just being knowledgeable and sensitive to the issues is one of the simplest ways real estate service providers can take part in the environmental movement. Other ways to make the green choice include: becoming a paperless or a reduced paper office, switching to electronic faxes, supporting Eco programs, etc.

One can speak "green" everywhere, but at the same time we should appreciate the fact that a work style or office that is devoid of evidence that the occupant is knowledgeable or sensitive to green issues delivers a very distinct and loud message.

ENGAGING TODAY'S CONSUMER

With today's consumer calling the shots relative to where they want to find the provider, when they want to find the provider and their media of choice for that interaction, the arrogant voice message—"I return my calls between this hour and that time"—is no longer acceptable to the contemporary consumer. They want to reach and to be reached on their schedule and on their media or device of choice. So, when today's real estate service provider goes fishing and tosses out a line it better be on the right "pole" and be equipped with an

CIVICS/SILENT GENERATION

The Civic or Silent generation is slowly disappearing from housing arena as most have already entered retirement or are busy doing so. Born before the end of WWII, Civics have always valued the success of the team over the individual. They respect self-sacrificing with a hard work ethic and respond well to authoritarian figures who explain "The Best Way" or "The Ideal Solution" to any challenge. This approach also requires a high level of respect in both presentation and service delivery.

This wide range of generations, ages, perspectives, values, expectations and demands in today's real estate marketplace is presenting a number of significant challenges that must be met. Real estate service providers who "get it" will make themselves familiar with the demographic most interested in their marketplace and services while at the same time making sure their image, presentation and style are appropriate to the consumer and do everything possible to appropriately present themselves.

BOOMERS

This is probably the best-known—and generally "disliked"—generation in American history. This 74 million strong, self-obsessed generation was born between 1946 and 1964. They examined themselves in the mirror of life and in the end declared themselves pretty and perfect. Idealistic and self-motivated, Boomers have a strong passion for career and individual advancement.

Real estate service providers would do well to market to Boomers with benefits-focused presentations that frame the material in terms of how it will improve their lives. Boomers like to view things in context, so explaining how you differentiate yourself and where your service package and consumer experience fits into the larger picture will go a long way with this generation. Present the Boomer with the answer to his or her questions and you may just survive the experience.

GEN X

Gen X'ers were born between 1965 and 1976. After a lifetime of being disappointed by media stars, public figures and personal heroes, they have learned to rely on no one but themselves. They have come to expect to work hard for what they have and they expect you to work hard for them. They anticipate spending more time developing a relationship and therefore you're encountering a mindset that initially distrusts most things, but one that is willing to work with you to reach a mutually agreeable decision.

Personal connection is important to Gen X'ers. They like to be recognized as individuals and place great emphasis on forming connections with colleagues and peers. This is where individual agents really have to shine. If they or the brokerage don't connect with the Gen X consumer they will go somewhere else; they aren't big on second chances.

"amazing and attractive lure."

Here are some recommendations that reflect the current industry wisdom regarding engaging today's consumer.

Providing a Compelling Story

Research indicates that consumers place a large value on learning through stories. The conventional wisdom regarding real estate marketing is therefore all about storytelling. The consumers love hearing, telling and learning through stories, especially on subjects that resonate with their current real estate challenges.

How can brokers and agents tell a story with their marketing? The answer is simple; create great content. Whether it's a blog post, how-to video, product photos or programs and services, in order to reach this new consumer it must contain content that drives their target audience to take action. Evergreen content, or educational content that is not time-sensitive, is safe to frequently share on blogs and Social Media; it generates a lot of "likes" and shares from consumers. But, decision-making content, like a product spotlight, promotional content or a special offer has to entice site visits and conversions or it has failed.

Learn to Listen and Hear

It's important to listen across Social Media sites to see how consumers are responding to, engaging with and sharing brokerage content. Metrics such as engagements, likes, comments and site visits can help determine how your content is being received. Sophisticated service providers are also using Social Media as a forum to ask questions and conduct polls to see how consumers feel about the brand and business being marketed.

MILLENNIALS / GEN Y

The youngest generation to enter the housing market is Generation Y. Born after 1977 and now in their mid 20s to mid 30s, this group is incredibly technology savvy, skeptical and accept almost nothing without verification. Service providers will have to prove themselves more than the previous generation did. Gen Y expects an environment of comprehensive, instant and verifiable information. This group responds well to short, focused presentations and they are heavy on the benefits and short on sales fluff.

Brand loyalty is almost unheard of among this group. Brokerages and agents that want to create long-term lasting relationships with this generation will have to bring their "A" game. No more "good old boy" or "fraternity brother" here; proving and validating oneself as the best choice for the Millennials' real estate transaction is the name of the game.

Brokerages and agents should be aware of and prepare for another unique aspect of working with the members of this generation. Each of the four generations currently functioning within the marketplace has experienced unique challenges that were created by the times in which they came of age. The Civic Generation was greeted by WWII, the Boomers were greeted by the atomic threat and Gen X was welcomed by the overwhelming wash of the Boomers.

The fate of the Millennials was cast by the fact that, by and large, they came into the ruins of the real estate market after the ravages of the crash in 2005, the mortgage meltdown of 2006 and the recession of 2007. This regrettably timed arrival, coupled with a crushing debt load from educational pursuits and deferred employment, means that for this generation the realization of the American dream of owning their own home is going to be delayed. (Read more in Trend #8—Rescuing Homeownership. Is Government For or Against It?)

What this means to the industry is that at the very moment in time this generation will want to seal their maturity with parenthood and homeownership they will find that historic blockades have been placed in the way of their being able to do so. Even the popular Mortgage Interest Deduction may prove elusive. While the specifics of this conundrum are too complicated to explain here it is sufficient to say that they are already presenting a huge challenge to the real estate industry.

This challenge has already begun, initiated by the fact that Millennials will likely have to engage in a longer than normal rental lifestyle than either of their predecessors; the Boomer and X Generations. With the specifics of this situation having been discussed earlier, it is sufficient to say here that while they are willing to accept the rental lifestyle for the time being they are definitely going to want to raise their children in single-family homes, reminiscent of their childhood. This situation is being exacerbated by the fact that many agents are declining to get involved in the rental practice and therefore the decision is in turn driving many Millennials to seek services outside the Realtor® community. Given the unique propensities of this generation they may not return to the Realtor® sphere when they can finally purchase a home.

3 | The Gentle Revolution

Changing Mindset of Generations

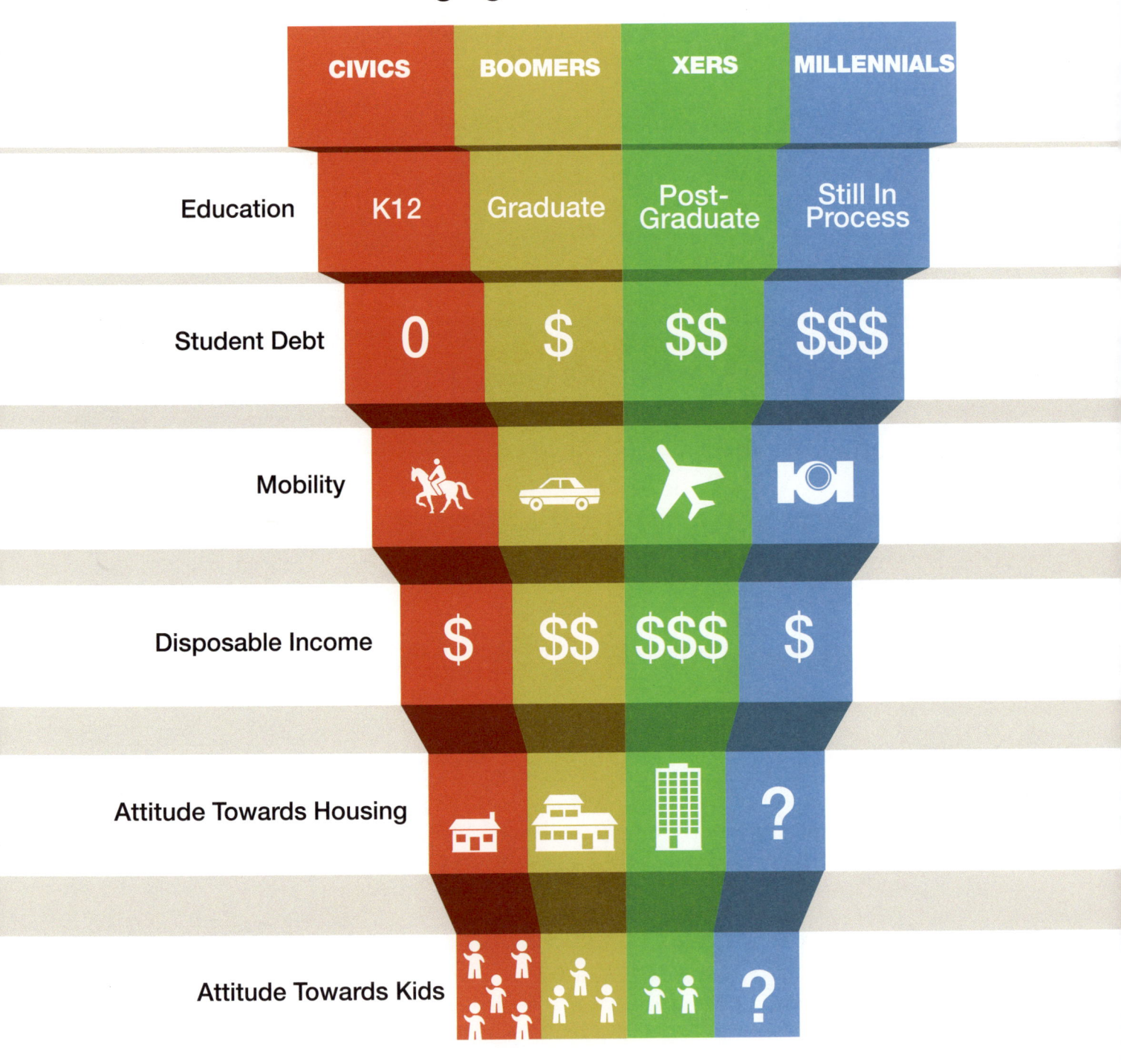

	CIVICS	BOOMERS	XERS	MILLENNIALS
Education	K12	Graduate	Post-Graduate	Still In Process
Student Debt	0	$	$$	$$$
Mobility	🐎	🚗	✈️	📡
Disposable Income	$	$$	$$$	$
Attitude Towards Housing	🏠	🏡	🏢	?
Attitude Towards Kids	👨‍👩‍👧‍👦	👨‍👧‍👦	👫	?

Based upon the information gained from this process, they can then respond with the types of marketing and messages that consumers acknowledge activates them to action. The key is not only to "listen" to the message but to "hear" and "try to "understand" what it means.

With this in mind we need to ask ourselves if there is a generational reference point to engineering appropriate interactions, communications and marketing touches with today's consumer.

UNDERSTANDING GENERATIONAL DIFFERENCES

The subject of generations and generational differences has been a popular one over the past few years.

©2012 RealSure, Inc.

Authors, speakers, consultants and industry observers have sought to draw clear lines of delineation between the four generations that are active in today's real estate marketplace—Civic, Boomer, X and Millennial.

Experience suggests that many of the differences, initially articulated five years ago, dealt with the use of technology, information and Social Media. Today the evidence is clear that all four generations have significantly mastered their abilities to use these technologies. While it may well be that the Millennials present the profile of a more sophisticated user, the other generations have caught up to a point where it would no longer be prudent to assume that the older and more mature consumers are not well connected and tech savvy. A more pertinent question, however, may be whether today's real estate brokers and agents have achieved the same or higher level of techno-literacy that the average home buying consumer has.

During the middle decades of the 20th century real estate buying power was concentrated within a relatively narrow range of years. The vast majority of real estate transactions took place between the ages of 25 and 55, that being the period of time necessary from "settling down" after graduating from high school to begin to prepare for retirement. In that environment a mass-market "one-size-fits-all" strategy worked fairly effectively, but by 2012 the range has widened from 25 to 75, increasing the range with 50% and adding, or keeping another generation in the mix for another generation.

Within the new economic, social and demographic boundaries of today's real estate marketplace all four generations are currently engaged in the residential real estate space at the same time making it more complex than ever before as each generation requires a different marketing and relational approach. It's important to remember that not only are consumers members of these generations but agents are also sprinkled among them as well.

SUMMARY

Picture a bright-eyed computer savvy individual that has just entered the real world and whose new, naïve natural delight at the prospect of purchasing a home is confronted with a number of traditional practices that may be, by comparison to his world, obsolete, secretive and even primitive.

Picture a disillusioned wise and experienced agent fighting for survival, one that has done things a certain way for decades and feels the need for immediate, transparent and online relationship building is a waste of time.

These two meet. How long before the "revolution" leaves someone lying on the battlefield?

The quiet evolution of the consumer resulted in the real estate revolution that had to take place. In the process consumers are beginning to discover they can force the change they desire. Failure of traditional brokerage companies, agents and associations to recognize this and move fast to position themselves at the leading edge of the shift will certainly result in something other than a "gentle revolution."

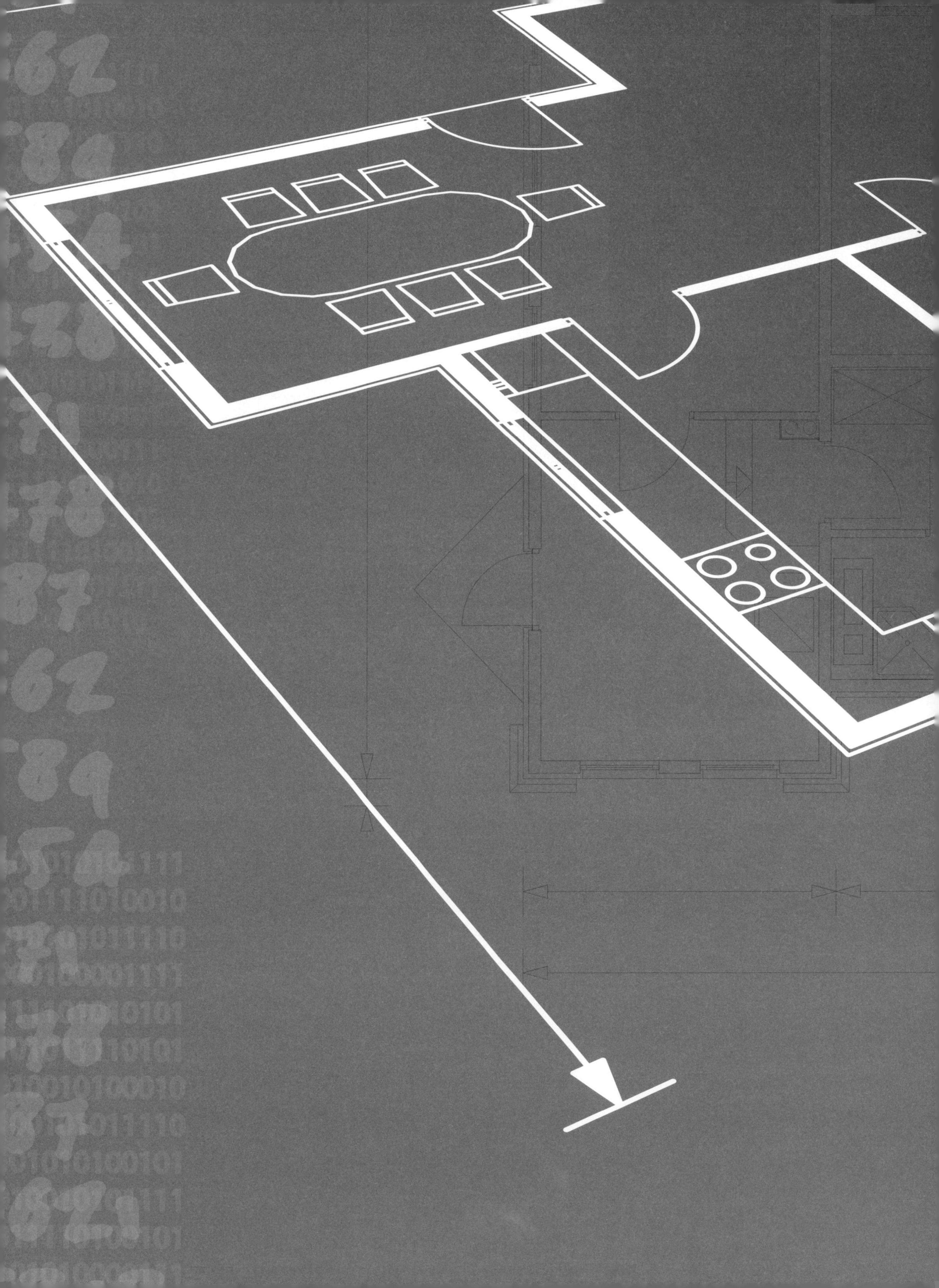

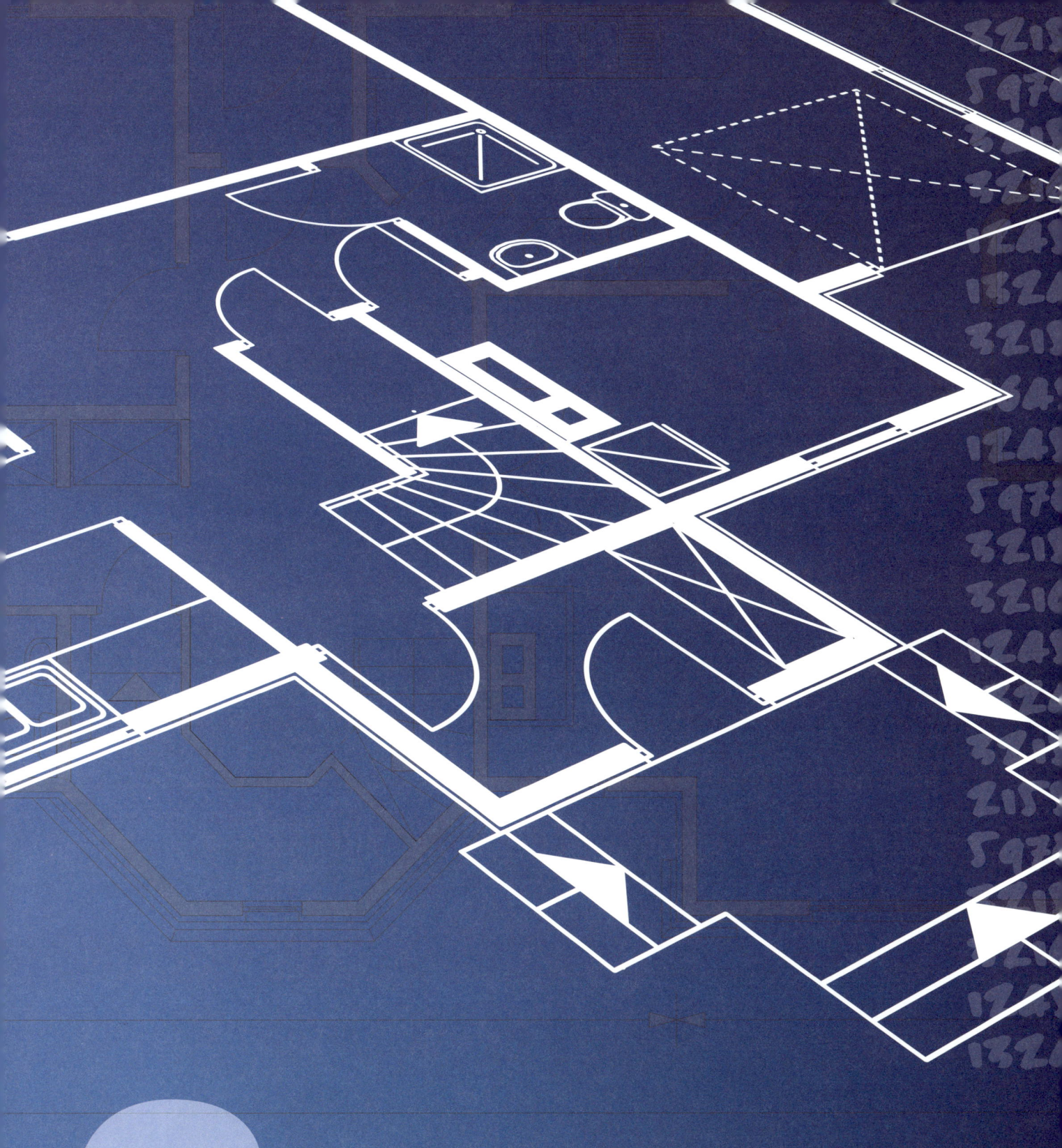

2
THE REAL ESTATE OFFICE OF THE FUTURE
The Options: Target, Starbucks, or Amazon.com?

The Real Estate Office of the Future

"While some consumers would rather meet their broker at Starbucks and save a little money, others may want the full-service experience of using the bricks and mortar office and seeing their home in a local newspaper. That's free enterprise." This statement made by Blanche Evans, then editor of Realty Times, was included in the 2006 edition of the *Swanepoel TRENDS Report*.

So what's changed in seven years? Well, homes are generally no longer featured in newspapers but on the web and consumers don't really have to go into bricks and mortar offices, they're increasingly meeting anywhere that is convenient.

And that's excellent!

In an advancing and shifting industry (today's residential real estate brokerage) the prevailing business model will evolve and different companies will evolve at different stages and speeds. Those that don't will see their existing model fade as new entrants find better, more efficient and more innovative ways to deliver the same service cheaper or offer a more expanded service for the same price.

As a rule it's incredibly hard for players in any industry to reinvent themselves and often, before they do, someone snatches away the opportunity. Maybe because the real estate business is so fragmented or maybe it's because so many have been reading our Reports for the past 15 years, either way it appears that the industry, or at least some major players, have taken innovation to heart and are adapting their business models to the changing market.

In previous editions we discussed the franchise brand war (#7 in 2007) and the influence of the Internet on the start-ups in real estate (#4 in 2011). This year we analyzed what is happening to the actual bricks and mortar offices that have been the industry's foundation since the beginning.

Some say they're no longer necessary and you can operate without a physical office while many others say offices will stay for around for decades to come. We found

Office Model Options for Brokers
Four Primary Choices

OPTION 1 — Stay the Same
OPTION 2 — Go Big or Go Home
OPTION 3 — Go Small and be Economical and Inviting
OPTION 4 — Go into the Cloud and Go

From the Vault: Swanepoel Trends Report (2006)

Competition in the residential real estate brokerage industry is immense and intense. New business models are increasingly being created and existing models redefined. As franchising dominated the 70s, the 100% concept the 80s and technology the 90s, there is little doubt that something new will again cause a major shift in the industry.

truth in both of those statements and decided to look for the options available today should they decide to reinvent their office. Here seem to be today's primary options:

1. Stay the same
2. Go big
3. Go café-lounge
4. Go virtual

If you have selected #1, and are happy with that option, then you don't have to read any further. Move on to Trend chapter #1 and read about what Warren Buffet is up to in the real estate industry. On the other hand, if you know you have to do something with your company and aren't sure which direction to take, are considering going on your own, want to join another company or are a leader at a vendor, MLS or association, then you are going to enjoy this chapter.

Let's look at three exciting office models of the future.

THE SUPERSTORE OPPORTUNITY

Go big or go home! We've heard it so many times, in all walks of life, and we've seen it in business and retail. Some people say big boxes are a failing model and with a smile point to online companies such as Amazon.com who we actually highlight as analogous to one of other models. Supersotores such as Wal-Mart and Target are extremely successful companies. Both are more profitable than Amazon, however, and Target's operating revenue is 500% larger and Wal-Mart's is 3,000% larger than Amazon.

But that's not the point. In almost every single vertical—industry or profession—consolidation has led to the creation of ever larger corporations. Economies of scale are a very powerful driver of profitability. Even though Amazon is a cloud-based company it of course still operates significant bricks and mortar structures (approximately 70,000 employees and 30 huge regional distribution centers across the country). It's not having "bricks and mortar" that is the downfall of a company but it's finding the right ratio of people, offices space and other expenses in relationship to revenue that determines success.

We refer to this as the "Target" model. We could have also referenced Walmart but on several levels Target is as impressive and its success is not only as a result of its size, but also an assortment of interesting successful business strategies. In 2010 Target was ranked #22 in Fortune Magazine's "World's Most Admired Companies."

The Real Estate Superstore

So what does a "superstore" real estate office, or mega market center as Keller Williams Realty (KW; kw.com) calls them, look like?

Obviously size varies as a result of space opportunities and limitations but a KW mega market center can blossom to an astounding 30,000 square feet; 400 to 500 percent larger than a traditional real estate office.

In the M&A world we live in, folding together other operations to create a high-volume, low-margin mega market center is a very appealing proposition. But this option is not feasible for many companies as it requires considerable capital, many agents and great systems.

The Real Estate Office of The Future

Operating a traditional office has always been tough and managing the expenses is a major part of the broker's burden. For years KW experimented to find the optimal framework for large-format market centers and it seems they have found an ingenious solution; having the agent population in an office partake in managing and sharing the burden of accountability through a Agent Leadership Council and profit sharing.

Today KW has 665 market centers across the country of which 90+ percent were profitable in 2012. Their top five market centers (two in Austin, two in San Antonio and one in Roseville, California) serve between 420 and 550 agents each, making the office space per agent between 55 to 70 square feet. That is considerably lower than the traditional office, which comes in around 100 to 125 square feet per agent. A good example of how economies of scale result in bringing the office cost per agent down by 45 to 60 percent.

However, recent efficiencies are enabling KW to keep the agent count very high (425 in Austin NW and 525 in San Antonio) yet modernize the market center down to around 15,000 square feet; bringing the space per agent down to an astounding 30 to 35 square feet. These large mega centers of course are not suitable for every city and therefore they depend on many factors, including the number and median price of transactions, the prospective agent base and the influence and production of the core group of agents.

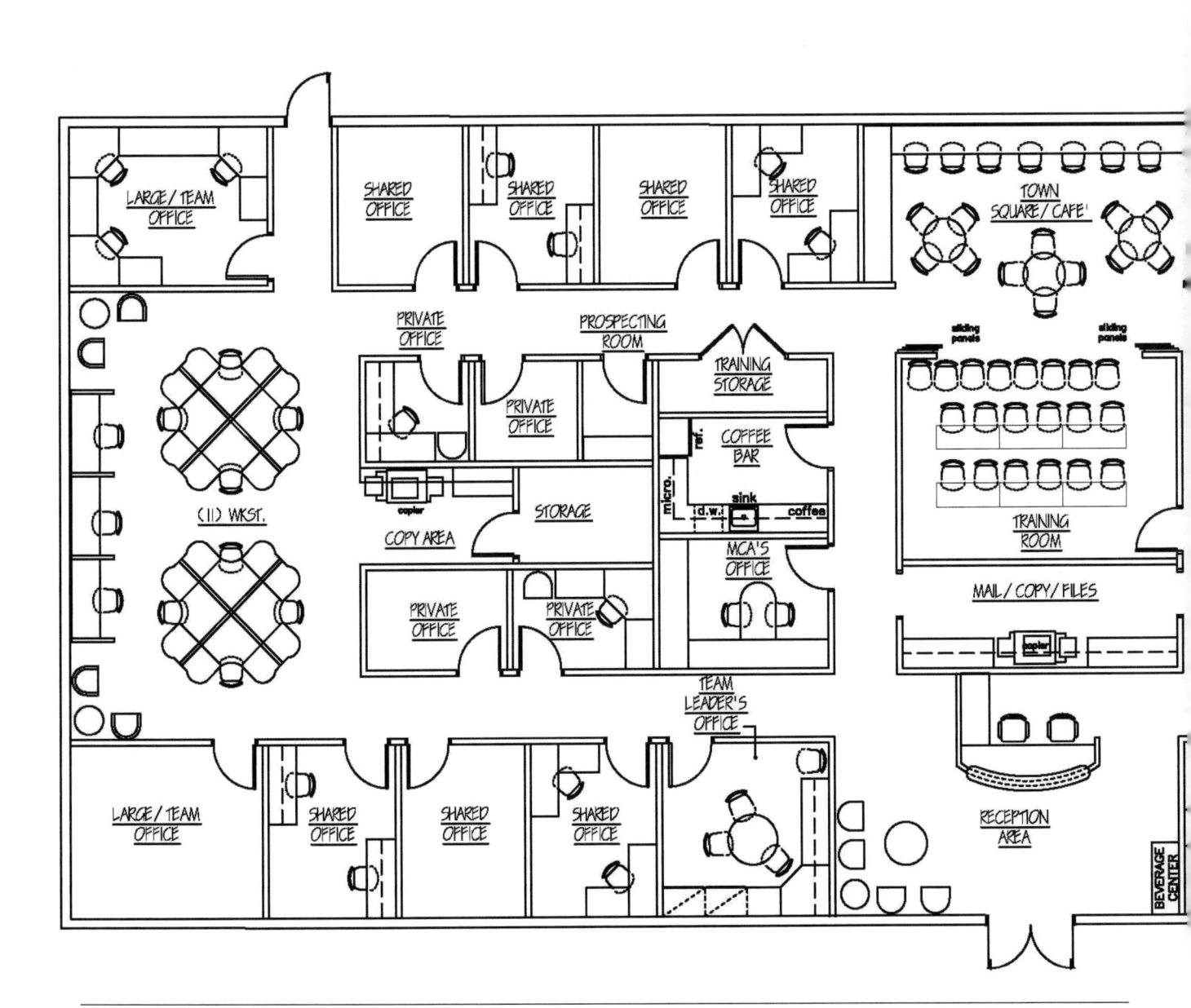

Obviously not all KW locations are that large and some consider the 8,000 square-foot centers the optimum size. This is still significantly larger than a traditional office of around 5,000 to 6,000 square feet.

Although most brokerage offices obviously need the same basic set of elements, the KW mega center especially focuses on a warm, welcoming reception/waiting area that projects a strong image and culture, generating a positive and lasting impression with visitors. There are flexible meeting spaces equipped with state-of-the-art technology that agents can use with their clients. The training facilities are at the heart of each market center and serve as the "town square"—an informal multifunction space that encourages collaboration and serves as a mobile work area and a supportive space for sharing and creativity.

Advantages

- By making the market center a hub of activity, office managers are able to offer high-quality, high-touch interaction training and programming year-round.

- The market center brings to individual associates the team's culture and sense of camaraderie. It reinforces the culture and keeps agents engaged with the office decisions and assists with overall retention and recruiting.

- Associates gain motivation and encouragement from participating in group activities like lead generation and prospecting. Market center staff assists agents with productivity tools and other resources.

- KW believes that market center agents are able to accomplish more in less time, paying dividends in terms of productivity, training and morale. Being in frequent contact with other associates encourages team members to give generously when colleagues and family members are in need.

- Economies of scale reduce the cost on many levels, such as technology and training and allow for the offering of higher quality services.

Challenges

- A concern for mega market centers (if you are one of the owners) is of course the financial burden and risk associated with launching and operating a space of this magnitude.

- As the model encourages highly visible and well-placed locations with ample parking, so the costs are higher than average.

- Mega size also means it needs to be mega flexible as many agents usually require many ongoing changes.

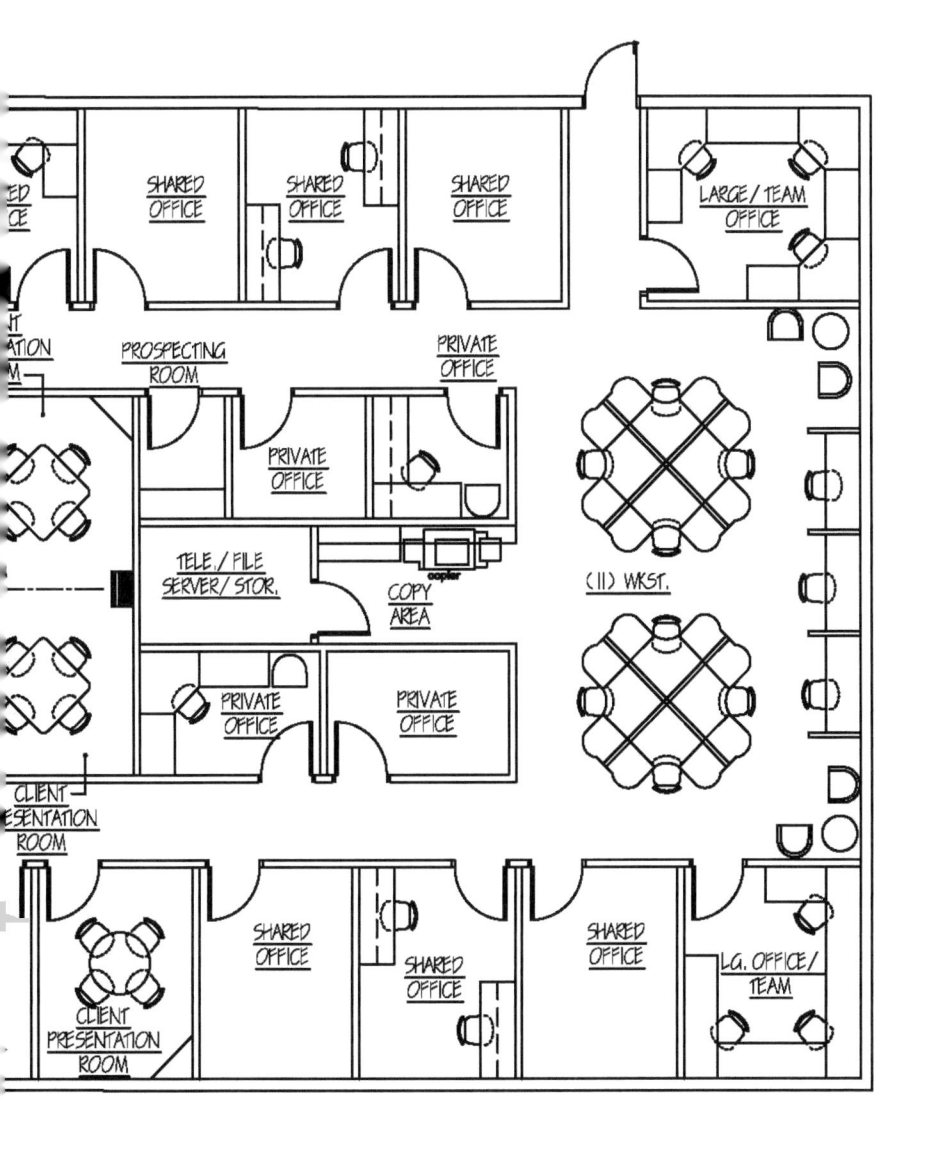

Corporate America

According to the Corporate Real Estate Group (corporaterealestate.com) 90 percent of corporate America intends spending heavily in the future in technology, 78 percent expect to use their space more effectively and 54 percent see Social Media impacting the way they will need to operate. Their answer is to design offices to be a place where workers engage their colleagues. Accordingly, CoreNetGlobal (corenetglobal.org) reports that the square footage per worker has already decreased from 225 square feet in 2010 to 176 square feet today and they predict that average will fall to 100 square feet or less within five years. Jones Lang LaSalle (joneslanglasalle.com) agrees and has identified a number of keydrivers of change including the increasing importance of sustainability, technological advancements like cloud computing and mobile technologies and collaborative working.

Even the government seems to be getting in on the shift. For example the General Services Administration (GSA; gsa.gov), which owns and leases 354 million square feet in 9,600 buildings in the Washington, D.C. area, is also renovating its headquarters to increase the number of workers it will support from 2,000 to 4,500, taking advantage of shared workspaces and telecommunicating.

THE CAFÉ OR LOUNGE OPPORTUNITY

Starbucks wasn't always successful. As a matter of fact it took more than 20 years from 1971 through the mid 90s to begin its meteoric rise. Most point to 1995 as the year it exploded after Starbucks formed a "stores of the future" project to raise store design to a higher level and come up with the next generation stores.

They focused on high-traffic, high-visibility locations with fireplaces, leather chairs, newspapers, couches and lots of ambience in creating their flagship stores. Special seating areas were added to help make Starbucks a place where customers could meet and chat or simply enjoy a peaceful interlude in their day.

Soon this became more cookie cutter and the company affected centralized buying, developed standard contracts and fixed fees for certain items. Basic layouts were developed on a computer with software that allowed the costs to be estimated as the design evolved. The team researched the art and literature of coffee throughout the ages, studied coffee-growing and coffee-making techniques and looked at how Starbucks stores had already evolved in terms of design, logos, colors and mood. The team came up with four store designs. There is one for each of the four stages of coffee making: growing, roasting, brewing and aroma; each with its own color combinations, lighting scheme and component materials. Architects and designers worked together to ensure that each store would convey the right image and character, which was often a challenge as stores had to be custom-designed because the company doesn't buy real estate.

Starbucks also entered into a number of key licensing agreements for store locations in areas where it didn't have the ability to locate its own outlets. For example, with Marriott Host International for airport locations, Aramark Food and Services for university campuses, Barnes and Nobles for bookstores and United Airlines for United flights.

The Real Estate Lounge or Cybercafé

According to our research Bill Wendel in 1995 pioneered the first walk-in, Internet-based housing information center near the Harvard campus in Cambridge, MA. Aptly named the Real Estate Café, it invited buyers to search properties on the MLS at a time when it was not publicly accessible on the Internet and other real estate agencies were still using property listing books.

In 1998 the Pacific Union Real Estate Group opened a prototype named SOMA Living, an acronym for South of Market, referring to areas south of Market Street in San Francisco. The boutique-like storefront had many Internet kiosks for customers to browse for homes or chart their house searches. SOMA was solely a buyer brokerage, did not take listings and agents were paid as employees rather than as commissioned independent contractors. An announced national expansion stalled with the stock market crashed in 2000.

In 2007 Thaddeus Wong, co-founder of @Properties, took the approach in a different direction in Chicago's River North neighborhood by going into partnership with a Starbucks-style coffee shop. Patrons logging into the cafe's free Wi-Fi service gained access to the brokerage website and were able to browse for properties for sale and rent.

In 2009 Jimmy Dulin advanced the real estate café concept with co-RE/MAX brokers at a conference in Toronto. Since then it is believed that hundreds of RE/MAX brokers have implemented some elements of the café concept. So as this is the first nationwide implementation of the café-lounge concept we decided to research this in more detail.

The RE/MAX Café
The RE/MAX café-lounge is akin to the SOMA prototype, which clearly was ahead of its time in 1997. Now, more than 15 years later, the maturity of technology, the emancipation of the consumer and the advancement of the mobile agent makes timing significantly more suitable.

We found various RE/MAX believers in the café-lounge concept. The first was Debra Meredith-Peters, the broker/owner owner of RE/MAX Anchor Realty in Punta Gorda, FL. "If you were going to take a plain, vanilla box and turn it into a traditional office, it would probably cost you $80 per square foot," she said. "If you were to create an office café it would cost you about $50 per foot." She estimates that a traditional office allocates about 120 square feet per agent, but with an office café agents thrive with around 50 square feet. In this office café concept agents don't even notice that the space per agent has dropped by almost 60 percent.

Another example is RE/MAX Heritage Green in Somerville, MA. The owner, Linda O'Koniewski, embraced the real estate café concept because it allowed her to have a much smaller footprint. In her flagship RE/MAX office in Melrose, MA she had 29 agents in approximately 2,100 square feet based on the traditional model. With the café-lounge concept she estimates she can double the number of agents to between 60 and 70, bringing the space per agent down to an incredibly effective 30-35 square feet.

Dulin himself is now also pulling out all the stops with his first built-from-scratch real estate café that is scheduled to open in the first quarter of 2013. The new 5,600-square-foot office will be similar in size to a traditional office save that he is dedicating about one-third of the office (1,800 square feet) to the café-lounge. Although the size feels very much like a traditional brokerage company the café design includes some less traditional features such as numerous video monitors, a video studio, multiple banquet areas for private meetings, and luxurious 30-foot ceilings.

In Canada one RE/MAX office has taken the concept even further by combining the café-lounge into a permanent showroom utilizing the latest in user-friendly interactive technology with over 20 large digital displays and touch screens to facilitate property searches and video tours. There is a team of onsite agents available seven days a week to provide professional consulting services as well as supplemental services including legal, financing, taxation and interior design. Consumer-friendliness is accomplished by providing a multimedia experience at the consumers' fingertips.

The United Lounge

In previous editions of the *Swanepoel TRENDS Report* we documented United Country Real Estate (unitedcountry.com) and their unique position as the country's only nationwide rural real estate organization with some 700 offices in the small towns and cities of rural America.

For more than 80 years they focused predominantly on farms, ranches, recreational property and country homes. Now they're expanding into the residential market by using the new café-lounge model combined with the 100 percent commission concept (created by Realty Executives in 1965 and made prominent by RE/MAX during the 80s and 90s). United refers to themselves as a new paradigm 'Freedom Model' offering full brokerage services.

United opened their first café-lounge location in Dallas, TX (see the floor plan), which served as a testing ground to refine space planning, agent recruiting and lead generation systems. Thereafter they rolled out United lounges in Houston, TX, Chicago, IL, Philadelphia, PA and Washington DC.

The company has targeted another 102 suitable Metropolitan Statistical Areas (urban areas of 50,000 people or more) in which they believe the café-lounge will work and have set an aggressive expansion plan to include:

- 17 Tier I Company owned offices
- 13 Tier I JV/franchise offices
- 72 Tier II Franchised offices

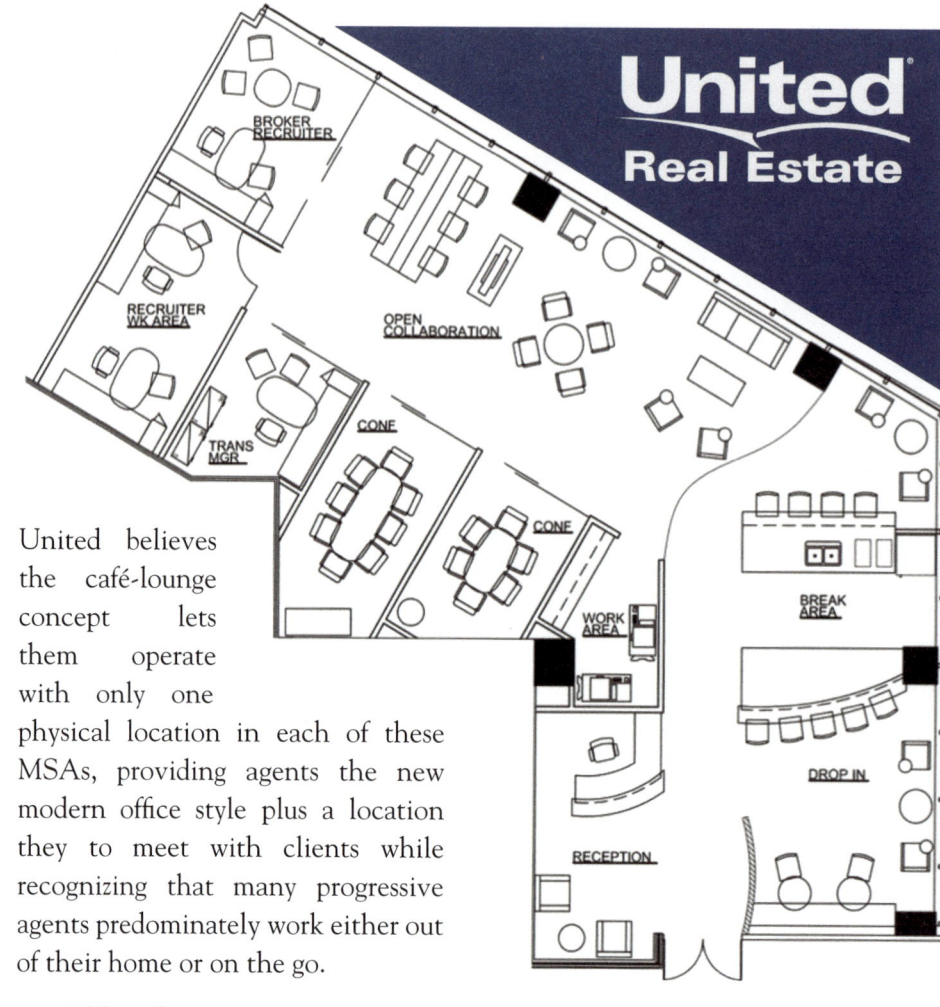

United believes the café-lounge concept lets them operate with only one physical location in each of these MSAs, providing agents the new modern office style plus a location they to meet with clients while recognizing that many progressive agents predominately work either out of their home or on the go.

Although various existing brokerages are considering or have started to implement some elements of the café-lounge concept, we believe United is the first franchise company to officially adopt the model and roll it out nationwide.

Advantages

- Lower operating cost, less space needed per agent and the opportunity to operate in a more energy-efficient office.
- Because of shared communal space there is an automatic tendency to keep the space cleaner and more organized.
- The hip, new-styled 21st century feel provides customers with a big "wow" factor. At the same time it exudes a homey, comfortable and non-threatening feel. It's also a great selling tool to attract new agents, especially tech-savvy ones.

Challenges

- Like Starbucks, location is key, and the café-lounge needs to be placed in a good central location with preferably good foot traffic and/or easy access, otherwise it defeats the purpose of making it easy for consumers to visit.

- With limited or no opportunities to have the agents together in the café-lounge space on a regular basis it will be difficult to build strong team spirit and culture.

THE CLOUD-BASED OPPORTUNITY

The growing number of Millennials in the work force is definitely one of the largest drivers reshaping the office of the future. They have little interest in the corner office, for them its become passé. Since most of them live in the online world they prefer to work off-site from home or their favorite Wi-Fi stop. At the office they want an "open atmosphere" with maximum flexibility for interaction with their contemporaries. One of their growing preferences is the new co-location facility where people from varying industries share common amenities like Wi-Fi, printers, phones, conference rooms, kitchen facilities and secretarial services. Office space no longer means a separate private office, just a Smartphone or laptop, an Internet connection and ear buds.

The bottom line is that there is an undeniable generational shift in how young people today perceive their living, social and working spaces. As Robert Lang, professor of urban affairs at the University of Nevada-Las Vegas put it: "There are other markers for status. It's not the turf. It's your network power."

Amazon is of course a well-known new paradigm electronic commerce company that started as an online bookstore before diversifying into movies, music, software, electronics, apparel, furniture, food, toys and jewelry. Today they sell almost everything, and with revenues over $48 billion they are already the size of Best Buy and 70 percent the size of Target, the second largest discount retailer in the country.

We cite this company as a comparison for the model because it's an e-commerce business that facilitates the buying and selling of products or services over electronic systems such as the Internet and other computer networks. There is a difference between those companies that are cloud-based—a "pure-click" company—and those that are "brick and click channel system" companies.

According to Wikipedia a pure-click company is one that has launched an online business without any previous existence as a bricks firm and does not operate brick locations. Brick and Click companies are those existing companies that have added an online website for e-commerce. So Amazon, although operating many warehouses across the country, is a cloud-based model and served as a great example for the real estate company we went hunting for.

The Real Estate Office in the Cloud

For two decades industry pundits have been debating when it will be possible to build a genuine full service real estate brokerage online.

Well today, 20 years after the arrival of the Internet in real estate, many agents have evolved into a fairly technology-savvy, mobile sales force that has a decreasing dependency on location. The growth of broadband, high-speed and the wireless Internet

The Real Estate Office of The Future

has removed the limitations of the virtual and suddenly most major real estate offices are racing to move certain components of their company to the online world. Today, virtually all real estate brokerages have significant online capabilities, allowing their agents to connect to their offices virtually and execute some level of a paperless transaction. But that, although valid and viable, is of course not a true virtual model. It's only the adaptation of an existing model using new virtual tools.

To find an actual virtual real estate example we went hunting in the cloud and found eXp Realty (exprealty.com), a virtual company built from the ground up, and like Amazon it's a true pure-click company.

The Model

The cloud-based model is unique in that there are no physical offices other than those legally required to operate in a given state (or by the MLS). eXp utilizes a 3D immersive work environment to create a cloud-based office ecosystem. Everyone in the company, including the corporate staff and state and provincial managing brokers, are all cloud-based as are all the documents. Brokers, agents and staff can now truly collaborate from anywhere at any time. For those agents who require an office environment eXp partnered with a global Executive Office Solutions company to provide drop-in space or a conference room in over 500 markets across the U.S.

Entering eXp in the cloud is a bit like sitting down to play a video game—one with realistic and extensive interaction—often referred to in the gaming world as a "massive multiplayer online role-playing game." This is of course not a game, it's a real workplace with a reception area, boardrooms, training centers, transaction rooms, a Wordpress design studio, a business plan development space, a coffee club, an administration office and so on. There are rooms for

132   www.RETrends.com

©2012 RealSure, Inc.

teams of agents or meetings between the state broker and the agents in his/her state. Being 3D Immersive you can literally walk around the offices just like you would in a physical office and drop in and join whatever discussion is taking place. All it takes are a headset, webcam and the ability to share your screen so everyone can see what you're sharing.

It does feel strange, and did to us, the first time we toured the offices. However, after a while you become more at ease with the process, your Avatar and the functionality of the site. And then you start to really appreciate the power of "anywhere" and "anytime." The first thing you do is set up your Avatar, your alter ego, inside of the virtual work environment. It's a graphical representation in the shape of a person that has your photo for a head. Interaction is very similar to what you do in the real world. In the virtual office you locate who you want to talk with and then sit down at their desk or meet in a conference room.

People entering and leaving the room are announced and while in the room you can move around, change seats, walk up to the podium, turn your head, walk around and so on. It's an environment in which agents enjoy socialization, broker support, web development support, training, coaching, transaction support and camaraderie like they would in a physical office.

Advantages

- The major benefit of the virtual office is of course the ability to collaborate from anywhere and still be part of a larger organization with all the support you expect from a more traditional brokerage office. Support is literally a mouse click away.

- The closest you can get to totally paperless. All contracts are either executed electronically between buyer, seller and the agent or, if the transaction starts on paper, it is scanned into the company's back office and the transaction moves to cloud.

- With eXp's virtual office model the expense normally associated with opening up in new markets is greatly reduced. Expansion doesn't involve any more work than a few lines of new code and managing the paperwork and legal issues according to the respective state requirements and eXp is up and running.

Challenges

- One of the biggest challenges facing any totally virtual company is the fact that brokers and agents obviously do not have the same level of personal interaction that you have in an IRL (In Real Life) environment. eXp strives to overcome this through its Chief Cultural Officer who acts as the internal glue that keep agents, brokers and staff connected by facilitating virtual classes, regular breakout sessions and private Facebook groups.

- Current software restrictions only allow for a maximum of 50 people that can be in any one online office at a given time. Technology will however overcome this restriction in the not to distant future.

SUMMARY

Over the past two decades residential real estate brokerage has undergone an evolving

Real Estate Office Type Comparisons

Brokerage Office	Tiers	Office Size (sq ft)	Agent Count	Space Per Agent (sq ft)
Brokerage Size Averages					
Traditional	Conventional	4,000 – 6,000	40 - 100	100 – 125
	Large	10,000 – 12,000		
Superstore	Starter	8,000 – 12,000	200 - 500	35 – 70
	Mega	16,000 – 30,000		
Café-Lounge	Boutique	2,000 – 3,000	40 -100	35 – 70
	Mini	1,500 – 2,000		

SOURCE REALSURE AND COMPENSATION MASTER

reorganization. Part of that process provides for the restructuring of the home buying process, the introduction of new technologies and players and the reengineering of the real estate office.

What is evident is that the traditional office model created a half a century ago has run its course and is no longer cost effective in the new economy. Office space per agent must decrease to make real estate offices more cost effective.

The three office models featured in this year's Report—the superstore, the café-lounge and the cloud-based virtual model—address the challenges, especially downsizing of square feet per agent, very efficiently (the virtual model of course does so in spades). Many ask which model will win. We think it is inconsequential as the real estate market is large enough to sustain all three models comfortably — probably more than one of each. These are all very stimulating and healthy business models and their growth will be less at the expensive of each other than at the expense of the traditional office that resists change.

People often say that big is bad, or that bricks and mortar is dead. Neither statement is valid. There are literally thousands of examples to dispel both of those fallacies. Size does matter and most of us enjoy the fruits of economies of scale every day—why would we not extend that benefit to homebuyers. KW is and it's working very well.

In 1998 industry analysts saw Starbucks as being well on its way to becoming the Nike or Coca-Cola of the specialty coffee segment. So who will be the "Starbucks" of the real estate industry? People often say that change will come from the outside.

Our guess is that it will actually be an "insider" that has the knowledge, vision and financial ability to roll out this new model successfully. At the moment no one has really snatched the lead spot but we think RE/MAX and United Real Estate are the frontrunners.

The virtual office model requires the biggest change to the traditional model and will therefore meet with the most resistance from traditional agents. But that's exactly what innovation does—it makes many people uncomfortable. However, history has repeatedly shown us that it takes innovation to become an industry leader. For example, Century 21 did it when they rolled out the franchising concept, RE/MAX did it when they introduced the 100 percent commission concept and HFS (now Realogy) did it when they perfected the M&A consolidation. Cloud-based real estate is no different. It's showing all the promise of being a powerful new innovation and eXp is leading that charge.

And as Victor Hugo said: "Nothing is as powerful as *an idea whose time has come*."

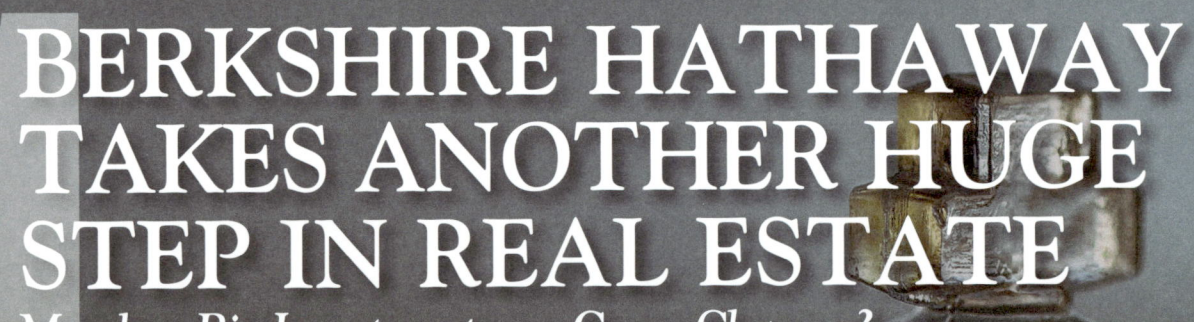

1 BERKSHIRE HATHAWAY TAKES ANOTHER HUGE STEP IN REAL ESTATE
Merely a Big Investment or a Game Changer?

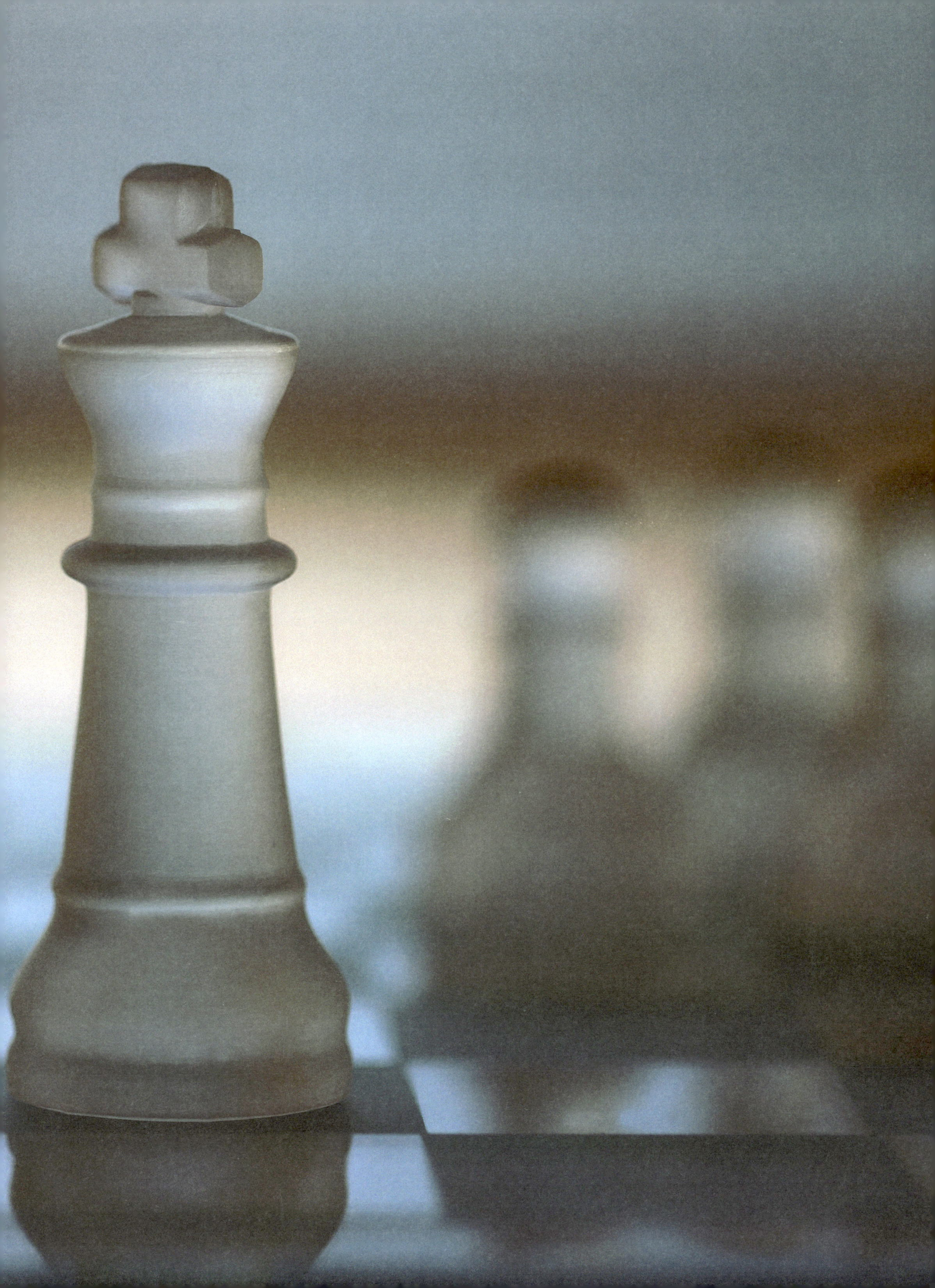

Berkshire Hathaway Takes Another Huge Step Into Real Estate

Before delving into our number one Trend this year we want to make sure that you have read the following Trend chapters as they help frame and clarify the significance of this Trend:

- Trend #6 — *Redefining Real Estate Professionalism: Hello, Capital. Are You Coming In?*
- Trend #5 — *The Value Proposition of Brands: Do Brands Still Matter in Real Estate?*
- Trend #3 — *The Gentle Revolution: What Happens When Smart Young Buyers Connect with Wise Old Realtors®?*

In residential real estate, consolidation is happening on two fronts simultaneously—the technology and data side of our industry and the brokerage and franchising side. Around 80 percent of the top 10 largest players have already consolidated, been acquired or become public entities, half of them during the last 12 months.

In October 2012 Canada's Brookfield Residential Property Services (Brookfield; brookfieldrps.com), a division of 100-year old conglomerate Brookfield Asset Management (NYSE: BAM; brookfield.com), announced the sale of Prudential (prudentialrealestate.com) and Real Living (realliving.com), including GMAC Real Estate, to HomeServices of America Inc. (HS; homeservices.com), a Berkshire Hathaway (BH; berkshirehathaway.com) company. The announcement stunned the real estate business community. Firstly because it involved Warren Buffet (one of the richest men in the world) and secondly because it involved multiple national franchise networks.

Berkshire Hathaway was already on that list of public companies active in the residential real estate industry through their subsidiary company MidAmerican Energy Holdings Company. MidAmerican is the parent of HomeServices of America that in turn owns and operates the nation's second largest, full-service residential brokerage firm and is one of the largest U.S. providers of integrated real estate services operating in 21 states. So their most recent acquisition isn't by any means their first as they already own 26 large regional brokerage operations.

But we think there is more—much more to this acquisition.

After analyzing the strategy of the transaction and making some logical and fair assumptions regarding the consequences of what is being created here, a more interesting picture emerges that affirms the consolidation and reengineering of the real estate brokerage business. When we look back on this acquisition in the years ahead it may well be listed as a pivotal move in the industry.

23 From the Vault: Real Estate Confronts Reality (1997)

Many [brokerages] will disappear as they are purchased by or incorporated into the national franchises; others will themselves buy other large independents in an effort to compete with the national franchises; and some will utilize franchising themselves as a method for expansion.

This is not an official position but here's how we see it.

BACKGROUND
Twenty years ago (let's say 1990) only about 20 percent of the top 10 major residential real estate brokerage brands were owned by public entities; Better Homes and Gardens (subsidiary of Meredith Corporation NYSE: MDP) and Prudential Real Estate Affiliates (subsidiary of Prudential Financial NYSE:PRU). In 2012 that number exploded to 80 percent (see chart).

Actually, oddly enough both companies through a series of acquisitions and name changes are the two companies that have been purchased by Warren Buffet to form the foundation of Berkshire Hathaway HomeServices; BHHS. The timeline depicts the flow of ownership, name changes and re-licensing agreements; note that Better Homes and Gardens Real Estate (BH&G) appears both above and below the timeline.

However, set aside who owns who and how they ended up in whichever portfolio for a moment. Today some 80 percent of the Top 10 real estate companies, including the biggest brands in the industry, have access to large sums of capital; far more than traditional companies have ever had.

Those of you that have attended any of my presentations will recall a phrase I have used: "If you and I were to compete, and had similarly matched intellect, abilities and comparable capital, it would be a very fair but prolonged battle. However, if tomorrow you gained access to a billion dollars—I lose."

Well, that is fundamentally what has happened to residential brokerage over the last two decades. Eighty percent of the largest players/

BERKSHIRE HATHAWAY HomeServices®

brands haven't had, and still don't have, access to large amounts of capital. And that's the first thing we need to understand as we take this journey; that a group of companies can now implement strategies and solutions that have not been possible for "traditional" brokers to consider because they have not had access to the capital markets.

Now, with that in mind, let's return to the portfolio and see who and how many of these companies got where they are today (see timeline).

THE LEADERSHIP SCOREBOARD
On the brokerage side, the publically owned entities are Realogy (NYSE: RLGY) and Berkshire Hathaway. For a complete list of their huge residential real estate brokerage holdings refer to the table on this page.

Making up the "Fab Four" are two other noteworthy groups, both privately held; Keller Williams Realty and RE/MAX. Both companies are still owned (there are a few minor shareholders in both corporations) and in large part headed by one of the orginal co-founders; Gary Keller and Dave Liniger. Collectively the "Fab Four" have an estimated 375,000 – 400,000 agents, representing approximately 40 percent of the one million Realtors® who are members of NAR.

On the other side of the ledger the primary third-party service providers of aggregated listings, property data, web services and technology tools

The New Berkshire Hathaway HomeServices Structure

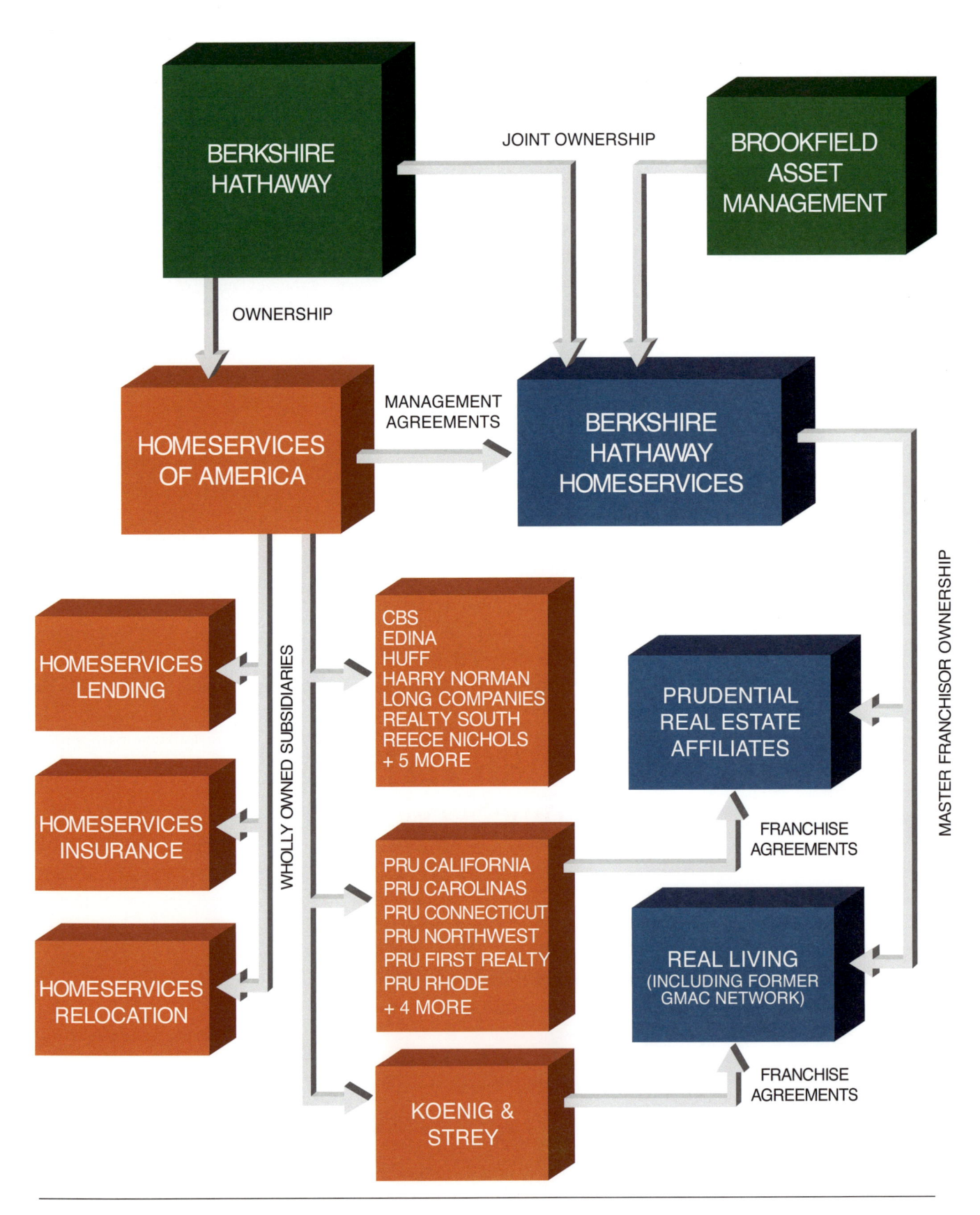

BERKSHIRE HATHAWAY —[JOINT OWNERSHIP]— **BROOKFIELD ASSET MANAGEMENT**

Berkshire Hathaway —[OWNERSHIP]→ **HOMESERVICES OF AMERICA**

Berkshire Hathaway & Brookfield Asset Management —[JOINT OWNERSHIP]→ **BERKSHIRE HATHAWAY HOMESERVICES**

HomeServices of America —[MANAGEMENT AGREEMENTS]→ Berkshire Hathaway HomeServices

Wholly Owned Subsidiaries of HomeServices of America:
- HOMESERVICES LENDING
- HOMESERVICES INSURANCE
- HOMESERVICES RELOCATION
- CBS, EDINA, HUFF, HARRY NORMAN, LONG COMPANIES, REALTY SOUTH, REECE NICHOLS + 5 MORE
- PRU CALIFORNIA, PRU CAROLINAS, PRU CONNECTICUT, PRU NORTHWEST, PRU FIRST REALTY, PRU RHODE + 4 MORE
- KOENIG & STREY

Berkshire Hathaway HomeServices — Master Franchisor Ownership:
- PRUDENTIAL REAL ESTATE AFFILIATES
- REAL LIVING (INCLUDING FORMER GMAC NETWORK)

PRU companies —[FRANCHISE AGREEMENTS]→ Prudential Real Estate Affiliates

Koenig & Strey —[FRANCHISE AGREEMENTS]→ Real Living

are also all public companies (in alphabetical order):

- Corelogic (NYSE: CLGX)
- Lender Processing Services (NYSE: LPS)
- Marketleader (NASDAQ: LEDR)
- Move (NASDAQ: MOVE)
- Trulia (NYSE: TRLA)
- Zillow (NASDAQ: Z)

Corporate consolidation has long been a staple in the evolution of American business and the engine through which professions and industries are transformed. We have seen this in manufacturing, engineering, law, medicine, construction, etc. (see graph) and now it's in full force in the residential real estate brokerage industry.

THE ANNOUNCEMENT

In reading past the actual announcement, the real interesting part is the creation of a new real estate brand; Berkshire Hathaway HomeServices.

MINNEAPOLIS, MINN. (Oct. 30, 2012) — HomeServices of America, Inc.™, a Berkshire Hathaway affiliate, and Brookfield Asset Management, announced today that they have partnered to introduce Berkshire Hathaway HomeServices®—a new franchise brand that joins the existing brands and affiliate networks of Prudential Real Estate and Real Living Real Estate.

Berkshire Hathaway HomeServices® combines the financial strength of both organizations, coupled with the operational excellence of HomeServices and superior real estate franchising experience of Brookfield.

The combined networks of more than 53,000 Prudential Real Estate and Real Living Real Estate agents generated in excess of $72 billion in residential real estate sales volume in 2011, and operate across more than 1,700 U.S. locations.

"Berkshire Hathaway HomeServices is a new franchise brand built upon the financial strength and leadership of Brookfield and HomeServices," said Warren Buffett, chairman and CEO of Berkshire Hathaway Inc. "I am confident that these partners will deliver value to the residential real estate industry, and I am pleased to have Berkshire Hathaway be a part of the new brand."

"We are honored and proud to be entrusted with the use of the Berkshire Hathaway name as our new real estate franchise brand," said Ron Peltier, chairman and CEO of HomeServices. "We will convey the strength of Berkshire Hathaway's reputation and its associated principles of integrity and financial stability in everything we do."

A new global real estate consumer brand! Definitely an attention-grabber!

Realogy — formerly Cendant, formerly HFS—didn't create a new real estate consumer brand when they acquired Coldwell Banker, Century 21, ERA, Sotheby's and Better Homes and Gardens. These were all existing brands, excepting some logo redesigning and modernization as in the case of ERA and BH&G, and the brand identities are for the most part still exactly the same. That's why they could change their name so frequently (HFS to Cendant to Realogy) as it was merely the name of the parent company and not the operating and/or consumer brands.

> **Today some 80 percent of the Top 10 real estate companies, including the biggest brands in the industry, have access to large sums of capital; far more than traditional companies have ever had.**

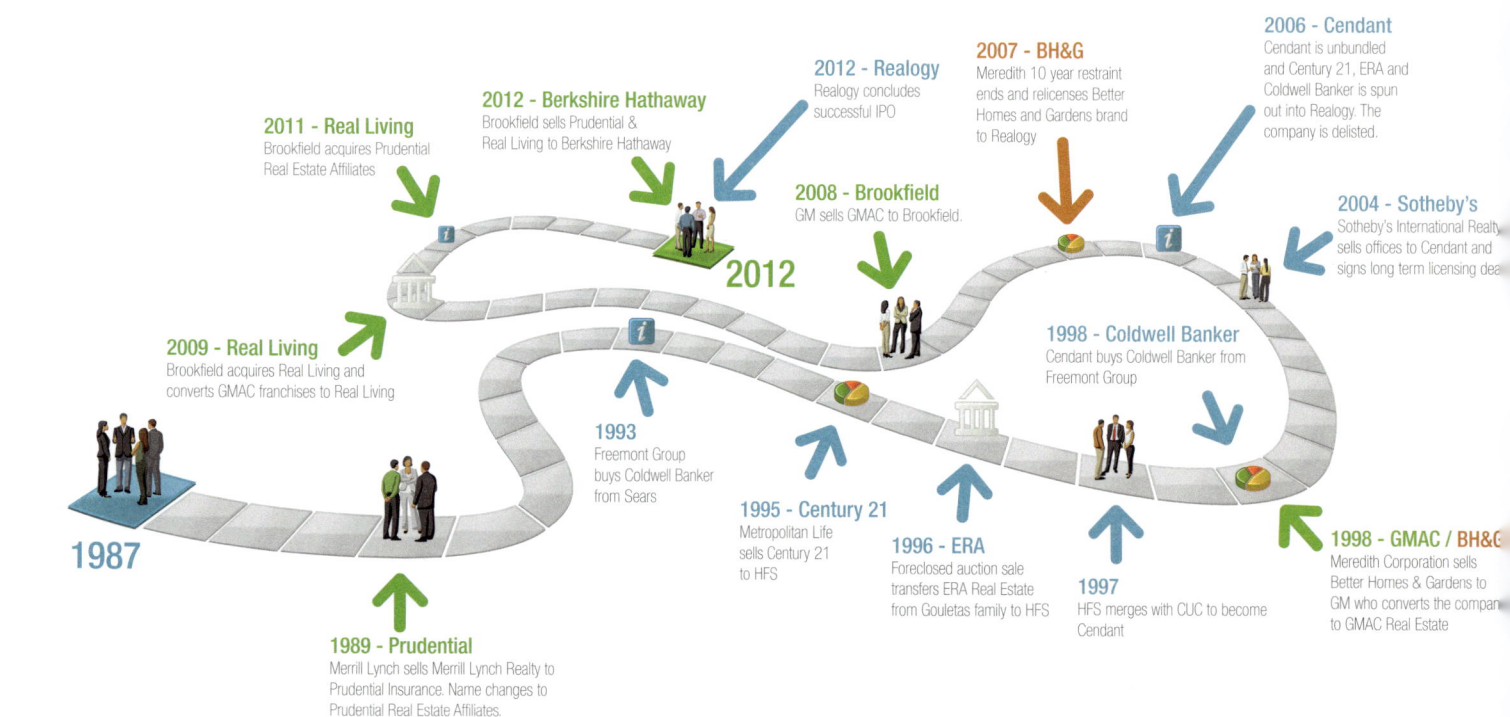

1 | Berkshire Hathaway Takes Another Huge Step Into Real Estate

2011 - Real Living
Brookfield acquires Prudential Real Estate Affiliates

2012 - Berkshire Hathaway
Brookfield sells Prudential & Real Living to Berkshire Hathaway

2012 - Realogy
Realogy concludes successful IPO

2007 - BH&G
Meredith 10 year restraint ends and relicenses Better Homes and Gardens brand to Realogy

2006 - Cendant
Cendant is unbundled and Century 21, ERA and Coldwell Banker is spun out into Realogy. The company is delisted.

2008 - Brookfield
GM sells GMAC to Brookfield.

2004 - Sotheby's
Sotheby's International Realty sells offices to Cendant and signs long term licensing deal

2009 - Real Living
Brookfield acquires Real Living and converts GMAC franchises to Real Living

1998 - Coldwell Banker
Cendant buys Coldwell Banker from Freemont Group

1993
Freemont Group buys Coldwell Banker from Sears

1995 - Century 21
Metropolitan Life sells Century 21 to HFS

1996 - ERA
Foreclosed auction sale transfers ERA Real Estate from Gouletas family to HFS

1997
HFS merges with CUC to become Cendant

1998 - GMAC / BH&G
Meredith Corporation sells Better Homes & Gardens to GM who converts the company to GMAC Real Estate

1989 - Prudential
Merrill Lynch sells Merrill Lynch Realty to Prudential Insurance. Name changes to Prudential Real Estate Affiliates.

1987

2012

Early Warning Signs

Would you have liked some warning that these changes were under way? Well, if you have been getting the *Swanepoel TRENDS Report* for the past 8 years you would have seen several tell tale signs. For example:

- Since the mid 90s a revitalized interest in franchising has resurfaced in the form of consolidation. Prior to 1996 Franchisors were separate. Then the unthinkable happened and HFS forever changed the dynamics of real estate franchising and the resurgence began (Trend #10: *Swanepoel Trends Report 2006*).

- The opportunity to gain dominance has been minimal, but with the advent of market share being owned by single entities, a door has opened for third-parties to enter the real estate brokerage industry. (Trend #9: *Swanepoel Trends Report 2006*).

- The race, more than ever, is to achieve critical mass and create a consumer recognizable national real estate brand (Trend #7: *Swanepoel Trends Report 2007*). Two of the most underutilized brands in real estate are HomeServices and GMAC (Trend #7: *Swanepoel Trends Report 2007*).

- What makes previous HomeServices acquisitions even more interesting is that not only have they purchased what are commonly referred to as "independents"—companies not affiliated with a national franchise—they have also included franchise companies such as Prudential and GMAC as part of their expansion (Trend #8: *Swanepoel Trends Report 2008*).

- Entire franchise networks don't change hands very often. 2010 was the year when it started to come together for Canada's Brookfield Residential Property Services after their acquisition of the GMAC franchise network in 2008 and the RealLiving Network in 2009 (Trend #1: *Swanepoel Trends Report 2011*).

- We are now down to five major players that rule the residential industry and they are: Brookfield, HomeServices, Keller Williams, RE/MAX and Realogy (Trend #4: *Swanepoel Trends Report 2012*).

A "NEW" BRAND

The creation of a new brand as the result of this transaction is noteworthy on two different levels.

The First Level – The Creation of a New National Brand and the Large-scale Conversion

This is not a first as other

142 www.RETrends.com ©2012 RealSure, Inc.

companies have done it before, but this time it's a fairly large and time consuming undertaking. Others on a national level that we can recall would include Merrill Lynch to Prudential back in 1989, the switch from BH&G to GMAC Real Estate in 1998 and then the switch from GMAC Real Estate to Real Living over the last two years.

But wait… these conversions involve the same two brands that are again part of this acquisition. Definitely out of the ordinary so we looked deeper, but found no unexplained phenomena.

The Second Level – Bestowing the Mantle of the Berkshire Hathaway Brand

Now, in our opinion, gaining the right to use this brand is big and again, there are two primary reasons:

- First, although by no means a well-known consumer brand, there are very few in the business world that haven't heard of Berkshire Hathaway and immediately associate the name with Warren Buffet. In 2012 Fortune Magazine (fortune.com) ranked the company 7th on its list of most admired companies and Buffet 7th on its list of top CEOs.

- And the second reason is that it's not really a brand, it's a company name. Look at the huge list of private and public companies Berkshire Hathaway owns and/or in which he has a significant investment. The Berkshire Hathaway name is very seldom attached to an actual company,

Berkshire Hathaway Inc. Public Holdings
Only Interests Exceeding $200M Are Listed.
Estimated value and holding as of 12/12/12

Company	Percentage	Value
Coca-Cola	8.9%	$ 15.0 B
Wells Fargo	8.0%	$ 14.0 B
IBM American Express	6.0%	$ 13.0 B
American Express	3.3%	$ 8.5 B
Proctor and Gamble	2.4%	$ 3.6 B
Wal-Mart Stores	1.4%	$ 3.3 B
US Bancorp	3.3%	$ 2.0 B
Phillips 66	4.3%	$ 1.5 B
DaVita	14.3%	$ 1.5 B
DirecTV	4.9%	$ 1.5 B
ConocoPhillips	2.0%	$ 1.4 B
12. Moody's	12.8%	$ 1.5 B
Mondelez International Inc	1.7%	$ 800 M
Johnson and Johnson	0.4%	$ 700 M
Washington Post	23.4%	$ 600 M
Liberty Media Corp	4.6%	$ 600 M
Bank of New York Mellon	1.7%	$ 500 M
Kraft Foods	1.7%	$ 500 M
M&T Bank Corp	4.2%	$ 500 M
USG Corp	15.9%	$ 450 M
Viacom	1.5%	$ 400 M
Costco	15.0%	$ 400 M
Deere & Co	1.0%	$ 350 M
General Motors Co	1.0%	$ 350 M
General Dynamics Corp	1.1%	$ 250 M
National Oilwell Varco, Inc	1.0%	$ 250 M
Precision Castparts Corp	4.5%	$ 230 M
Torchmark Corp	0.8%	$ 200 M
MasterCard, Inc	0.3%	$ 200 M

SOURCE ALEX POLLOCK, AMERICAN ENTERPRISE INSTITUTE 2010

1 | Berkshire Hathaway Takes Another Huge Step Into Real Estate

Berkshire Hathaway Inc. Public Holdings
Most But Not All Non-public Companies Owned/And Or Controlled

Acme Brick Company	Applied Underwriters Inc.	Ben Bridge Jewelers
Benjamin Moore Paints	Berkshire Hathaway Assurance	Berkshire Hathaway HomeServices
Berkshire Hathaway Homestate	Blue Chip Stamps	BoatUS
Borsheim's Fine Jewelry	Brooks Sports, Inc.	Burlington Northern Santa Fe Corp
Business Wire	Campbell Hausfeld	Cavalier Homes
CBT Inc.	Central States Indemnity Company	Clayton Homes
Cort Furniture	Dairy Queen	Duval
Fechheimer Brothers Company	FlightSafety International	Forest River
Fruit of the Loom	Garan Inc.	Gateway Underwriters Agency
GEICO	General Re	Helzberg Diamonds
HH Brown Shoe Group	HomeServices of America	International Dairy Queen
Iscar Metalworking Companies	Johns Manville	Jordan's Furniture
Justin Brands Inc.	Kansas Bankers Surety Company	Kirby Company
Larson-Juhl	Lubrizol Corporation	Marmon Holdings, Inc.
McLane Company	Medical Protective	MidAmerican Energy Holdings
MiTek	Mouser Electronics	National Indemnity Company
Nebraska Furniture Mart	Nederlandse Reassurantie Groep	NetJets
Netjets Europe	Omaha World-Herald	Oriental Trading Company
Precision Steel Warehouse	Prudential Real Estate Affiliates	RC Willey Home Furnishings
Real Living	Richline Group	Russell Corporation
Scott Fetzer Companies	SE Homes	See's Candies
Shaw Industries	Star Furniture	R.C. Willey Home Furnishings
The Buffalo News	The Pampered Chef	TTI, Inc.
United States Liability Insurance	Wayne Water Systems	Wesco Financial Corporation
World Book	XTRA Corporation	

and as far as we know it has never been attached to a product or professional service.

According to Earl Lee, the new CEO of Berkshire Hathaway Franchise Affiliates, using the Berkshire Hathaway brand will have a huge impact as it will attract the best companies and the best agents because of what it stands for and what it has accomplished. Historically, agents have generally not attributed a great deal of value to branding, but with the injection of such a high value brand Lee believes the value-add will be significant. And not surprisingly, the initial response from affiliates has been overwhelmingly positive.

Lee furthermore says that their goal is to become the most "highly valued" franchise system and brand in the real estate industry. And that means operating the company in a manner consistent with the tradition of the brand: "If we are going to become a household name and be able to attract the best we will have to have a uniformity and consistency in our operations and systems that is in keeping with the quality of the Berkshire Hathaway brand.

The Leadership Team
The new senior executive leadership team at Berkshire Hathaway HomeServices consists of three people. Ron Peltier (originally Edina Realty CEO and most recently CEO of HomeServices of America) becomes the new CEO of Berkshire Hathaway HomeServices, Robert Moline heads up the company owned operations as president and COO of HomeServices and Earl Lee heads up the new franchise operations that includes the Prudential and Real Living brands. Lee has been President of Prudential Real Estate and Relocation Services at Prudential Financial Inc. since December 2008 and has served in numerous roles and later President of Prudential Real Estate Affiliates (PREA) from 1978 through 2000.

Some Background on the Buffett Empire
Born August 30, 1930, Warren Edward Buffett is an American business magnate, investor and philanthropist. He is widely considered the most successful investor of the 20th century. Buffett is consistently ranked among the world's wealthiest people and is variously called the "Wizard of Omaha," the "Oracle of Omaha" or

Warren Buffet

the "Sage of Omaha." In 2012 Time magazine named him one of the most influential people in the world and specifically the world's wealthiest person in 2008.

Buffet is noted for his adherence to the value investing philosophy and for his personal frugality, despite his immense wealth. Buffett is also a notable philanthropist, having pledged to give away 99 percent of his fortune to philanthropic causes, primarily via the Gates Foundation. On April 11, 2012, he was diagnosed with prostate cancer, for which he completed treatment in September 2012. (Wikipedia).

In the world of business Buffet is known for his role as the primary shareholder, chairman and CEO of Berkshire Hathaway, one of the top 10 U.S. companies with the largest market cap. Valued at over $210 billion at the time of going to print, Berkshire Hathaway is more valuable than IBM, AT&T, Coca-Cola or Well Fargo (see table).

Earl Lee

1 | Berkshire Hathaway Takes Another Huge Step Into Real Estate

Shift from Private to Public Entities by Top Real Estate Brands

Public **Private**

Note: Companies are not listed in ranking order

1990	2012
BH&G Real Estate Group (via Meredith Corp.)	BH&G Real Estate (via Realogy)
Prudential Real Estate (via Prudential)	Prudential Real Estate (via Berkshire Hathaway)
Coldwell Banker	Coldwell Banker (via Realogy)
Century 21	Century 21 (via Realogy)
Electronic Realty Associates	ERA Real Estate (via Realogy)
Realty World	Realtor.com (via Move)
Realty Executives	Sothebys Real Estate (via Realogy)
Red Carpet	Home Services of America (via Berkshire Hathaway)
Gallery of Homes	Zillow (via Zillow)
	Trulia (via Trulia)
Help U Sell	
RE/MAX	RE/MAX
RELO	Keller Williams Realty

146 www.RETrends.com   ©2012 RealSure, Inc.

Very impressive, but let's not forget the other real estate giant, especially since it had a momentous year in 2012.

REALOGY

REALOGY

Realogy was created in 2005 when Cendant, in an effort to appeal to shareholders, decided to split into four separate companies. This was followed in late 2006 by a $6.8 billion leveraged buyout of Realogy with Apollo Global Management chipping in $1.05 billion. Unfortunately the timing couldn't have been worse as home prices peaked at the same time and the following years were awful to real estate in general and Realogy's cash flow in particular. And in the midst of this severe cash squeeze ruthless "corporate raider" and billionaire Carl Icahn filed suit against Realogy over a proposed debt swap and in 2008 the company found itself fighting for its life.

But Apollo stuck with Realogy, facilitated a successful restructuring that blocked Icahn and brought in $1 billion through a new debt purchase. The industry was full of rumors concerning the demise of the company at the time, but this skillful move bought Realogy the much needed time to stay afloat.

In 2012 Realogy Holdings Corp. (NYSE: RLGY) filed for and completed a successful IPO, selling some 40 million shares at $27. Share prices climbed to $34.20 on the first day of trading giving Realogy a market value of almost $3.5 billion. This enabled the company to reduce its debt by roughly a third; $7 billion down to $4.5 billion. According to Richard Smith, Realogy's CEO, the company plans to further reduce its debt by approximately $1 billion a year as the housing market recovers.

Realogy owns and operates the following brands: Better Homes and Gardens Real Estate, CENTURY 21, Coldwell Banker, The Corcoran Group, ERA and Sotheby's International Realty. They are active in over 100 countries and have approximately 13,500 offices with 240,000 agents, approximately four times larger than the combined number of Prudential and Real Living agents that have just been folded in under the Berkshire Hathaway tent.

Realogy also own NRT, Inc., which in turn owns and operates approximately 725 offices with 42,000 agents. This would be comparable to HomeServices of America referred to earlier that has approximately 16,000 agents. Both of these entities manage the wholly owned real estate brokerage companies within their respective groups.

Berkshire Hathaway HomeServices is exciting and has significant potential, but remember residential real estate is still very much a Realogy world with approximately one in four buyers or sellers being represented by a brand in the its stable.

SUMMARY

In the real estate industry there has been much debate and significant competition has been built around

> Let's not forget the other real estate giant, who also had a momentous year in 2012.

the necessity and value of brands (Trend #5: The Value Proposition of Brands: *Do Brands Still Matter in Real Estate?*). And with the majority of consumers' perception of the industry at or near the bottom in most polls we now have one of the richest men in the world deciding to attach his brand to real estate agents, bringing with him huge credibility based upon an incredibly successful track record across a broad spectrum of businesses. That's significant!

However, Berkshire Hathaway hasn't just come in as a parent company; it's actually putting its brand on the "For Sale" signs in front lawns. Realtors® will be carrying a business card that says they're working for Berkshire Hathaway HomeServices. That's big!

Although Berkshire Hathaway is, just like Realogy, a stable of multiple brands it will most likely remain so for a number of years as there are hundreds of franchise agreements in place that can legally keep the Prudential and Real Living brand in play until 2024. But think about the opportunity: consolidating all those brands into one single, powerful corporate identity. That's huge!

Realogy doesn't have that option available as it has extremely well known and strong brands like Century 21 and Coldwell Banker, and it also has very long-term licensing agreements to manage other brands; BH&G and Sotheby's. In addition, it is their stated vision to be a multiple brand stable of options, which of course has many unique advantages.

Setting the benefits of a multi brand strategy aside (not discarding them), there are also huge benefits in a powerful, single global brand. Berkshire Hathaway may actually be able to pull it off as the Real Living brand is still quite unknown as a national brand and the Prudential brand, although credible, is still often associated with the insurance company and needs to be phased out at some future date.

Most new growth will likely take place under the new Berkshire Hathaway HomeServices brand, and one would suspect so would most consolidations within the group. After a year or two of positioning this is going to become a very attractive alternative. Earl Lee agrees and says that "It is a compelling opportunity to join a brand with a compelling proposition."

However, a potentially large stumbling block is whether or not the hundreds of franchisee owners (many Prudential) and the many presidents of the company-owned HomeServices subsidiaries that all still operate under the same name as when the where acquired during the last decade (such as Edina, Harry Norman, Reece and Nichols, etc.) will want to switch to the new Berkshire Hathaway HomeServices brand, or stay with what they have. In most cases what they have is, almost without exception, the same name that was placed on the front door when the company was founded half a century ago; a very strong local brand.

We have unofficially learned that the President of each separate brokerage company will be given the right to decide whether or not to keep their existing branding, and if they decide to switch, when to do so. With so many people involved and without getting input from over 60,000 agents the decision to consolidate under one brand any time soon is very, very unlikely. Transitioning multiple brands (Prudential, Real Living and HomeServices) under one new flag is going to require standardization, cooperation and lots of capital.

But with that said, real estate brokerage has only a handful of "Hotspots"—I'd say about five—and this is most certainly one of them. So is this merely a big investment or is it a game changer? We say Game Changer, but don't expect big changes in 2013 or 2014—it's a big undertaking.

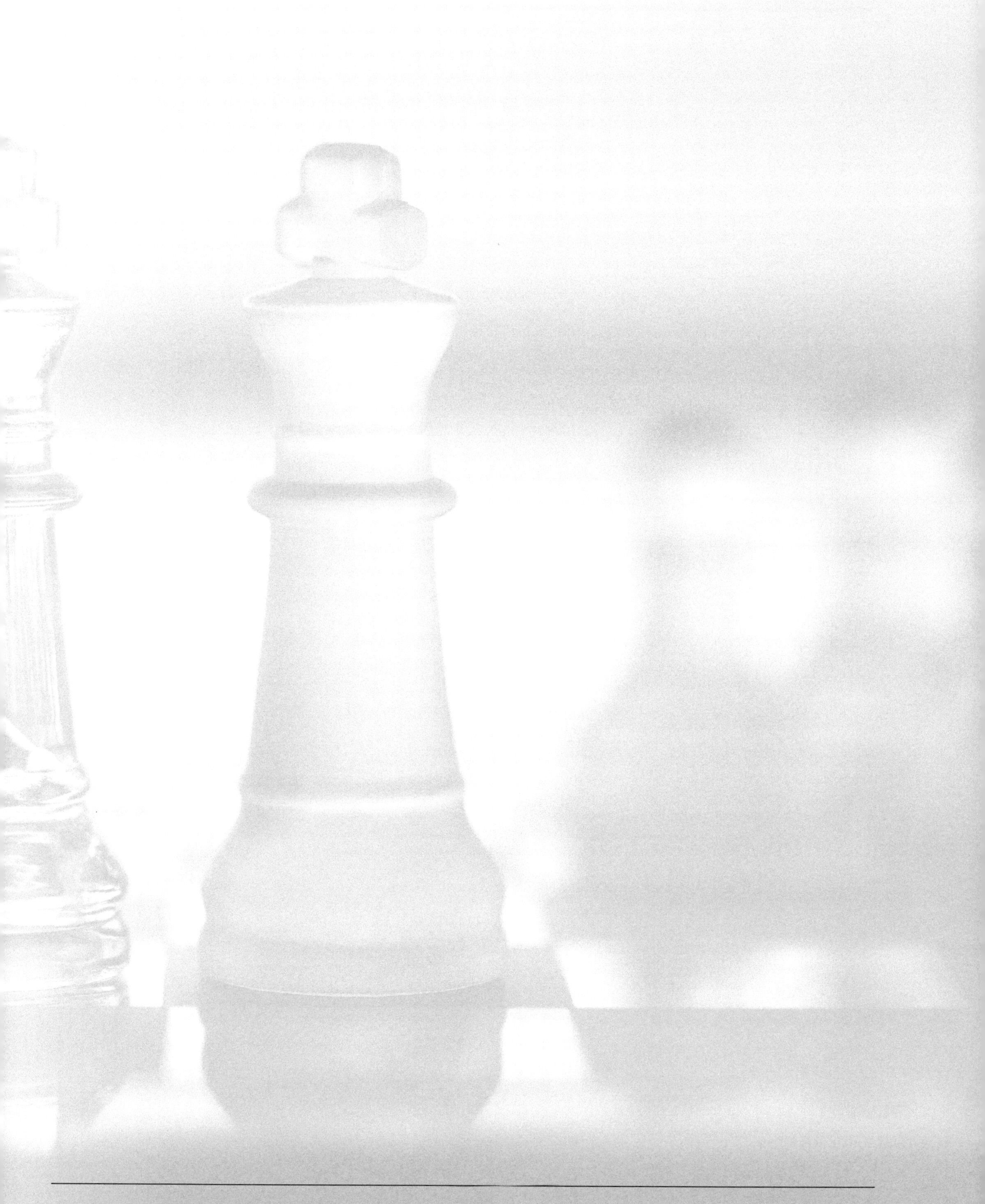

References

2011: A Year In Review, ERA Real Estate. 2011

2012 Has Real Opportunity, But There is a Long Way to Go, Ross, Joel. April 15, 2012

2012 Home Buyer/Seller Satisfaction Study Results, J.D. Power. August 15, 2012

3 Million of America's Most Vulnerable Homeowners Are On The Brink Of Foreclosure, Woodruff, Madi. Business Insider. July 30, 2012

3.8% Tax – Real Estate Scenarios and Examples. National Association of REALTORS. 2012

69 real estate companies make Incs fastest growing list, INMAN News. August 20, 2012

A Strong Close to 2011 Confirms Improving Outlook for 2012, Nadji, Hassam. Marcus & Millichap. January 26, 2012

A Tale of Two Housing Markets: Single and Multifamily, Olick, Diana. CNBC. April 17, 2012

Academics Look to Foreign Countries for Mortgage System Guidance, Brookings Institution. February 24, 2011

America's Gen Y, Metropolitan Life Insurance Company. 2010

American Business Awards Recognize National Association of Realtors, Singer, Stephanie. National Association of REALTORS. June 19, 2012

Apartment Market Hot Streak Continues, NMHC. July 2012

Apartment Production Up Strongly Year Over Year, Eye On Housing. August 20, 2012

Apartment Rental In The US, Kelly, Doug. IBISWorld. September 2012

Are High Homeownership Countries Wealthier? Davies, Alan. June 17, 2012

Back To The Future: Real Estate Search Centers 2.0, Counter Intelligence: The Real Estate Café Weblog. December 21, 2007

Berkshire Hathaway unit takes stake in Real Living, Ball, Brian R. Business First. October 29, 2012

Big Data and the Evolution of Smart Systems, The Economist. June 5, 2012

Bob Floss Former CAR President Speaks Out on Impeachment, Ricci, Peter. Chicago Agent Magazine. August 20, 2012

Brand in the Real Estate Business – Concept, Idea, Value? Viitanen, Kauko. 2004

Break in EU Clouds Welcome News, But Volatility Far From Over, Nadji, Hassam. Marcus & Millichap. July 3, 2012

Budget Again Includes Unpopular Curb on MID and Other Deductions, Freedman, Robert. National Association of REALTORS. February 14, 2012

Building a Shared Future, Huffington Post. May 20, 2012

Buying A La Carte Bill Wendel's Latest Venture, The Real Estate Café, Aims to be the Buyer's Guardian Angel, Sit, Mary. Boston Globe. September 10, 1995

Case Shiller Home Prices Rise By More Than 2 Percent, Wall Street Journal. July 31, 2012

Chicago Association of Realtors Ousts President, Matthews, David Lee. Chicago Real Estate Daily. August 24, 2012

Comparison of Real Estate Franchises, National Association of Realtors. August 2011

Consumer Webinar, The Pinnacle Group. October 18, 2012

CoreLogic Monthly Foreclosure Reports, CoreLogic. January to December 2012

Co-working spaces: the real estate office of the future? Merritt, Tina. February 14, 2012

Customer Centricity The Focus At Hear It Direct, Chamberlain, Audie. October 3, 2012

Debate Rages Over Principal Forgiveness at Fannie and Freddie, Olick, Diana. CNBC. April 10, 2012

Depressed US Birthrates Are Undermining The Housing Recovery, Shedlock, Mike. Global Trend Analysis. July 27, 2012

Despite High Affordability, Renter Nation Reigns, Olick, Diana. CNBC. April 30, 2012

Dodd Frank Could New Rules Derail the Housing Recovery? RISMedia. August 5, 2012

Does the US Government Really Want to Help You Stop Your Foreclosure? Jensen, M. J. August 2, 2012

Don't Be Confused by Conflicting Reports Focus on the Consensus, Kelly, Margaret. RE/MAX. May 31, 2012

Due North: Canada's Marvelous Mortgage and Banking System, Perry, University of Michigan. Mark J. February 26, 2010

Echo boomers still want a home, but only when they're ready, Market Watch. October 22, 2012

Economic Growth Resembles a Recovery, Not a Head Fake, Nadji, Hassam. Marcus & Millichap. March 4, 2012

Economists Hop on Recovery Bandwagon, Cook, Steve. Real Estate Economy Watch. August 18, 2012

Edina Realty Pulls the Plug on Realtor.com, INMAN News. May 22, 2012

Europe and the Summer of Uncertainty, Raymond James. June 14, 2012

Family Incomes Down in Recent Years, McClatchy Washington Bureau. June 12, 2012

Feds Rethink Policies That Encourage Home Ownership, Wiseman, Paul. USA TODAY. August 11, 2012

FHA Turns To Investors As Losses Continue To Rise, Olick, Diana. CNBC. June 8, 2012

Flood of Foreclosures Still Fails to Materialize, Olick, Diana. CNBC. May 2, 2012

Fort Lauderdale Realtor Group Sues Miami Realtor Group, Gale, Kevin. South Florida Business Journal. December 20, 2011

Freddie Mac Attack, Angry Bear Blog. January 30, 2012

Freddie Mac Bets Against American Homeowners, Eisinger, Jesse, Arnold, Chris. NPR News. January 30, 2012

Free Fall: How Government Policies Brought Down The Housing Market, Wallison, Peter J. American Enterprise Institute. April 26, 2012

Generation Y Going Nowhere, And They're Fine With That, Lutz, Bob. Forbes. July 6, 2012

Generation Y, Walter, Ekaterina. January 21, 2012

Generation Y – Their Attitudes Towards Work and Life, English Online. 2012

Generation Y Chooses to Rent, Hartwell, Sharalyn. February 6, 2010

Gen Y, The Largest age demographic in the country's history, Pulte Group. July 11, 2012

Gen Y Home Buying is Motivated by Quality of Life, ERA Real Estate. August 14, 2012

Generation Rent: Slamming Door of Homeownership., Neuman, Scott. June 7, 2012

Generation "Y" is Generation"Rent", Coupal, Joseph. July 22, 2012

Generation Y: I'm Sure Not Looking for my Parents' Home, EPMSonline. February 6, 2012

Getting To Know Generation X, NAS Insights. 2006

Global Outlook Summary, The Economist. August 13, 2012

Have Home Prices Hit Bottom? Olick, Diana. CNBC. June 26, 2012

Hispanic Group Reveals Latinos Are Super Consumers, MarketWire. February 1, 2012

Home Prices Have Found A Floor, Housing Wire. June 28, 2012

Homeownership Rates: A Global Perspective, Proxenos, Soula. Fannie Mae. March 11, 2007

Homeownership Trends Worldwide, Munjee, Nasser. May 23, 2007

HomeServices and Brookfield Announce a New Residential Real Estate Franchise Brand-Berkshire Hathaway HomeServices, Marketwire. October 30, 2012

Household Formation Not Job Growth Key to Apartment Sector, Friedman, Jeffrey L. June 21, 2012

Housing Remains Bright Despite Overall Slowdown, Fannie Mae. July 25, 2012

Housing Starts Up 23.6 Percent Over Last Year, MSN Real Estate. July 18, 2012

Housing: Bottom, Reversal or Just Noisy Numbers? Olick, Diana. CNBC. April 205, 2012

How Long Can Seniors Work? Miller, Jonathan D. July 11, 2012

How Much Office Space Do You Need? Buck, James. About.com.

Howard Hanna Invests 1M Plus to Enhance Real Estate Listings, Carter, Matt. INMAN News. February 21, 2012

HUD Accepting Applications for Entities to Purchase Troubled Mortgages, HUD. July 18, 2012

Improving Foreclosure Prices Drive Recovery, Cook, Steve. Real Estate Economy Watch. June 5, 2012

Industries in 2012, The Economist. 2011

Investment Outlook An Economy on the Rise, Lereah, David. Real Estate Economy Watch. March 23, 2012

Investors Get Creative With Hot Rental Market, Olick, Diana. CNBC. June 20, 2012

Is Housing Recovery Real, Not Everyone Is Convinced, Noguchi, Yuki. NPR. July 31, 2012

Is The Apartment Rental Market Overheating? Olick, Diana. CNBC. July 5, 2012

Is Your Future in the Industry Crucible, Conaway, Jeremy. September 11, 2012

Keller Williams Sues Iowa Realty Over Commissions, Eller, Donnelle. Des Moines Register. June 27, 2012

Lack of Distressed Supply Continues To Hit Home Sales, Olick, Diana. CNBC. May 30, 2012

Lack of Distressed Supply Pushes Home Sales Lower, Olick, Diana. CNBC. April 19, 2012

Last Generation of Homeowners May Just Be on Hold, Walsh, Meghan. Bloomberg BusinessWeek. July 16, 2012

Lawsuit alleges improper spending by former Realtor's association executive, McGarry, Caitlin. Las Vegas Review Journal. June 1, 2012

Local Realtor Sues Association Member for Internet Comments, AGBeat. September 6, 2012

Looking Beyond This Summer Drag, CRE Maintains its Luster, Nadji, Hassam. Marcus & Millichap. June 12, 2012

Miami Association of Realtors Sued for False and Deceptive Advertising, Barkett, Richard W. PRLog. December 20, 2012

Miami Association of Realtors; Fort Lauderdale Realtor Suit "Disappointing," Britell, Alexander. Imperial Real Estate Group. December 22, 2011

Millennials and the Shared Economy, US Chamber of Commerce. December 26, 2011

Millennials May Not Be The Key To Growth, Carranza, Sule Aygoren. Globe Street. August 20, 2012

Mixed Messages from the Housing Market Data, NAHB. August 6, 2012

Moneyball Lessons For The Sharing Economy, Savitz, Eric. Forbes. February 8, 2012

Mortgage Interest Deduction: Understanding How it Works Today and the Proposed Changes, Paoli, Alison. Zillow Blog. December 28, 2010

Mortgage Lending Hit 16 Year Low in 2011, Philadelphia Inquirer. September 23, 2012

Mortgage Market Still Hampers Housing Recovery, Olick, Diana. CNBC. May 10, 2012

National Association of Realtors Member Profile 2012, National Association of REALTORS. 2012

Nearly One-Third of Mortgaged Homes Underwater, Scoggin, Andrew. HousingWire. May 23, 2012

Neighborhood City Hit With MLS Copyright Lawsuits, Brambila, Andrea. INMAN News. April 24, 2012

New Crop of Foreclosures is Coming, Olick, Diana. M. CNBC. July 26, 2012

New FHA Foreclosures Spike, Olick, Diana. CNBC. May 31, 2012

New Listings With Your Decaf? Prevost, Lisa. New York Times. January 13, 2008

No Danger of Overbuilding in Multifamily Sector Until 2013, Misonzhnik, Elaine. NREI Online. January 18, 2012

Occupy Big Business: The Sharing Economy's Quiet Revolution, The Atlantic. December 6, 2011

Office of the future really isn't, Jacobson, Don. St. Paul Star Tribune. October 25, 2012

Plain and Simple, A Job Killer, Miller, Jonathan D. February 2, 2012

Profile of Home Buyers and Sellers 2012, National Association of REALTORS. 2012

Property Management in The US, Schmidt, Dale. IBISWorld. May 2012

Reaching Generation Y & Turning Them Into Homeowners, Guaranty Mortgage. August 13, 2012

Real Estate – All You Need To Know, UBS Global Asset Management. August 2012

Real Estate Café: A Residential Repast, Wollam, Allison. Houston Business Journal. April 14, 2005

Real Estate Debt From Crisis Comes Opportunity, Mercer. October 29, 2010

Real Estate Hits Top 10 List of Consumer Complaints, Waters, Jennifer. MarketWatch. August 1, 2012

Real Estate In The Networked Economy: Big Changes in When, Where and How Business Works, Lyne, Jack. SiteNet. 1998

Real Estate Search Stores – Coming Soon, Burslem, Joel. Inman/Next. December 19, 2007

Real Estate Trade Group Seek Control of Internet Domains .Realtor, .MLS, Brambila, Andrea V. INMAN News. June 18, 2012

Realogy Announces IPO, RealTrends. June 8, 2012

Realtor Association of Fort Lauderdale Sues Miami Association of Realtors, Hoyos, Patricia. Miami Today News. December 22, 2011

Realty One Group Expands Into Franchising, Hagey, Paul. INMA News. August 15, 2012

Re-examining The Mortgage Interest Deduction, Reuters. November 14, 2010

Refinance Applications Reach Highest Level Since 2009, Mortgage Bankers Association. July 30, 2012

Renting Is Becoming More Popular, But Only Up To A Point. The Economist. March 3, 2011

Sharing – Culture and Economy in the Internet Age, Schafer, Mirko Tobias. 2012

Shifting Demographics and Housing Choice: A Whole New World, Copeland, Brian. Realtor.org. May 18, 2012

Single Family Rentals Ignite Management Boom, Real Estate Economy Watch. July 28, 2012

Spat over commissions as KW enters Des Moines market. Wahlgren, Lisa. INMAN News. June 18, 2012

The Allure of Apartments, Lynn, David. NREI Online. January 17, 2012

The Bank Settlement Solved Little, Ross, Joel. February 12, 2012

The Café Concept, Immobliler Lifestyle Real Estate. L'Espace. 2012

The Debt Crisis and Real Estate, Conaway, Jeremy. July 26, 2011

The Fiscal Cliff What It Means For Housing and Home Builders, NAHB. May 28, 2012

The Future of the Real Estate Office… and Company. Dollinger, Matt. TheYouFactor

The Gadget Generation, E-Marketer, March 2011

The Market Pulse; CoreLogic. January to December 2012

The Recent Employment Numbers Raise Some Flags, Ross, Joel. April 8, 2012

The Recent MLS BreakIn, Cohen, Matt. Clareity Consulting. August 1, 2012

The recession may be contributing to poor job outcomes for the younger generation, Weiss, Debra Cassesns. March 14, 2012

The Rise of the Sharing Economy, Mashable.com. February 7, 2012

The Sharing Economy, Sacks, Danielle. FastCompany.com. April 18 2011

The Untold Debt Story, Deloitte University Press. 2012

The Virtual Assistant Model, Myers, Christopher, Armstrong, Aaron, Reger, Craig, Campbell, Seth.

The World's First Daily Deal for Real Estate, PRNewswire. July 12, 2012

There Is A Shortage Of Homes And Its Leading To Fierce Competition, Los Angeles Times. June 10, 2012

Three Demographic Trends That May Not Be True, Ascierto, Jerry. MFE Demographics. October 10, 2010

Three Secrets Third-Party Aggregators Don't Want You To Know, Balduf, Brian. VHT Inc. August 8, 2012

Trulia Files to go Public, Boero, Brian. 1000Watt Consulting. 2012

Trust and the Sharing Economy: A New Business Model, Green, Charles H. Trusted Advisor. March 23, 2012

US Growth Stalling at 2% Into Fiscal Cliff, Englund, Michael. Reuters. June 18, 2012

US Housing The Unlikely Silver Lining, Englund, Michael. Reuters. July 24, 2012

US Real Estate Market – Quarterly Outlook, UBS Asset Management. May 2012

US Treasury Hastens Demise of GSEs, Morphy, Erika. August 19, 2012

US Widens Bulk Home Loan Sales Program, Reuters. July 18, 2012

Watch the Ten Year Yield, Ross, Joel. June 3, 2012

Weak Jobs Report Another Bump in Road to Recovery, Nadji, Hassam. Marcus & Millichap. May 16, 2012

Weak Jobs Report Drives Misreading of Tem Hiring Gains, Chandan, Sam. July 9, 2012

What Does Gen Y Want When It Comes To Home Buying? Los Angeles Times. August 22, 2012

What Does Generation Y Want? Sichelman, Lew. October 17, 2012

What the Brookfield Purchase of Prudential Means for Brokers, Agents and Consumers, RISMedia. August 2012

What Renters Want – Four Reasons Millennials DO Want to Buy, Flur, Jessica. Multi Housing News. July 3, 2012

What's Next? Real Estate In The New Economy, Urban Land Institute. 2011

What's The Future Of The Sharing Economy, Scorpio, Jessica. Co.Exist.com. June 5, 2012

When Foreclosure Supplies Fall, The Bottom Falls Out of Housing, Olick, Diana. CNBC. 2012

Where Are the Generation Y Home Buyers? KCM Crew. December 12, 2011

Where Are The Move Up Buyers? Olick, Diana. CNBC. August 1, 2012

Where Do We Go From Here, Gleckman, Howard. Urban Brookings Tax Policy Center. March 2, 2011

Where The Jobs Are, Chandan, Sam. January 16, 2012

Why Millennials Will Never Be Homeowners, Lewis, Marilyn. MSN Real Estate. August 20, 2012

Why Purchase Shares in Realogy's IPO When you Can Purchase Shares in ZonincRealty.com Direct Public Offering, Veracrest Capital Partners. June 2012

Why Shopping Will Never Be The Same, USA Today. August 8, 2012

With Completions Near Historic Low, Apartment Pipeline Growing Rapidly, Chandan, Sam. February 27, 2012

Zell Talks Politics Debt International Market and How He's Investing Today, National Real Estate Online. Bodamer, David. January 25, 2012

Zillow Sues Trulia Over Home Valuations, INMAN News. September 13, 2012

About the Authors and Contributors

STEFAN SWANEPOEL

Stefan is widely recognized as the leading visionary on real estate business trends in the Unites States. He has given over 700 talks in 8 countries and 44 states to over 500,000 people and has penned 24 books and reports including:

The Amazon.com bestseller *Real Estate Confronts Reality* (1997), the highly acclaimed annual *Swanepoel TRENDS Report* (2006, 07, 08, 09, 10, 11, 12 & 13), the most recent addition to the family, the *Swanepoel TECHNOLOGY Report* (2013), and the New York Times, Wall Street Journal & USA Today bestseller *Surviving Your Serengeti: 7 Skills to Master Business & Life*.

His academic accomplishments include a bachelor's in science, a master's in business economics and diplomas in arbitration, mergers and acquisitions, real estate, computer science and marketing. His life has been a "Serengeti journey"—from his birth in Kenya to schooling in Hong Kong and South Africa to running a New York-based global franchise network with 25,000 sales associates in 30 countries. He has served as president of seven companies and two non-profit organizations.

Stefan writes, blogs and tweets throughout the year. To stay current with the latest information, where he is speaking and to reach out to him connect through one of the following sites:

Trends and Technology in Real Estate
- Website: www.retrends.com
- Twitter: www.twitter.com/retrends
- Facebook: www.facebook.com/realestatetrends

Business Fables
- Website: www.serengetibook.com
- Twitter: www.twitter.com/serengeti
- Facebook: www.facebook.com/serengeti
- YouTube: www.youtube.com/serengetibook

Speaking Engagements
- Website: www.swanepoel.com
- Twitter: www.twitter.com/swanepoel
- Facebook: www.facebook.com/swanepoel

About the Authors and Contributors

JEREMY CONAWAY

Designer, facilitator and strategic architect Jeremy Conaway was born in July of 1948 in Traverse City, Michigan. His first job occurred when he was thirteen years old and worked as a pinsetter in his parent's bowling alley. He earned a BA in Economics from California State University, an MBA from the University of Maryland (FED) and a JD from the University of the Pacific, McGeorge School of Law. Jeremy was a fellow with the Robert Wood Johnson Foundation and in that capacity served on the staff of the California Senate, The U.S. Senate and the Connecticut Legislature.

Today Jeremy he serves as President of RECON Intelligence Services. RECON's clients include many of the most progressive brokerages and franchises in the North American real estate industry including to firms in nine different countries. With RECON's assistance its clients are focusing on a new generation brokerage business model that emphasizes profitability, investor centricity, consumer focus, strategic management, engaged leadership, standardized services delivery, comprehensive data provision and universal accountability. Jeremy can be reached at jeremy.conaway@reconis.com.

ROBH HAHN

Rob is a graduate of Yale University and NYU School of Law where he earned his JD in International Bankruptcy. In 2003 he served as Senior Director, Interactive Marketing at Realogy until he founded 7DS Associates in 2009 where he assists institutional clients in real estate and related industries develop and implement corporate strategy.

Rob is a Change Agent and is at his best shaking things up by starting new strategic initiatives, whether as small as a new corporate website or as large as major changes in business models. He understands the limits of new techniques, whether social media, online communities, technology products or business models and utilizes his blog—Notorious ROB—to opine about various topics in marketing, technology and real estate. Rob can be reached at rhahn@7DSAssociates.com.

About the Authors and Contributors

MATT COHEN

Matt Cohen, Clareity Consulting's Chief Technologist, has over fifteen years of extensive real estate technology experience. Matt has consulted for many of the top Associations, regional MLSs, MLS software vendors, large brokerages and a wide variety of information and technology companies that service the real estate industry. Matt also serves as Clareity's lead Multiple Listing Service and Transaction Management System analyst and facilitates the system and vendor selection and contract negotiation process for several organizations each year.

He also leads Clareity's online survey practice, performing market research for software providers and member satisfaction surveys for associations and MLSs. Real estate software and technology providers look to Matt for assistance with strategic planning, market research, product planning, software design, quality assurance and usability and security assessments. Matt has helped establish Clareity as the most experienced real estate information security consulting company in the United States. Matt can be reached at matt.cohen@callclareity.com.

MARC DAVISON

As a partner of 1000Watt Consulting Marc brings more than twenty five years of experience in advertising, marketing and entrepreneurship. A native of New York City, Marc attended Princeton University and completed his education at NYU, after which he joined the legendary advertising agency Young and Rubicam. In 1984 he founded DGE entertainment, a full service PR agency focused on the music industry. In 1998 Marc founded Access Media Group to provide marketing and strategic consulting services to clients across the country where through one of his clients, Inman News, Marc was introduced to the world of real estate.

Subsequently he founded VREO, Inc., a technology company delivering software solutions to real estate agents and brokers. While there, he defined the company's strategic direction, built their brand and established the firm as an industry leader. Marc is a regular columnist for Inman News and speaks to real estate audiences across the country. Marc can be reached at marc@1000watt.net.

About the Authors and Contributors

THOMAS MITCHELL

Tom holds a BS degree in Business Administration from Colorado State University with majors in accounting and finance and advanced studies in finance. Upon completion of his degree he became a Naval Officer with extensive combat experience in operational fighter aircraft operating off of aircraft carriers in Viet Nam and is a decorated veteran. After leaving the military Tom has had a very successful consulting career involving numerous industries in the fields of renewable energy, telecommunications, education and technology. He also spent 20 years involved in various aspects of commercial real estate; brokerage, development, investment and syndication having founded Eagle National Development Company in 1972.

As a partner with Stefan Swanepoel in RealSure Inc., Tom serves as Managing Partner where he utilizes his extensive teaching, writing and editing expertise as published author and ghost writer, serving as head of research and managing editor of the *Swanepoel TRENDS Report* and other books, white papers and reports published by RealSure Publishing. Tom can be reached at mitchell@realsure.com.

Fifteen Years of Trends and Tracking
Real Estate Trends Research and Publication by Stefan Swanepoel

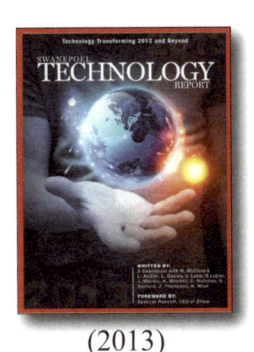

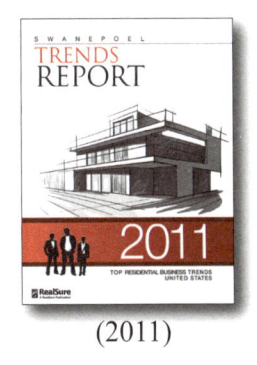

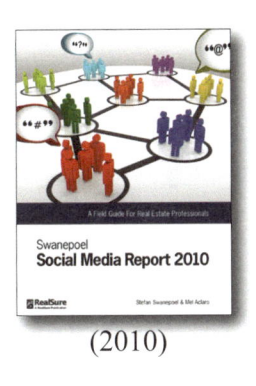

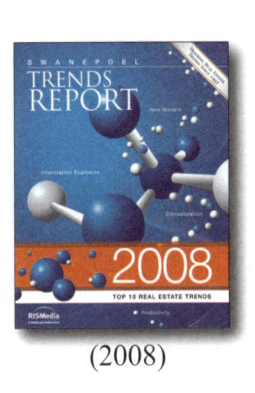

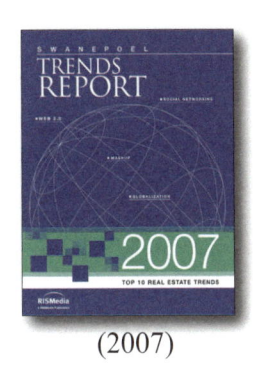

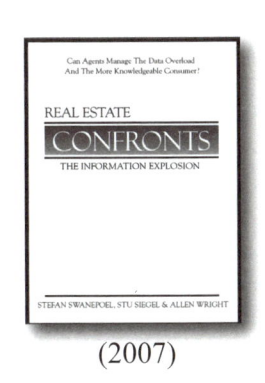

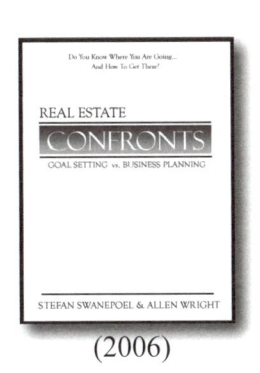

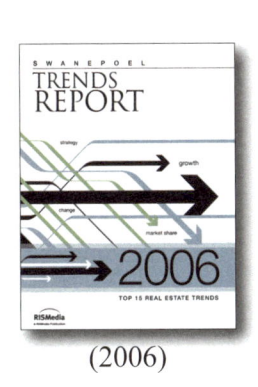

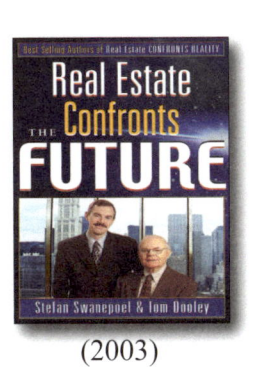

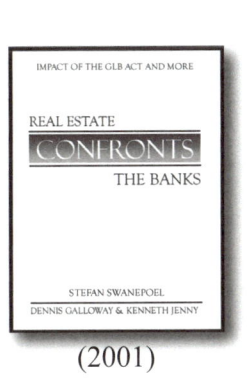

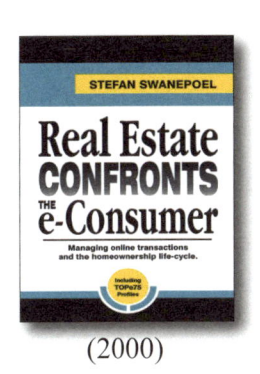

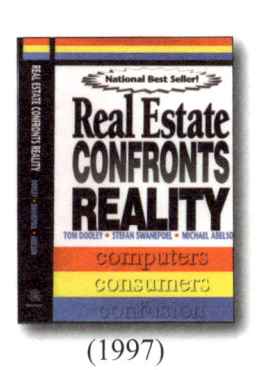

(2013) (2013) (2012) (2011) (2010)

(2010) (2009) (2008) (2007) (2007)

(2006) (2006) (2005) (2004) (2003)

(2003) (2001) (2000) (1999) (1997)

© 2012 RealSure, Inc. www.RETrends.com 161

TWO
AND THEN THERE WERE TWO

Words	**80,000**
Hours of Research and Writing	**1,500**
Chapters	**20**
Authors	**15**
Reports	**2**
Source of Information	**1**

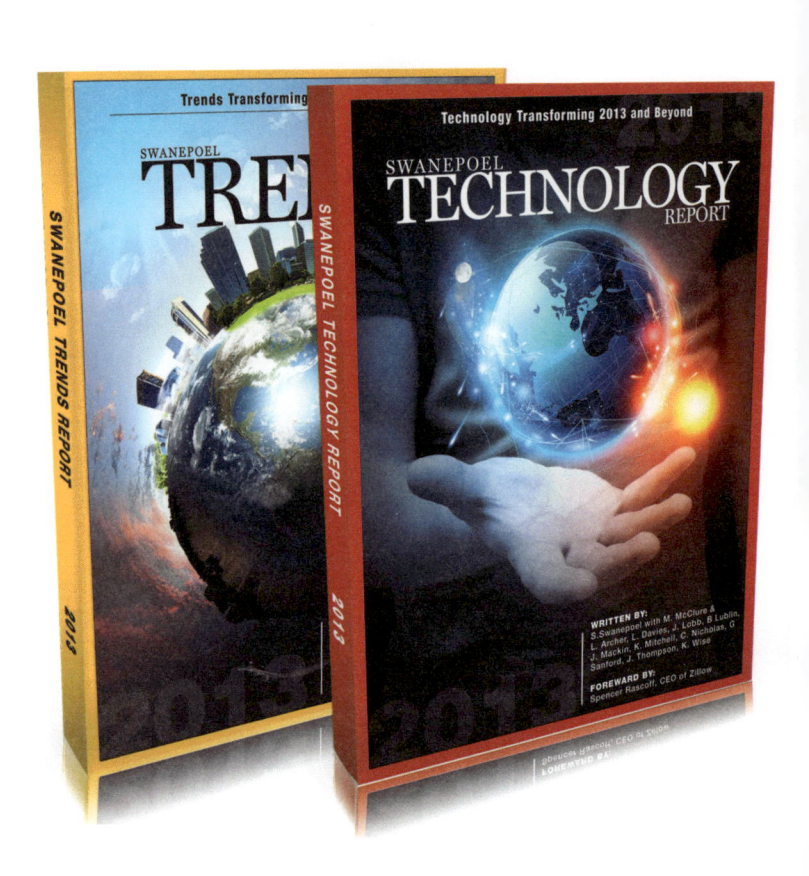

The extent, speed and volume of change, innovation, shifting business models, technology and mobile advancement has resultzed in the RealSure team expanding its lineup to 2 annual reports.

SWANEPOEL TRENDS REPORT (160+ PAGES)

SWANEPOEL TECHNOLOGY REPORT (160+ PAGES)

April 17-19, 2013

SWANEPOEL
T3 SUMMIT
TRENDS | TECHNOLOGY | THOUGHT

- **Tracking Trends**
- **Analyzing Impact**

- **Innovating Solutions**
- **Making A Profit**

TRANSFORMING AN INDUSTRY

Stefan Swanepoel has become the custodian of American Real Estate and now also hosts the industy's premier brainstorming event.

No exhibitors. No sponsors. Only movers and shakers, leaders and rainmakers. If you like to be in the driving seat, make a difference or be the leader of the pack - we will see you there!

" The Best Way to Predict the Future, is to Invent it. "
- Alan Curtis Kay

T3Summit.com

serengeti institute
| live | learn | survive | thrive

THE BOOK

A riveting business parable recognized as a national best seller by the New York Times, Wall Street Journal and 20 other publications and organizations. Whether you are overcoming the hardships of a brutal business environment or the struggles of life itself, you will enjoy this life fable written against the Africa safari. Published by Wiley & Sons it is available in print, audio and on the Kindle and Nook. Get your copy at www.Amazon.com

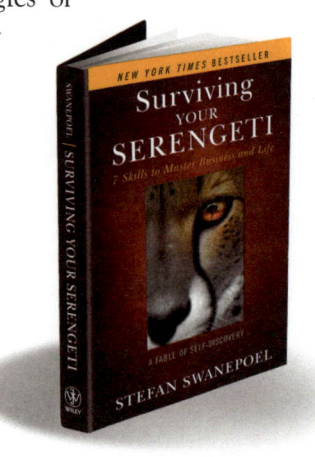

SKILLS ASSESSMENT

Over 125,000 people have taken the "What Animal Am I?" quiz. Take the first step on your journey of self-discovery with this surprisingly accurate 3-minute quiz. Discover your strongest, innate, survival skill. This free quiz can be taken at any time and as many times as you wish — online, your smartphone or via Facebook. Take the quiz at www.WhatAnimalAmI.com

TEAM BUILDING WORKSHOPS

"The Safari of Self Discovery" is a journey of introspection and personal improvement. Learning interesting behavioral and strengths about your office colleagues, team members and friends invariably leads to a fun and extensive non-threatening discussions about how people work together and why we often take decisions the way we do. This fully packed, face-to-face two-day workshop is facilitated live and includes hands-on learning with many practical exercises and extensive small- group interaction. For more information visit www.SerengetiBook.com

KEYNOTE TALKS

The 90-minute keynote presentation by Stefan Swanepoel is more than a talk. It's a high-energy, stimulating experience that transports attendees into an "African Safari" with awe-inspiring visuals, stimulating stories and revealing breakthroughs. Any of the seven skills — being strategic, taking risks, being efficient, enduring, being enterprising, being good at communication and being graceful — are easily incorporated into any event and conference. To book Stefan, visit www.Swanepoel.com

LEADERSHIP SAFARIS AND RETREATS

Custom leadership retreats held according to clients' needs in both the U.S. and in the Serengeti in East Africa. Numerous retreats have already been held in the U.S. and the first retreat in the Serengeti is scheduled for February 2013.